"This is my new go-to playbook when working with neurodivergent clients. What a gem of a resource!"

—Scott Barry Kaufman, Ph.D.,
author of *Twice Exceptional,*
Ungifted, Transcend, and *Rise Above*

The Neurodivergent Playbook *is a giant deep breath for anyone who is neurodivergent themselves or wants to better connect with people who experience the world differently. With humor and compassion, Dr. Zakreski unravels the complexities of ADHD and other diagnoses, mixing his own experiences and real-life case studies with scientific evidence. The result is a guide that is equal parts heartfelt and data-driven—and an absolute must-read for anyone who has ever wondered, whether for themselves or a loved one, Why do the "easy" things feel so hard?*

—Caitlin Moscatello, author and journalist

Dr. Matt is the real deal. His authenticity is engaging and contagious, allowing us to fully accept ourselves for who we are, while inspiring us to be better. Drawing on his experiences in life, teaching, and therapy, he not only breaks down the "code" in a way we can understand, but also teaches us the foundational skills needed for life. Affirming and compassionate, The Neurodivergent Playbook *is a beacon and guide for all who are wired differently and those who raise, teach, supervise, and coach them.*

—Dan Peters, Ph.D., licensed psychologist,
co-founder and Executive Director, Summit Center,
author, *Make Your Warrior a Warrior* and *From Warrior to Warrior,*
co-author, *Boosting Your Child's Natural Creativity* and *Bright, Complex Kids*

Dr. Zakreski is one of the country's leading experts on neurodivergence, and I have had the pleasure of attending many of his talks. His forthright, knowledgeable approach always helps me learn more about this and other important topics, and I was excited to read his new book. It does not disappoint! His passion and expertise regarding neurodivergence jump off every page, and he includes a plethora of practical information and advice for individuals interested in how and why some of us see the world so differently than others.

—Johnathan Plucker, Ph.D., professor at Johns Hopkins University
and former president of the NAGC

The Neurodivergent Playbook

How Neurodivergent People Can Crack the Code of a World Not Built for Us

Dr. Matt Zakreski

Edited by: William D. Beuscher
Interior design: The Printed Page
Cover design: Kelly Crimi

Published by
Gifted Unlimited, LLC
12340 U.S. Highway 42, No. 453
Goshen, KY 40026
www.giftedunlimitedllc.com

© 2024 by Dr. Matt Zakreski

ISBN: 978-1-953360-36-6

Dedication

To my families. The one that I was born into.
The one that I married into. The one we created.
And the ones that I found along the way.
Thanks for supporting me and making this wild ride worth it.
I love you all more than I can say.

—MJZ

Acknowledgements

Writing a book is HARD! You really cannot do it yourself. I would be remiss if I didn't take a moment to thank everyone who helped me along with this process. Molly and her team at Gifted Unlimited Press. My assistant Julia is and has been amazing. I got great coaching from real writers like Kris Jansma and Alyssa Biber Colman, who acted as sounding boards and kept me from spinning out.

I was honored to receive much support from many people in the neurodivergent community, like Dr. Emily King, Brian Housand, EKM, Julie, Debbie Reber, Nicole Tetrault, Susan Baum, Edward Amend, Katie Anderson, Matt Fugate, Rena Subotnik, Tilj, Femke, Dr. Sharon Saline, Barry Gelston, SBK, Gordon Smith, Gail Post, Richard Cash, Charlton Wolfgang, Seth Perler, Dave Mendell and the PAGE family, Elaine Chesboro and the NJAGC family, and others. You have all made me feel like I belong in this community as a professional, not just as a person. I am honored to share these spaces with you and hope to continue to work alongside you to help change the world for neurodivergent folks.

Thanks for the love and support from my friends—Gutsy, Ben Whiting, the other Ben W(right), Kelli, Locco, Mitchell, Jon and Ashley Schorah, Nelly, Chris Rockwood, Rich, Courtney, Allie, Cainna, Chardsy, Crezzie, Alarico, Kasi, Zach, Grant, Jason, Dave, Ashley, and so many more. You're the ones who helped me hone these skills over the years, whether you know that you were doing it or not. When you've been through times in your life with no friends (as I certainly have), you come to know in your heart what friends mean and what they're worth. Time and distance can never change what we have and how much you mean to me. You changed my life in innumerable ways; in all honesty, you probably saved it.

To the Godparents—Paul and Rachel, Dan and Jennie, Jon Margolick (CTY 4eva) and Katie, and Abbie and Adam. Thank you for being a part of our family, earning the honorific of "Uncle" and "Aunt." I've been asked to be a godfather twice in my life; both times it was utterly humbling because I think that there is no greater honor than to be told by someone, "This is my child, and I trust you to watch over them." The second-best honor is to realize that you have people in your life that you can say that sentence to. You all remind me every day how lucky we are to have amazing friends in our lives that have chosen to be active in the lives of our kids. And a special thank you to my godkids—Katie and Molly.

To my mentors—almost too many to name! But Dr. Cassano, Dr. Zarabba, Dr. Salter (RIP), Dr. Mesquita, Dr. Mendes, Dr. Peterson, and Dr. Postma. Thank you for your wisdom and patience. Dr. Postma, in particular, was the first person to look at me and say, "You need to be speaking more. I can give you those opportunities. Now can you go get me a Pepsi?" (If you know Mike Postma, that's exactly how he said it).

To my siblings (Laura and Katie)—I love you both so much and I'm so proud of you. We have taken different paths towards success, but I've watched every step you've taken with such pride and joy. You're both incredible professionals who serve your communities with dignity, wisdom, and compassion. And somehow, you're even better people. Thanks for putting up with an aggressively weird brother all your lives. I hope that I've taught you half as much as you've taught me.

To my siblings-in-law (Erin and Leah) and my brothers-in-law (Wyeth and Sean)—You inspire me to be a better person because each of you have skills that I wish that I had. Thank you for bringing so much richness to my life. I love having more brothers and sisters in my life; it's an honor to share this journey with you. Thanks for welcoming me and my family into your lives.

And to my amazing in-laws, Garry and Mary, thank you for letting me be a part of your family and sharing your love, home, and traditions with me."

Mom and Dad—thank you for everything. I cannot even begin to express how much you've meant to me and what your unconditional love and support has meant as I grew through all the twists and turns into the man I am today. I'm honored to be a part of your legacy. All the kids that I have helped and will help are a direct reflection on how much you taught all of us how important it is to help others and to use your powers for good. I can't imagine that it was easy, raising me, but look at me now!!

Emerson and Sten—I hope that this book helps to create a world that is kinder and more compassionate for brains like yours. I love you so much, Moo and Duck. Thank you for letting me be your dad; it's the biggest honor of my life. You both inspire me to be better every single day. I'm not always going to get it right, but I'm going to be right there with you every step of the way. Remember my #1 job…

Julia—I love you. There aren't enough words to explain why and how much (and this book is plenty long enough as it is). Simply, you're my everything. Without you, none of this would be possible. Thanks for deciding to introduce yourself to me that first day of IGCP. You've been my cheerleader, my editor, my shoulder to cry on, and my fierce advocate throughout not just this writing process, but my whole life. In a world of chaos, you bring peace, grace, wisdom, and love into my heart. I'll spend the rest of my life trying to do the same for you.

Contents

Foreword

The first time I heard Dr. Matt Zakreski speak was early in the COVID pandemic. I attended a webinar on kids, mental health, and suicidality, in which Matt led a powerful conversation with a group of teens and young adults who'd survived attempts. With care and compassion, he helped them share their hard-won insights so parents, educators, and mental health professionals could better protect the kids in their lives.

It was a powerful hour, so much so that shortly afterwards, I reached out to Matt and asked him to join me in conversation for my *Tilt Parenting* podcast. As someone who leads a community of parents raising neurodivergent kids—kids like mine who are impacted by things like ADHD, autism, learning disabilities, giftedness…kids who I refer to as "differently wired"—I knew how badly our children were struggling. I was (and am) grateful for Matt's ability to tackle these tough topics with a deep love and regard for kids who struggle in ways that are often unseen and/or misunderstood.

When I launched Tilt in 2016, my mission was to offer a positive, empowering home base for parents like me. I saw Tilt as part of a revolution aimed at shifting the way the world sees and supports exceptional children so they can thrive in schools, in their families, and in life. Over the years, this mission has led me to seek out like-minded revolutionaries. I know them when I see them. And I knew right away that Dr. Matt was one of "my people."

Since that first webinar, I've seen Matt speak to both large and small audiences. I've been in conversation with him during heartfelt virtual events. Once we even swapped stories about our childhood foibles over tacos in Reno. I see Matt as that quirky, engaging therapist every parent wishes their kid had access to, the one who has instant cred by humorously and honestly sharing the highs, lows, and in-betweens of going through life as a differently wired person. I'm continuously struck by his unique ability to connect with and inspire kids and adults alike. It's a gift that parents like me, parents in the trenches trying to navigate schools, systems, and communities that weren't designed with our kids' wiring in mind, need so very much.

In my book *Differently Wired*, I encourage parents to become "fluent" in their children's language, a.k.a. get curious about what their words and behaviors are communicating (and how they interpret ours) so we can be on the same, respectful page. This is because one of the hardest parts about parenting an outside-the-box kid is reconciling the mismatch between our expectations and the reality of who our children inherently are. This was certainly the case for me, the parent of a twice-exceptional child who recently discovered her own twice-exceptionality.

Of course, what I didn't have access to as I fumbled through the first twenty years of my child's life, and what I would have given just about anything for, was an honest, useful, and optimistic playbook to help me better understand my child's experience. And that's why I'm so excited about *The Neurodivergent Playbook*. In it, Matt offers readers a "code" to unlock a world designed for neurotypical people, not by prescribing a set of "rules" for fitting in, but rather by suggesting empowering ways for interacting with systems and communities that may not appreciate the fullness and complexity of neurodiversity.

As a podcaster and community wrangler, I'm always seeking resources that align with Tilt's positive, strengths-based, "there's nothing broken or in need of fixing" philosophy. Matt's book fits perfectly into this ethos. What's more, Matt has an extraordinary ability to break down the neuroscience of neurodivergence into simple, accessible language, whether the topic is asynchronous development, executive functioning, imposter syndrome, emotional regulation, anxiety, or social emotional learning. Matt draws on his lived experience and his extensive work with clients in sharing the concepts, which results in a book that's both relatable and digestible. We'll see our kids, maybe even ourselves, in the pages to come and feel understood in a way we might not have before.

Ultimately, *The Neurodivergent Playbook* feels like an extended and incredibly helpful conversation with a wise, funny, not to mention unapologetically-nostalgic-for-the-'90s friend. Matt gives us permission to embrace the full range of the neurodivergent experience, while offering unwavering understanding and validation, as well as a plethora of practical ideas to help "crack the code" so readers can design a life on their own terms.

If I shared everything I appreciate about *The Neurodivergent Playbook* here, the book would be twice as long. So I'll just say this: In a neuro-normative world that reinforces the message that there's something "wrong" with who our kids (and we) inherently are, this book is the warmest "welcome to the Club" we could want. In writing the book he needed for himself, Matt has gifted the rest of us a wise and practical guide to being a complex human in a conventional world. Whether you're raising a differently wired child, sharing life with a neuro-divergent partner, are yourself neurodivergent, or all of the above, *The Neurodivergent Playbook* will not only help you feel seen, informed, and confident—it will fill you with HOPE.

—Debbie Reber, CEO & Founder,
Tilt Parenting, author *Differently Wired*

Prologue

The seeds for this book were planted a long time ago, on a beach in Sea Bright, New Jersey in the summer of 1998. I had gone to the beach with my sister Laura and a family friend and their kids, enjoying the sun, surf, and sweet freedom of no longer being in middle school. We were gathered in our beach chairs, seated a loose circle, reading our books (who remembers summer reading? BOOOO) when a commotion caught our attention.

Our beach had a small playground in the middle and there were two boys (I'd say probably 10 years old) who had commandeered the platform at the top of the slide. They were pointing and shouting down to another, smaller boy standing on the beach. "You can't come up!" they shouted, "You don't know the code!"

"Then just tell me the code!" the other boy shouted, clearly near tears. "Tell me the code and then I can play with you guys."

"No way! You should just *know* the code." They laughed. "*Everyone* knows the code!" This exchange went back and forth for a while, with increasing desperation from below and increasing arrogance from above. Eventually, the smaller boy turned and fled, disappearing into the beach blankets and umbrellas. Having claimed another victim, the two boys on the slide high-fived and gloated about the "power of the code." I'm sure that they were planning to kick puppies or pollute the ocean on their way home. I bet they leave shopping carts in the middle of parking lots to this day.

From across the beach, I felt righteous anger while watching this exchange. I looked over at my sister Laura, who was feeling similarly aggrieved. Stuff like that—namely social injustice—had always bothered us. Our family friends saw our frustration: "C'mon, lighten up, you two!" their mom said with a grin. She was often telling us to lighten up, which showed how little she understood us, even if we were capable of doing it. Owen, one of her kids, agreed: "Those kids are just having fun." It should be noted that while all members of my birth family are various flavors of neurodivergent, these family friends were neurotypical, and definitely more socially adept than the five of us (or at least Laura and me). Social stakes probably felt lower to them because friendships came more easily; but since we two Zakreskis had both taken some serious blows in the friendship department, our awareness of the challenges of socializing raised our emotional stakes and kept us tethered to the issue at hand.

"It's not fair!" I said. "They're bullying him!"

"Well, all he needs is the code," Owen pointed out.

"But that's just it!" Laura shouted, "They never told him the code! How can he play if they never told him? All they had to do was tell him."

"I'm sure they told him at some point, he just forgot. It happens," their mom responded, probably regretting looking up from her Jodi Piccoult beach novel. "It's not worth worrying about, honestly."

"*I* never feel like I know the code," Laura said, miserably.

In that moment, my sister had articulated something that I had long felt but never found the words for. It often felt like everyone else had "the code" —an understanding of the unwritten set of behaviors detailing what to do, when to do it, and what not to do (somehow the most important part) in social interactions. I had always felt a little offbeat compared to my friends, but the feeling of difference had worsened by the end of middle school to the point where I felt utterly socially adrift and miserable. Everyone seemed to be getting a lot more out of middle school than I was. At least socially: my grades had been good until my mental energy went to trying to figure out where I went wrong with people, and I could not determine why or how for the life of me.

The best way to describe the feeling that had been dominating my thoughts is that it felt like missing the in-class review of the material the day before a pop quiz, coming into the quiz cold. You look fine on the outside, but there's this unshakeable feeling that everyone else knows something that *you don't,* and if you don't figure it out something bad is going to happen. As a gifted kid, I had the confidence that my brain could catch me up on missed information; but the social process was fundamentally different. It was looser, more nebulous, more closely guarded. Anyone could read a textbook, but the social protocol felt designed to keep people out. It's like they only wanted *some* people to "pass" their test.

Why would they want to keep me out? I'm very likeable! I'm very smart! Why can't I figure this out? Did everyone go to a review without me? Did my invitation get lost in the mail? Did they send the details through that newfangled electronic mail on the computer that everyone was talking about, and I had just missed it because the angry modem noise totally freaked me out? (Remember, it was 1998! Parents, please explain this reference to your kids.)

If "the code" existed, it has surely been taught at the review that I hadn't been invited to. I had good reason to believe that "the code" *did* exist and covered a lot of things. All I had to do was watch my peers at lunch and recess engage in suspiciously large amounts of handholding when there hadn't been any before; I desperately wanted to know what it was all about, but no one was telling me "The code!!"

Not knowing "the code" had contributed to a spectacularly awful eighth grade year. I showed up after the summer ready for the same old school scene that had been the case since kindergarten. When you grow up in a small town, the rhythms are wonderfully predictable; you talk about who went where during the summer and gossip openly about who got the meanest teachers. Maybe some new friendships bloomed over the summer, or maybe someone was trying a new sport, but that was all part of growing up, right? By Halloween, things would be running along smoothly.

But in eighth grade everything was suddenly different. People didn't just have new shirts for the first day of school; they had outfits. And were people wearing **bras**? What is this, *90210*? (Parents, please explain this reference as well). There was facial hair, whispers of parties and whiffs of cigarette smoke, none of which made any sense to me. Interpersonally, things were no better. I laughed at the wrong jokes or at the wrong times. I didn't have the same interests as other people, even though I felt like we had shared those interests very recently: "Star Wars?! That's so lame!" said one former friend who still had my Yoda t-shirt from when he borrowed it at a sleepover over that summer, before everything changed.

I didn't actively resist these changes, but I certainly spun out emotionally while trying to catch up to my peers and understand just what the heck was going on. I'm sure that I got increasingly shrill and desperate. Before long, my former friends had abandoned me, mocking me in private (and then very much in public) for being "a freak" and "a loser."I just couldn't figure out what had changed! Yes, I was a gifted kid and kind of a nerd, but I had always gotten along with everyone. I wasn't at the top of the social food chain, but I was comfortably far away from the bottom—or at least I had been. Now everyone seemed to have learned new rules over the summer and shared them…with everyone but me. I felt socially radioactive.

The event that sealed my social fate was sticking up for the new kid. I'll call him Scott (for the purposes of this story), and he lived right down the street from me (my town was literally a square mile). Zach had a sleepover with lots of guys from the neighborhood, and though I wasn't invited, I certainly heard about it. Specifically, I heard that Scott had two dogs he really loved, and they were running around during the sleepover, the way dogs will do. Fast forward a week and word spreads that Scott had developed mono. Obviously, he's not going to be in school for a while, but missing school isn't the worst thing in the world. I remember thinking that mono is just one of those things that happens and figured it would be life as usual. I even offered to bring his work to him from school.

But the new social rules meant that nothing was usual. Suddenly, there was a rumor that Scott got mono because "he totally made out with his dogs." The rumor was spread by a kid named George (not his real name, of course) who had been a friend of mine, but now wanted to climb to the top of the social food chain, apparently at any cost. I remember hearing the rumor on the playground and feeling flabbergasted, that it was not only ridiculous but didn't even make sense! A different kid might have seen this as an opportunity to step on someone else to climb the social ladder, but not me. I'd like to say that it's because of my personality, but I also didn't know that "the code" dictated that you social climbed to survive; so, y'know, I was not like George. I piped up, "Guys, that's stupid. Scott doesn't make out with his dogs and, even if he did, that's not how you get mono!"

A thunderstruck silence. Then (so inevitable, in retrospect) the response: "You only know that because you guys are gay together and you gave it to him!" Calling someone or something "gay" was the peak of social critique in the late 1990s; in high school I was called gay for dating a girl from our rival school...just let that sink in for a moment. Regardless, the die had been cast; I had defended the weird new kid who wasn't there to defend himself or even clarify what had happened and thrown myself in with him. There were peals of laughter from the students and, ultimately, more loneliness for me.

As an interesting side note, I went home and told my parents about this incident. My dad (who like my mom is a clinical psychologist) said, "Well, you could have done the mean thing there to be cool." To be clear, he wasn't suggesting that I *should* have done so, he was just talking about my options. I responded, "Dad, if that means that you have to be mean to be cool, then that's just not me. I'd rather be nice." My dad gave me a hug. Later, I would find out that my dad told this story to hundreds of kids in his therapy practice over the years, as other kids like me navigated similar social minefields. I'm quite proud of taking that morally elevated stance now, though it definitely didn't help me then.

Those kids in my parents' offices are part of the reason why I wrote this book. Looking back at it now, I was lucky! Things could have been much worse. (At the time I did not believe that it would ever get better; it still feels surreal even now that I did end up with friends and a successful high school experience). In high school I made a new group of friends, fell in love with musical theatre, played soccer, did a million extracurriculars, and even became Student Government Vice President. Eventually some of the bad feelings faded. I recovered from a year of pain to re-enter the social milieu as someone more comfortable in his own skin, but also much more wary of others.

Moving forward, I paid constant attention to the things that seemed to be social norms and tried to find enough snippets of data to get by. I felt like an anthropologist studying a foreign tribe with utterly unique customs and language. (Or, perhaps more accurately, I felt like Sheldon Cooper in the episode of *The Big Bang Theory* when he dresses up as a *Star Trek* ensign to document the historical inaccuracies at his local Renaissance Faire). I wanted to learn what they knew and knew they wouldn't tell me, so I kept my ears open for moments that I could translate or decipher. While I never did quite figure out "the code," I learned enough about it to mask when needed, faking it until I made it. Additionally, I found people who were willing to be outsiders with me; we created our own "code." One of them was Zach from down the street; he was my best friend for many years.

But I'm not writing this book to gloat or pat myself on the back. As a clinical psychologist who specializes in working with neurodivergent people (i.e., other people who would craft an elaborate metaphor about not being invited to a training where people learn a bespoke social "code" of behavior), I hear versions of this story dozens of times a year. The pain of these people always takes me back to that school year, and those boys on that summer playground screaming about their precious "code." Life seems to be no fairer today than it was then; the world still runs on who is "in" and who is not. I can listen to my clients and reflect their pain from an empathetic place; I'm really good at that part of the job. Lately, however, I've been asking myself if it isn't time that I do something about the social disconnect around "the code."

The world is built by and for neurotypical people; they represent about 80% of the population, so it makes sense that they would craft and maintain a world that fits their needs. Neurodivergent people don't know the "code" because we weren't the target audience. And since "the code" is part of that broader macro-culture, it doesn't feel like a thing that can or should be explained to an outsider, it's a thing that you should *just know*. I got lucky and survived not knowing it because I found friends and activities that allowed me to be me; many kids are not so lucky. Lots of people are still carrying around the pain of feeling like a freak and a failure. Some people aren't here anymore because of it. I'm not being melodramatic, the stakes of social exclusion can be that high to include suicidality (van Geel, Goemans, Zwaanswijk, & Vedder, 2022).

I can't say that this book is completely "the code" that you were looking for (cue Obi-Wan Kenobi voice); it's not a Rosetta Stone (or even Duolingo!). I don't speak neurotypical enough to fully decipher their rules and norms, and I'm not Indiana Jones-esque enough to spirit their rulebook away from their temple (which in my mind is a giant country club) and avoid the rolling boulder (which is probably a luxury SUV, to further the metaphor). But this book is my attempt at unpacking social norms and giving you, my dear readers, the skills to navigate those challenges through the lens of your neurodivergence. I want to make you feel comfortable enough with "the code" to recognize it when you see it and adapt your behaviors appropriately.

And language is not enough! We need context to understand the hows and whys of neurotypical behavior and contrast that to our own neurodivergent experiences. As such, we will cover the neuropsychology of neurodivergence and the psychology of emotional regulation, social connection, and self-confidence, through case examples from my practice, incidents from my own life, and anecdotes from my various travels and cohorts of friends. I will attach skills and exercises to try and make this process as tangible as possible; I want you to know what I know ("The hard-won wisdom I have earned" sings Curtis Jackson as George Washington in *Hamilton*) so you can use these lessons and make it your own.

Because ultimately that's the point. If you're neurodivergent, neuroqueer, neurospicy, or neurospiky, ultimately you need to find or create your own community where your quirks, interests, info-dumps, and foibles are not just tolerated; they are loved. We all must navigate neurotypical people, but it isn't their world, it's just their macro-culture, and we must abide within it. To do so most effectively—whether on a blind date, at a job interview, or at a co-worker's wedding—you need to know "the code." But "the code" is not the be-all end-all of socializing; it is a piece of the puzzle, an approach to connecting, a common set of tools and skills. When I explained the concept of this book to my neurodivergent colleague Emily, she said that my metaphor feels like ketchup to her. Ketchup is the condiment of the macro-culture; it's everywhere. But she doesn't like it very much; she prefers more exotic sauces. As she's gotten older, she has come to grips with the fact that sometimes ketchup is her only option, and she must make do. She doesn't abandon

The neurotypical "code" is no better or worse than whatever guides your neurodivergence. But we cannot deny that the neurotypical "code" has value. We can fight that reality, or we can put on our thinking caps and embrace the challenge of trying to debug as much of their behavioral Linux as possible. Knowledge is power, after all, and aren't we good at knowledge? So come join me! Pull up a beanbag (or a standing desk), put on your noise-cancelling headphones, get your comfiest nerdy hoodie (mine currently reads: "Storm Trooper Target Practice" and there's not a blaster mark on me LOL), and we'll learn this together.

And to that kid who didn't get to go up on the slide that day, I hope this book makes its way into your hands. I hope that life has been kind to you. I hope that you debugged "the code" and navigated the world with grace, humility, and compassion. Because once you've been on the outside, you never forget the isolation and loneliness. Many neurodivergent people are ostracized, which is why my therapy practice exists. Some people harden their hearts after they're hurt and use that pain to hurt others. I can't begrudge you that choice, but it's not the only way. Many of us, perhaps even most of us, use our past pain as a reason to open doors to others and welcome them in, making the world a kinder and more transparent place. Because since I had to go through the pain of being socially excluded without an understanding of what happened or why, I will do whatever is in my power to keep you from feeling such pain. If nothing else, you can use this book as a guide to navigate these painful interpersonal situations, should (OK, *when*) they arise.

And if this book helps anyone—including you—do that, then I'll be happy.

—MJZ

CHAPTER 1
Introduction

Pop quiz, hotshot. (Yet another pop culture reference, in this case the classic popcorn movie *Speed* with Keanu Reeves and Sandra Bullock. Be warned; there are many more coming.)

Why do we go to school?

Simple question, right? You go to school to learn. ABC, 123, state capitols, the periodic table, C++, and all that jazz (including, perhaps, learning jazz...if your school district hasn't cut music yet to fund another "Assistant Vice Principal of Strategic Planning" in the district office). You do your 13 years (at least) of hard time, they stick a cap and gown on your head, shove a diploma in your hand, and send you off into the world or work.

So...Why do we go to work?

Because of capitalism! You go to work to make money. You go to work to put a roof over your head, food on the table, and gas in the car. You strive towards turning your education into something tangible and productive so you can contribute positively to the world. After 50 years or so (a concept that may age poorly if we're still reading this book in twenty years), you turn in your work ID, retire, and start taking increasingly long trips to Florida.

At least, that's how it used to be.

Traditionally, American education has focused on what we call "vertical in the thirteen years that we have them. Imagine each student in a classroom carrying a large bucket to be filled with knowledge; teachers have traditionally tried to pack that bucket with all the information that they can through didactic instruction (Reese, 2011). Thus, the students become informed citizens and, hopefully, productive members of society based on what we taught them. However, teacher are no longer the only meaningful sources of information, with the rise of social media, search engines, AI, ChatGPT, and more. If more people have more knowledge, then the differentiator is what one can *do* with what they know, not whether they know it in the first place. In order to show this "lateral learning," we need to have the interpersonal skills to communicate effectively and the intrapersonal skills necessary to manage ourselves (Kopnina, 2020). Increasingly, the research is showing us that effective teaching stems from shifting our focus to different kinds of learning to fully engage our students and help them develop as *people*, not just repositories of information (Kopnina, 2020).

To meet those shifting needs, there is an increased focus on mental health in schools that certainly wasn't there when I was a kid. You see Social-Emotional Learning (SEL) classes, schoolwide climate initiatives, and Diversity Equity and Inclusion (DEI) programs that honor the unique experiences of all varieties of people in the community (Dahunsi, Robinson, Parks, & Nittrouer, 2024). In the classroom there are more independent projects and project-based-learning (PBL) activities that involve the *application* of knowledge rather than just regurgitation. And these are all excellent trends which are great to see, because research overwhelmingly shows that this is how kids learn best, and how they like to learn (Olive, McCullick, Tomporowski, Gaudreault, & Simonton, 2020). The best practices in neurodivergent education are the best practices in education overall, whether in the classroom (Robinson, Shore, & Enersen, 2021) or in the office (Schlegler, 2022; Rao & Polepeddi, 2019).

We're also seeing these shifts in the workplace. Yes, many of us are overworked and underpaid, but there are glimmers of healthier jobs out there with better understanding of the *human* part of Human Resources. Many places let you work at least partially from home, or come in only for the most important meetings. I'm even seeing HR departments adapt IEP-style (Individualized Education Plan) menus of accommodations for employees, from different kinds of office space to voice-to-text apparatuses to allowing for different types of interviewing to opting out of the dreaded team-building activities (Rao & Polepeddi, 2019).

This stuff used to be done quietly, even off the books, but it's becoming more mainstream and acceptable. I was a guest on the "Gen Z at Work" podcast in 2024 and we talked about whether Gen Z is the most neurodivergent generation ever; I suggested that they were the most openly neurodivergent generation because they grew up in a society that allowed for their needs to be out in the open, whereas previous generations were asked to keep their diagnoses quiet. The best thing about Gen Z is that they were raised in a world where they didn't just ask for what they deserve, they expected it, and are not afraid to demand change. They were raised to be aware of their needs and the steps within society's systems to get those needs met. This is a generation who doesn't quietly whisper "therapy" when people ask them why they were late to school; this is a generation who livestreams their therapy sessions over Twitch. And, honestly, I think that we're all better for it. When one person says what they need, it becomes easier for other people to do so as well; soon we reach a critical mass and real change occurs.

The changes are happening everywhere! The internet has made it much easier to go out on your own to start a company (or companies! Hi, Etsy!) and thus make your own rules and standards. The gig economy allows people to opt out of traditional employment structures and craft professional mosaics that work for them. Big companies have been forced to adapt to keep pace, and those changes are largely for good. Fortune 500 Companies have groups for working parents, neurodivergent employees, and other social identity supports called ERGs (Employee Resource Groups) (Rodriguez, 2021). They help create a personal community within the broader one, and the created community is by choice. The micro-culture is shared within the broader company, providing everyone with best practices for effective problem-solving, strategic communication, and empathy.

Why are these shifts happening at school and at work? Because the powers-that-be are finally coming around to the idea that you don't have just students and workers, you have *people, individual* personalities with strengths, weaknesses, limitations, dreams, blind spots, identities, and neurodivergences. And those differences need programs that don't treat everyone monolithically; we have to honor the uniqueness of people in order to best serve them. Part of honoring that uniqueness is identifying when people need to be taught soft skills (like socializing, self-care, and emotional regulation) at school and work in addition to the overt skills that one needs to do their job. For example, one of the car repair shops by me in northern New Jersey recently asked me to come in and do a training for their staff on effective communication with customers. The staff were correctly identifying the problems with the customers' cars, but they were communicating those diagnoses in a way that felt condescending to the customers, which was leading to bad reviews online and an unhappy workforce. Their manager said to me, "Dr. Matt, all these guys can change a tire and fix a fan belt, but if they piss people off, then we'll all be outta work." I couldn't have said it better myself, and I'm not even a car guy.

Research overwhelmingly shows that organizations that meaningfully invest in the social and mental health of their employees (the pizza parties just aren't going to cut it anymore, sorry) perform better, retain more people, have more engaged communities, and attract higher quality workers to the team (Rodriguez, 2021; de Oliveira, Saka, Bone, & Jacobs, 2023). Schools that invest in SEL (social emotional learning) programs show similar improvement in student and staff wellness, including retention of good personnel (Gueldner, Feuerborn, & Merrell, 2020) and higher academic success (Hart, DiPerna, Lei, & Cheng, 2020). And since turnover is one of the biggest causes of "sunk costs" within any organization, these programs are worthwhile to invest in to protect the culture and the bottom line (Bilan, Mishchuk, Roshchyk, & Joshi, 2020).

With such data publicly available, you'd think that more organizations would make those soft skill investments. The programs not only save money, but they also increase profit for the organization in the long run (Bilan, et al., 2020). Alas, many of the people who hold the power to make those changes believe that "nobody wants to work" and "you can pull yourself up by your bootstraps" and "mental illness was created by TikTok." (This last one is an actual quote from a real administrator in a town with a highly rated school system. I nearly died on my feet when I heard it.) Excuses abound for why we should not invest in developing the soft skills of students and employees, especially a commonly-held belief amongst administrators that the world isn't changing all that much and "the good ol' ways" remain enough. And if you're looking for reasons that your preferred system is working, you're going to find them, especially when comparing that system with something like SEL, which is admittedly challenging to measure effectively. Personally, I see that it is a good investment in the schools and organizations that I work with, but if we need to convince more people to make this happen, so be it. Clearly, we need more help.

adequately support us. There's too much red tape, infrastructure, and inconsistency (and ignorance—can't forget that). We can and must agitate for change, but as the expression goes, "Pray for rain but dig a well while you do." The best soft skills work is done within oneself because it is highly personal in nature. It is an investment in yourself. We have to make our own way in this world, which means that we need to customize evidence-based strategies for each person and their unique needs, and provide work that understands and supports this. But how do you do it? That's probably why you bought this book! (Or borrowed it from your local library, which I wholeheartedly endorse).

I'm lucky in my career for the chance to give a lot of different talks to teachers. I come from a family of teachers, and I've always admired the profession. In another universe, I think that I'd be an amazing high school history teacher and JV soccer coach (Oh wait, I'm just copying what my friend Adam already does…maybe theoretical teacher me would direct the musical instead). While I don't have the training that teachers do, I try to maintain a fluency in educational lingo so I can amplify the amazing work that teachers are already doing. I leverage the things that I know are true in the overlap between mental health and productivity, including the science of learning, the psychology of how to engage people, and effective strategies on increasing motivation to get our people where we want them to go personally and professionally. Thankfully, those strategies are remarkably similar between school and the workplace (Rodriguez, 2021). Traditional, didactic learning is a necessary piece of the puzzle to raise the knowledge base of our audience, but it doesn't produce the engagement that we want for meaningful learning and achievement (Reese, 2011). It is not so much *what* we teach as *how* we teach it, and how our audiences, student or professional. Those are the best approaches to making meaningful change.

In the therapy space, didactic learning is only a small part of what the intervention ultimately entails. For example, I can tell you what a panic attack is; I can tell you what your sympathetic nervous system is doing, how anxiety functions in the brain, and why being in an elevator sometimes makes you feel like you're having a heart attack. But if you've had a panic attack, knowing exactly what it *is* only goes so far towards helping you get over the attack and *feel* better. You need intentional and strategic guided practice with the skills needed to navigate challenging situations; otherwise, it's all just theory. Theory is helpful, but it will never be as helpful as repetitions of the skill itself. I've had two panic attacks in my life, and in both cases knowing what was happening to me only helped me feel a little bit better, as I struggled to remind myself that I wasn't actually dying. The second panic attack thankfully went a little bit better than the first, because I had the experience of regulating myself through the first one.

Should I tell that story? Of course I should! I had my first panic attack during the final exam for my Philosophy 101 class at Wake Forest University, after pulling an all-nighter trying to study for it and my Biology 101 final, which of course were both on the same time. Suddenly, I felt like I couldn't breathe properly, the lights in the classroom were too bright, and my clothes felt like iron bands across my chest. I staggered out of the classroom to try and get my hyperventilation and flop sweat under control, and I ended up sitting under the water fountain to do so. I heard someone clearing their throat, and I looked up to see my professor standing there. Instead of offering basic human empathy, he coolly asked me if I was *entirely* sure that I wasn't faking it. That's when I knew he had never had a panic attack himself. I stammered that I needed a minute, and he left me alone. (I gave that class a terrible rating. He had tenure, so it didn't change anything, but it sure as heck made me feel better, even though he gave me a C-).

The most important thing in intervention is the experience of recovery. We want to create an engaging process where people experience not only the stressor (life does plenty of that on its own), but the *recovery* from that stressor. That's what the best education is, not telling someone that they'll feel and do better next time after flubbing a note in choir, but making sure that they practice hitting that note so much that the physical experience of prior success serves to carry them through towards accomplishing their goal. We wouldn't ask someone to tackle a chemistry lab without instruction around what chemistry is, how to work within its parameters, and what to do when something goes catastrophically wrong (I don't know about you, but I always find the eyewash station when I visit a school with a science lab). A chemistry lab with no guidance is all challenge and no skill-building, offering no personal pathways toward recovery from the stressors of not knowing what to do we shouldn't be surprised when it fails.

Telling someone to "go make friends" without giving them the confidence and competence to do so is similarly a fool's errand: we are setting them up to fail. Though we don't go to school or work primarily to make friends (Homer Simpson voice: "$20 can buy many friends!"), no one would say that having healthy relationships makes those places worse. You probably remember your favorite co-workers with a lot more fondness than the actual job you were there to do. Like-minded people (like in ERGs) create community and targeted support because people do better when they don't feel alone (Sullivan & Bendell, 2023). Organizations are putting emphasis on healthy workplace social dynamics and creating community, which is great in theory. But the best of intentions can fail in potentially dangerous ways if we push people to engage without the skills to do so comfortably and effectively. Not everyone starts from the same place with the same competence and confidence—that's to be expected. But if we meet each person with skills, structure, and practice opportunities, we can expect better results and happier people: they will know what to do and how to do it.

How do we accomplish this goal and avoid the situation with the boys on the slide that I mentioned above in the prologue? The "code" is real, after all, even if we can't write it down (though if someone from the neurotypical community would leak it to me, I think it would be an immediate best-seller). We have to find a way to make the process of socializing objective, concrete, practical, and intentional, using systems, lessons, and interventions that are designed to help people develop social skills in a way that they can use. That's where I parachute in to help organizations: the world of social-emotional learning (SEL). Social-emotional learning is a wonderful thing—*when it's done right*—because it represents a major shift in how we feel about the "soft skills" needed to survive.

I was once speaking to a public-school administrator, advocating for increased social-emotional programming in their school. I wasn't trying to sell him anything, I was simply suggesting that they use one study periods per week as an SEL instructional session. And with no small amount of condescension, he said to me, "Well, they'll just learn it organically, they'll be fine. You know, I learned that stuff, and you did too, of course, and most people will figure it out on their own if we just let them. We can't baby them and it's not our job to help them make friends. So, I don't see the point of making SEL a priority."

Pause for a moment and imagine if we taught math that way, just assuming kids would figure it out. Do division signs just speak to you? Do fractals share their secrets willingly? Do you think that you can just look at a calculus book and figure out how to do those equations? Some kids can: many of them are my clients; but most people cannot. We have to consider teaching social skills from the lens that everyone can benefit from instruction on how to interact more effectively and positively. Some people get these skills naturally and use them with little need for instruction; that's great for those people! But we cannot avoid or ignore those of us who need specific, repeated instruction on how to get along with others. If we do, we risk falling into the trap of survivorship bias, where we assume that those who came out of our programs successfully did so because of our instruction, not because of something that they already had (like personality) or something outside of our control (like luck) (Shermer, 2014). But organizations use this kind of thinking all the time to justify not investing in skill-building.

To repeat the example that I actually used in this conversation, imagine if we taught driver's education the way this administrator would have our kids learn social skills. *Kids see other people driving, they've seen movies (you, too, can drive like Vin Diesel! just watch all the "Fast and Furious" movies) and they've heard their peers share driving tips and tricks; today's kids don't need driving instruction; they'll just figure it out.* If that was true, we would see a 1000-fold increase in car fatalities, and nobody wants that. Kids must be taught how to drive so they can avoid danger and develop coping strategies and skills: it would be irresponsible to do otherwise. The administrator feebly sputtered that it wasn't a fair analogy.

No one has to learn to drive, but we all must learn to manage being around other people. Either way, driver's education is proof that codifying something that "everyone knows" is effective at translating that information effectively and efficiently for lots of different people with different experiences, skill levels, and motivations.

Yes, people (and especially kids) are going to learn social and emotional skills from being around peers, from streaming services and movies, and from social media. But not all those lessons are good ones, or generalizable, or even effective. So, it behooves all of us to teach our kids the best social skills overtly and intentionally. We want to give people the language to communicate about their feelings, the skills to manage them, and the awareness of when to get extra help. Having people with better social and emotional skills creates better cultures, and better cultures create much healthier organizations across the board.

To me that feels like good practice, and I'm not alone: the rise of SEL programs in many schools, workplaces, and other organizations corroborates it. But there's a problem: many social and emotional learning programs are built using a traditional "vertical learning" model of education: you come in, sit down, do a lesson, talk about feelings, do worksheets, and move on. There can be good content and certainly good intention in such lessons, but it's not enough. People need to be engaged with the content and see meaningful connection to their own life for the lessons to be effective. One of the biggest mistakes in the implementation of these programs is to assume that people "should just want to" learn these things instinctively. There is no instinct to accept dry facts being shoved down our throats. Educators have to make these ideas authentically meaningful and individually accessible.

Returning to the driver's education example from above, I had a client who had an eidetic memory. He literally memorized the driver's manual for his state (I remember him saying, "There's a typo on page 46 when they talk about turn signals; it's not *tarn* signals"). Having memorized the manual, you'd think that he would be perfectly prepared to ace the driving test, right? Not so. He stalled the car in the starting box because he had never actually practiced starting a car before. And after he failed the test, he quit! He no longer saw the point of learning how to drive if it wasn't something based on mastering the rules. The process was no longer meaningful to him.

Driving didn't re-emerge as a priority for him until he joined a local LARP (live action role-play) group and needed independent transportation to get to events (have you ever tried to take a bus dressed as a Western Orc? I wouldn't recommend it). This time I suggested that he handle things differently. He should physically get behind the wheel of a car for actual driving practice; it is not a skill that can be learned theoretically. And *doing* that was difficult! It involved trying, failing, learning, and adapting. When he finally finished the process, with his license and its obligatory terrible photo, he was proud that he had done the work of developing physical skills, not just downloading what he was "supposed to" know. Social skills are the same way: if you memorize a script or rigid rules about what one is supposed to say, you will be much less able to adapt to your surroundings and translate knowledge into effective communication.

With those examples in mind, I am arguing for a continued shift in SEL toward a more experiential learning model at school and at work, for all people (but especially neurodivergent folks). Knowing what to do is important but knowing how to do it is even more important. "The code" is not just what to say, but how and when to say it. Sometimes those rules are clear, but far too often they're unspoken or communicated poorly. We need to give kids the opportunity to get meaningful practice where the stakes are lower, and the feedback is built-in and positive. The real world does not work with such protections, and so preparation is required. There's a reason most kids practice driving in parking lots and on back roads. I don't want their first driving lesson on I-95 at rush hour any more than I want your first difficult conversation to be when you're fighting to keep your job against a bullying supervisor. Practice matters. Make errors in training, where it's safe, before you go tearing off into the challenging real world.

For things to work in the real world, advice must come from a real place, so the following chapters have examples from my clinical practice and speaking engagements, as well as a guide on how to implement these skills and the programs that supported their growth. I am a clinical psychologist, so confidentiality is critically important; my stories are based on real clients, but identifying information has been changed. Whenever possible, I've gotten permission from the people involved to extrapolate from their stories.

This book has examples of interventions and strategies that work to develop the skills that people need. These examples are applicable and accessible in the real world. Most importantly, these techniques are viable because people actually *do* them in the lessons. They're getting meaningful repetition to build these skills, whether on the bus to softball, in the locker room at the YMCA, chatting with the administrative assistant at work, getting your first roommate, or infinite other possibilities. Social and emotional learning is not something that we can just *tell* people; our brains don't work like that. Being a social person, especially in the modern era, is far too complex to learn using only verbal instruction. You'll never crack "the code" that way.

In my therapy practice, I might have a session or two with a client working on social skills, after which they start to feel confident and prepared; so, they go out and try them at a party or in the cafeteria or on the bus. When they are out in the real world, the opportunities to implement the skills come fast and furious (cue Vin Diesel talking about "family"), they get stressed and don't perform very well, and they start to doubt themselves. Their self-talk is, "if I was any good at this, I wouldn't struggle at it." Failing at something hurts, *especially* something so important. But to be good at anything, we have to accept starting our development from wherever we are, which if (ever so painfully) often at the beginner stages.

The reality is that trying and failing easily leads to missing important context, because therapy (or SEL classes) can never meaningfully approximate the pace and complexity of the real world. While we can adjust to this pace as best as we can, there will always be a lag between practice and performance. If we acknowledge that reality, then we can prepare for it. The unfortunate stakes of existing in the real world, with the judgmental way that people can be and the social milieu that shapes peer relationships, means our people might have only one or two shots to get it right. We need to set them up for favorite outcomes before a situation demands that you succeed or suffer the consequences.

I want my people to come to social environments with as many skills and as much awareness as possible. I will repeat this phrase several times throughout this book: the fundamental reason that we work hard at SEL is that we want people to have competence and confidence. Competence is important because they need to know what to do, how to do it, and when to use the many different tools in their toolbox, which is their own way to hack "the code". Confidence is important because it affirms that the tools have worked, that they have found ways to use them effectively by making them their own. If you are doing SEL work in your school, office, or therapy practice, you must be sure that what you're doing is building authentic confidence and competence that can be used when the stakes are highest. If you're not, you need a new plan.

The interventions that we'll be going through are designed to address the core components of social and emotional skills. As things move along, the instructions for these activities will be illustrated with case examples. Seeing how these techniques play out in real time with real folks will help you understand our goals and how it works, while also highlighting my own errors so you don't have to troubleshoot as much as I did. Failing and struggling is a real part of this process, so please don't give up too quickly if things are hard. The chapters may contain a little bit of neuropsychology because, as you know, I am a brain nerd. Additionally, I will cite the concepts that I talk about in this book. Even if this isn't formal academic writing, it's important that you know where these ideas come from.

You can use this book as an entire treatise, or you can use just the chapters that work for you. My goal is that you gain more skills and more knowledge than you had when you picked up this book, as well as more confidence and competence. I want you to have your own "code" to support you personally, as you confront "the code" of the real world, from Wall Street to Wayside School.

Are you ready? Trick question! (Because this is a book and I can't hear you, though I'm sure you'll let me know on social media.) Let's jump in anyway.

Chapter 2
Background for
Social-Emotional Learning (SEL)

This is probably the graphic I use the most often in all my talks. Sharing this image with you makes me feel like I'm introducing an old friend.

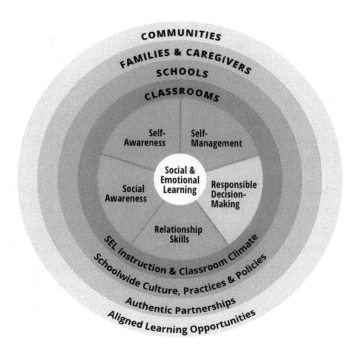

If we're going to talk about social emotional learning (SEL), it's vital to define it clearly. It may seem obvious, but it resists a clear definition because it is a broad topic. People call social and emotional skills different things, and they wouldn't be wrong, per se, because the variety of skills are inherently interrelated. In the interest of clarity and collaborative purpose, a shared definition will give us the best chance to work towards the same goals. Social-Emotional Learning is the process by which we learn, understand, and apply the skills, knowledge, and perspectives necessary to interact with other people in a prosocial manner (CASEL, 2018). OK? Good. I feel that one more definition seems appropriate.

What exactly is "prosocial?" The opposite of antisocial? Well, in a way. Prosocial behavior is intentionally designed to help other people and society, ideally creating a net benefit for both the person doing the act and the person receiving it (Wittek & Bekkers, 2015). Being prosocial is not defaulting to being *nice*. It may include being nice, but prosocial behavior is not primarily about good manners. It may involve uncomfortable conversations, because true prosocial behavior seeks to find the best outcome in a situation for everyone involved, *including yourself.* Being nice focuses only on other people. And while being nice may be a lovely idea, it often ends with nice people getting stepped all over while only the other people get their needs met. On the other hand, being selfish means that only *you* get what you want, which isn't helpful either (socially, at least: we get way too much reinforcement in this country for the idea that "I got mine!" is the only way to be).

Ergo, "prosocial" is a better word for a better approach. "Prosocial" covers a far wider range of behaviors and strategies that lead to better outcomes for all of us (Wittek & Bekkers, 2015). My favorite way to demonstrate the difference between "prosocial" and "nice" is an activity I use when I'm giving a talk. I explain the definitions and then illustrate the difference by picking someone at random who is drinking from a coffee cup or water bottle. I walk up to them, smile, introduce myself, and ask if I can take their drink.

The moment is always interesting, because you can see the competing impulses at play: it's nice to give your drink to someone, on the other hand, it's your drink and you brought it and why would you let someone just take it? People hem and haw, but usually end up giving me their drink even if they don't want to (unless I'm speaking in New York City, Philadelphia, New Jersey, or Boston, where social norms tend to be more on the, shall we say, *assertive* side). Why do they give it up? Because we are all trained to be nice.

Then I ask the person if they *wanted* to give me their drink. They usually blush and then haltingly explain that, no, they didn't. It's a great way to demonstrate the difference between nice and prosocial, because being nice sometimes means that you don't get what you want, but being prosocial allows you to express your own needs. I then give them their drink back and repeat the exercise. Usually, people now feel empowered enough to choose the prosocial response the second time around, and kindly say "no thank you".

So, if I ever ask you for your coffee cup, feel free to say no. I won't be offended, I promise. I don't need your coffee. I'm a very capable person; I can get my own. Really! Though, if you're buying, I'll take a large, iced coffee with milk and two sugars. Thanks.

One of the reasons that neurodivergent people, and especially Autistic people, are labeled "rude" is because they tend to choose prosocial responses, rather than defaulting to being nice (the traditional neurotypical response because of socialization) (Wittek & Bekkers, 2015). When I ask an Autistic person if I can have their drink, I know that their response is more likely to come from an authentic place because they're wired to consider their own needs as a priority, which is good, and probably healthier. Autistic people just need to figure out how to deliver those responses in a way that ruffles fewer feathers, because the effectiveness of our response depends, at least in part, on how it is delivered. Neurodivergent people in general tend to focus on their motivation for action—how *they* feel—rather than the impact—how it makes the recipient feel (i.e., "I'm not at fault because I didn't want to share my water! I'm thirsty and there's a water cooler over there for you, why should you just get to take my water?"). There is a middle ground to being prosocial where you're taking care of everyone's business without being (too) blunt.

Because being prosocial is important, let's talk about the skills that we need to get there. The CASEL group (www.casel.org) identifies five major components of social emotional learning. They are self-awareness, self-management, social awareness, relationship skills and responsible decision making. Each one of those components has its own skills and inherent aspects. You will notice that they overlap significantly.

Self-Awareness

The first SEL skill is self-awareness. Self-awareness is a combination of the various pieces of our self and understanding how we respond to the different things we experience in the world (Cain, 2020). How we interact with the world shapes how it responds to us, and therefore how we respond to ourselves. We want to have enough self-awareness so we're not flying blind, but not so much that we're just navel gazing. Developing self-awareness determines what works for you in pursuit of your specific goals. We're allowed to find our own paths towards success in different fields and define what that success is going to look like. But we must give ourselves the time to figure out what exactly we like and dislike as we engage the various arenas of life in the world.

Some examples:

○ If you're afraid of clowns (like me!!), then Halloween is probably tough for you.

○ If you love spicy food, then you're going to be drawn to certain restaurants and not others (looking at you, Cracker Barrel).

○ If you can't stand workout culture, then you're probably going to be unhappy doing CrossFit or going to a gym.

○ My mom has misophonia and cannot handle people chewing gum, so she's very thoughtful about where she sits on planes, in movie theaters, and basically anywhere there are people.

None of these things are inherently good or bad; every possible choice works for many other people. It might feel that there are some choices that are "better" for fitting in socially, but choosing your own way sometimes means going against the macro-culture. Take this from a guy who walks by all the weight benches at the gym and heads right for Zumba class. I honestly don't care if the gym bros judge me; that's the workout that works for me, and my needs come first.

We must figure out where *our* needs and likes are within these broad societal constructs. If you don't want to go to the gym and lift weights, then don't go lift weights. Can you go hiking or rock climbing or play ultimate Frisbee? That's all exercise. If you don't want to buy a car, get a bike. If you don't want to go to a Speed Dating event, download one of the various dating apps. You don't have to do what everyone does if it's not your journey, especially if you're neurodivergent. You're not like everyone anyway, so it makes sense that your needs, path, likes, and dislikes are different. But unless you take the time to figure out what *your* needs are, you might default repeatedly into following along with the macro-culture, even if it isn't meeting your needs and thus is failing to make you happy.

While it might seem paradoxical, connecting with others starts with connecting with yourself. To effectively connect with others, you must first have a sense of your strengths and your weaknesses, your likes and dislikes, your triggers and quirks, your areas of rigidity, your values and areas of potential growth. All these things matter a great deal while navigating the world and its various social iterations. You must understand and organize the sometimes disparate pieces of yourself to get into the best situations, to connect with others, to survive. And we've built a society where most people, especially kids, don't have that time.

The amount of free time that kids get in schools has decreased drastically, by about 50% over the last 10 years (Hodges, Centeio, & Morgan, 2022); it has, of course, largely been replaced with more classwork and academic content. With so much less free time, kids struggle to use it effectively. They don't understand unstructured time or how to be bored, which causes them to panic when they're faced with it, which leads to conflict with teachers, parents, and coaches. And how do those adults respond? Well, they tend to blame the free time as the problem and seek to diminish it further, which exacerbates the problem of kids knowing how to use it in the first place; it's become a vicious cycle (Hodges, et al., 2022).

Down time and unstructured time at school and work is psychologically beneficial (Hodges, et al., 2022), as well as being a crucible for burgeoning social development (Dirzyte, Patapas, & Perminas, 2022). Those unstructured spaces (the playground, the water cooler, the parking lot, etc.) are traditionally where kids develop the awareness and skills to understand themselves in relation to others. (Remember the administrator that said that kids "would just learn social skills on the playground?" Although he was right about the playground being a common place for social-emotional learning, his point was destroyed by the fact that he was actively working to diminish its role in the school setting by cutting recess by 75% for middle schoolers).

Kids who don't use free time become adults who can't use free time. Developmental skills need to be practiced or they become functionally vestigial (Dirzyte, et al., 2022); free time is no different. I have a distinct memory of walking across the quad in college and realizing that, for the first time in my life, I was completely in charge of how I used the rest of my day's free time. I ran back to the dorm and played *Halo* (XBox video game) with my hallmates for a while¬ and then studied for my French exam later on. Because my parents had allowed me to have free time as a kid, so I was proficient at using it effectively. If you have a bunch of free time, you're going to choose the activities that feel best to you, whether that is playing the guitar or doing video games or going for a run or making sidewalk chalk art. You need to have the time to learn these things and connect with these values. The more you learn about the activities that bring you joy, the more you can ultimately find people and communities to share values with.

What exactly are values? It's a term that you hear a lot in this kind of book, and it makes sense to move forward with a shared definition, otherwise the term is wishy-washy enough to devolve into nothingness. Values are the beliefs and attitudes that people have in their relationship with others (Shell, 2021). They start internally as principles and are expressed outwardly in the world as they guide our interactions, communication, and self-reflection (Kiamos & Lumme, 2020). Our values shape not only who we are internally in how we see ourselves but how we are seen by our peers and community.

When I do exercises with clients about finding their values, I often refer to a classic therapy exercise, "the miracle question." The Miracle Question is often associated with Solutions-Focused Therapy, but it can be used in any modality, including developing self-awareness (Neipp, Beyebach, Sanchez-Prada, & Delgado Álvarez, 2021). In this exercise, you describe the world as it would be if you woke up and a miracle had occurred overnight that made the world exactly what you'd want it to be. The therapist then asks you to describe that world in detail. It may seem silly at first, and the first few answers you give might be simply surface-level, capitalism fantasy porn: a big house, a nice car, lots of money in the bank, etc. The therapist might look at you, expecting more, and you simply raise an eyebrow, as if to say, "And this is helping me...how?"

Now, of course, those materialistic things are nice and reflect a deeper process: the desire for comfort. Who wouldn't want to be more comfortable? Life is hard!! And then you follow your fantasy: what would you use the money for? If you had to save some, who (or what) would you save it for? If you had to donate some, which are your favorite charities? The Red Cross? Goodwill? Meals on Wheels? 11th Hour Animal Rescue? The Jimmy Fund? Now we're getting into it, because the organizations that we would give our fictitious money to reveal our actual values.

You can go even deeper in this exercise. If you lived in a big house, would you be the only house on the block? No? Who else would live there? Why? While not everyone seeks the same kind of community, everyone wants their favorite people around. Who cares if it's not practical? This is a miracle universe! Additionally, a surprising number of people would choose to work in their perfect world, and the tasks they choose reveal a lot about their values. You find CEOs saying that they'd be high school math teachers; you find teachers wanting to be philanthropists. One client I worked with sheepishly said that all he's ever really wanted to do is drive a big rig truck cross-country (which of course is a big 10-4 from me). The answers are all inside us, but our practical lives get in the way of us reaching them. When we do this kind of exercise, our answers lead us to our values and start to shift our behavior towards our real self.

Getting to know ourselves through talk about self-awareness starts with this kind of self-inventory. Another good way to get to know yourself is through traditional icebreaker questions (I know, you hate small talk, but trust me, I'm going somewhere good with this). What's your favorite food? What's your favorite ice cream? What's your favorite movie? What's your dream job? What scares you? What's your worst injury? What's the most uninteresting thing about you? (That's a favorite question, and my answer is that I own over three dozen pairs of socks. Super uninteresting!) Who is your favorite celebrity? Who's your celebrity crush? Are they the same? Didn't I see you in the Lin-Manuel Miranda fan club meeting last week (Google him if you're not aware of his lyrical genius on stage and screen)?

All these things matter. They may seem shallow, but they connect to something much more fundamental about who we are. Things that we choose, when we are able to make choices, illustrate our likes and our values. For example, I hate pickles, so you'll never see me willingly eating pickles in any situation. (If you see me eating a pickle, I may be under duress and signaling for help). This opinion may seem arbitrary (it's not: for me, pickles are gross), but it connects to a series of memories, sensory input (ew, slimy), and choices I make to set and hold boundaries. These choices impacted the development of my sense of self, and being aware of my pickle hating anchors me to my own journey. Neurodivergent people tend to hate small talk because it feels inauthentic, but it can connect to something deeper. Self-awareness can point us towards things that we truly like and away from things that we dislike, because we took the time to understand how we really feel about the details.

To use another example, let's say that you want to talk about music. If you lump all music into a broad category, you may not be successful finding music you want to talk about. I love a good Broadway musical (shock again!). Give me *Hamilton*, or *Dear Evan Hansen*, or *Les Mis* all day. Many people don't like Broadway, and that's fine! I just happen to. On the flip side of the music world, I appreciate thrash metal, but it's not my scene. I would be much happier at a Broadway show than I would be at a thrash metal concert. That's not bad or good; it's just how I feel. But we can keep going. I would be happier at a thrash metal concert than I would be at a symphony. I would like an open mic night more than I would like opera. My values, dislikes, and likes all exist on a spectrum, which shows my complexity. Don't you think that other people want to experience that for themselves also?

It isn't just about liking music, per se. It's about understanding your likes and dislikes within the broader construct and connecting to the reasons for those preferences. Why do you like certain music? Is it a sensory thing, guidance from a parent, or perhaps a friend's influence? Was it the song playing in the background during your first make-out session in the back of a Honda Civic (you can call that exact song to mind now that I've brought it up, right)? Is it simply "bad vibes?" It doesn't matter what experiences shape your choices, as long as you take the time to connect the dots. When you understand how you feel about the realm (in this case, music), then you can intentionally put yourself in certain situations and avoid others. When you put yourself in the best situation for you, you're much more likely to enjoy yourself, and that positive energy makes you more likely to meet good people for you and make deeper connections.

These questions and answers take time. And one of the nice things about doing SEL work, whether at school, at work, or in your own therapy, is that it gives you time to not only ask those questions, but to answer them. I would much rather you take the time to sort your thoughts and feelings beforehand than to suddenly construct a values list on the fly. Grab a journal or some Post-It Notes and jot down some ideas: What's your comfort food? Favorite movie on a rainy day?

Least favorite TV show? What would you never put in your tea/coffee? Favorite superhero? Favorite *Real Housewives of CITY*

Self-Management

Self-management is understanding how our bodies react when exposed to certain things, and figuring out how to deal with those responses (Rolls, 2015). I mentioned clowns in the previous example—but to repeat, I am terrified of clowns. When I see a clown, my body gets panicky and sweaty, and I start breathing heavily. My mind races. My body wants to escape but my knees go all wiggly. These are very unpleasant physiological responses! I don't like them very much. But I know that about myself. The feelings can be unpleasant, but at least I am prepared for them, and I have practiced what to do when they arrive (other than sprinting for the exit of the Haunted House).

This is where self-awareness and self-management tie into each other. I know that there are some self-regulation strategies that work well for me, and some that don't work at all. For example, I'm not big into deep breathing. I know it works; I've seen the studies and watched experts use it to great effect. That's awesome for them! But it's not my go-to: I am allowed to feel that way. I do, however, like a guided meditation. My favorite is the "leaves on a stream" meditation. If you YouTube it, you'll find many good examples to see if it works for you. None of these options are inherently right or wrong, good or bad. If you don't like deep breathing don't do deep breathing, but you must find some sort of coping strategy. Nature may abhor a vacuum, but your anxiety loves one, seeking to fill you up with dread, hyperventilating, and fear. Find something that works and do it, even if it just makes things suck less.

Let's continue with deep breathing for a moment. "Take a deep breath" is one of the go-to self-management strategies in schools and workplaces all over the world. Many providers like it because it's simple, can be done anywhere, is relatively easy to do, and costs nothing (I'll give you two guesses which part is their favorite). The science behind the deep breathing is solid: when you take a deep breath, you force your body's sympathetic nervous response to slow down, flood your cells with oxygen, and activate your body's parasympathetic nervous system (Doyle, 2022). Deep breathing is an essential tool in many therapeutic tool kits, from middle schools to plane flights to performance anxiety. Great, right?

Well, if you ask a lot of people, they will say that they don't like deep breathing because it "doesn't work." To explore this claim, I asked more than 60 of my therapy clients about deep breathing, and 70% of them said it's not effective. And I've tried to teach it to many of them! But the science says it works, and lots of smart people agree with those studies, so where's the problem? Are my patients wrong or lying to me? I sure hope not! I think that when people say, "deep breathing doesn't work for me" what they're really saying is "people keep telling me to breathe deeply without telling me how to do it right, so I try it and it doesn't work, which sucks because I don't feel better and I would really like to feel better, so I'll just find another strategy, thank-you-very-much."

We aren't teaching the skill of deep breathing appropriately and we aren't pairing it effectively with real stressors in the world. If we say, "just breathe" without telling people the how or the why of deep breathing as a self-management strategy, it feels like another chapter of "the code" that we can't access. In effect, we're just adding another demand to a person who's already stressed out (like telling someone to "Relax!") and wondering why their distress isn't decreasing. Poorly delivered demands (awkward in tone and lacking in context) make people more upset, not calmer.

To put my money where my mouth is, I'm going to teach you a technique called Square Breathing. Point your right arm up and to the left. Breathe in for a count of four as you move slowly from left to right (1, 2, 3, 4). Then hold that breath as you move down in a straight line (1, 2, 3, 4). Then exhale as you move from right to left (4, 3, 2, 1). Then hold that non-breath for a count of four as you complete the Square. Repeat four times or for four minutes.

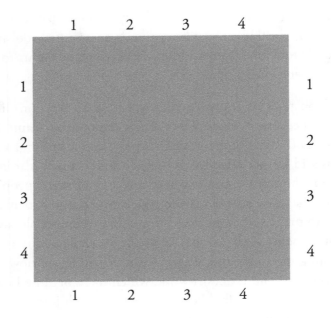

Self-regulation or self-management boils down to being exposed to and practicing many strategies and working on ways to make them personal so they tie into our own needs. If we think of succeeding in life as successfully managing a series of stressors that are increasing in intensity (and don't we all?) we should have a coping strategy or two to meet us at and regulate us through every challenge on the docket. Square Breathing is straightforward, concrete, and applicable to many different types of challenges, though usually on lower intensity stressors. It works biologically by activating our parasympathetic nervous system, and mentally by giving us a personalized way to respond to the "coded" demand to "calm down." The next time you feel anxious or agitated, do four rounds of Square Breathing. You'll feel better. Now you've got a real coping skill! (Only 153 more or so to go for you to feel like this book is worth it, right?).

Knowing the things in life that impact you allows you to proactively seek the positive stimuli and avoid the negatives when possible. Make a list, use an app—or tattoo it on yourself like the guy in the movie *Memento* if you must—but try and keep these thoughts in mind! It is extremely beneficial for us to have at least an idea of what's happening to us and what its impact is, so we can stay plugged in to our emotional reactions and use that knowledge to do better because we are now acting from an informed place.

The tendency in many people is to try to avoid their feelings, because they're unpleasant and dysregulating. But the reality is that we are not very successful at getting things to not happen to us (despite all the salt I threw over my shoulder as a kid). We can be much more successful when we accept that disruptive things are going to happen, and we will likely feel bad when they do. It might sound like giving up, but's not! (It would be a lousy self-help book if "give up" was my pitch!) Accepting the fact that uncomfortable emotions are a part of life means that they cannot surprise you! You know they're coming. If they show up in you, it's no longer "ARRGHHH!"; it's now, "Ah, there's that trigger." Then we attach a coping strategy to the triggers and feel the de-escalation.

You might have noticed earlier that I said that I was running away from clowns in the Haunted House; you might reasonably be wondering why I would go into a Haunted House if I'm afraid of clowns. My friends and I go to a haunted attraction every year at Halloween, and I genuinely love the experience of a good Haunted House (shout out to Eastern State Penitentiary). It's become a great venue to practice my self-regulation strategies because I *know* there's going to be a Clown Room (there's always a Clown Room). If I'm going to do this tradition with my friends, which is something that I value greatly, then I must be prepared. I don't get to choose how I feel, but I do get to choose how I respond. Since I expect the Clown Room, when it inevitably arrives, I work on my Square Breathing and get out of there as fast as possible.

Here's an interesting case example: One of my clients (I'll call him Mick) tends to bite the fleshy ball of his thumb when he feels dysregulated. This is not atypical behavior in the neurodivergent community; there are a lot of nerve endings in that part of your thumb, and it can be re-regulating when they are stimulated. Granted, most people don't stimulate those nerves by biting, but to each their own. But his teachers are freaked out by the biting! Ultimately, they called a meeting and seriously asked me if I thought Mick was a cannibal; I had to laugh because I've seen a lot of things in my career, but cannibalism is not on the list (not yet, anyway). I said, "No, he's trying to release some endorphins because that's an area of his body that has a lot of nerve endings, so there's a lot of stimulation that comes from that behavior. I know it looks weird, but he's honestly trying to help himself stay calm in class." They were floored; it had not occurred to them that Mick was biting himself to achieve a positive goal.

When his teachers saw the behavior as a coping strategy, they explored it from a place of curiosity, not judgement. After doing so, they realized that the biting behavior was almost always occurring when Mick was being asked to write anything more than a paragraph, which completely changed their reaction. Because Mick has dysgraphia, or a Specific Learning Disorder around Writing. The stress of that Disorder was leading to a coping strategy, in this case, the biting behavior. But since the behavior was uncomfortable for his peers and teachers to observe, we got Mick a laptop, so he didn't have to physically write as much. And the behavior rate went down! We also got Mick a fidget spinner, a chair band, and we wrote into his 504 plan that he can chew gum in class. Adding a lot of sensory tools to his toolbox helped him tremendously with his behavior in class. Everyone felt better for us taking the time to understand him, his behavior, and his triggers, and then craft interventions that worked for him.

In psychology, we call this kind of approach *harm reduction* (Logan & Marlatt, 2010). It's foundational to my work and it will be helpful in your self-advocacy. All behavior is communication, from staring out the window (I'm bored; there's an epic squirrel fight in the park) to being late to class (Did you get lost? Again?!) to sending emails to your boss after 10pm (Do I have poor boundaries or is it just bad time management?). Harm reduction says that we can take any behavior and move it increasingly towards safe, prosocial options (Marlatt, Larimer, & Witkiewitz, 2011). If you see these behaviors as coping strategies, it moves us from judging that person to being curious about them; our curiosity breeds empathy. Empathy then puts us in a position to work with them to add more coping skills to their toolbox.

These interventions (internal and external) allowed Mick to better regulate, and thus self-management has increased for him. It must be said that self-management comes from parts of the brain that are often weaker or underdeveloped in different mental health conditions and neurodivergences (Doyle, 2020). A lot of self-management comes from the prefrontal cortex (PFC) in the frontal lobe of the brain, specifically how the PFC uses dopamine (Berger, Kofman, Livneh, & Henik, 2007). This part of the brain is where executive functioning lives. It's where a lot of our coping strategies are, and they're closely tied into the emotional awareness systems that begin in our limbic system and end in that same frontal lobe (Perlman & Pelphrey, 2011).

The fact is that having coping skills is only part of the battle for self-management. They must be developed through practice, and we must build up this part of the brain to do so, because that's where the skills go. A good thing about this is that this part of the brain works like a muscle: the more we use at it, the stronger it gets, so we continue to "pump it up" (cue Arnold Schwarzenegger voice). We must carve out the time and space to work on it so it can get stronger. As you can imagine, this is where many people fall short; there's just not enough time to practice and not enough infrastructure support to do it effectively. The power of therapy and social emotional learning is that they carve out a space to work the brain and flex that skill.

Social Awareness

The next piece of the CASEL framework is social awareness, which includes observing what other people are doing, making theories for why they are acting (or not acting) in a particular way, determining what those behaviors mean for us, and assessing whether we are equipped or willing to have similar behaviors. Social awareness is a particularly challenging piece of development, in terms of social and emotional skills, because our brains are in general much more attentive to ourselves, and this phenomenon is heightened when one is neurodivergent (Hart, et al., 2020). We neurodivergent folks have what the kids call "main character energy" in our own brains.

Sometimes we're not always aware of what other people are doing or why they're doing it. But fundamentally, we are social creatures. There's always an interest in what other people do because we can glean a lot of information from them, even if that information only leads to, "wait, should I be doing that too?" Evolutionarily speaking, that social awareness kept us alive when we were cavemen (y'know, because saber-toothed tiger = run away). That same threat detection wiring exists today, but the threats are far more complex and nuanced (Al-Shawaf & Lewis, 2020). In the modern world, the threat would be that the saber-toothed tiger unfollowed you on Instagram and blocked you on Snapchat while definitely setting up a group chat that you're not involved with. That's certainly a *different* flavor of deadly, but our body doesn't know the difference in threat level (or actuality) without our brain's help to give context.

How do we help people do better in the spaces where they must interact with others? After all, they are surrounded by incoming data, but they may not know how to use it or be willing to do so. The social context clues can inform their behavior to do better, because at worst, you realize that this situation isn't for you, and at best you learn this situation's "code" and can play along. If people feel more empowered, they perform better in social spaces. Then they will feel more connected to their peers and do better at mapping into what other people are doing in various interpersonal situations. Competence breeds confidence, which leads to more experience, which will be more successful because of the previous iterations; we call this a virtuous cycle (as opposed to the vicious one that you're all too familiar with).

A classic example of this social awareness deficit conflict from the gifted community is what happens when you get a substitute teacher in school. The substitute teacher asks the room, "So what were we supposed to do today?" Now, it's the unwritten rule of basically every school in America that whatever you guys are doing in class, the substitute teacher can't know that, especially if it's something like a test or a pop quiz, because if they don't know the assignment, they can't make you do it and you can watch reruns of *Bill Nye the Science Guy* (obviously on the big wheeled-in TV stand!). Everyone else in the room sort of looks around and shrugs their shoulders. But to lean on a bit of a cliché, the gifted kid is going to say, "Well, we were supposed to have a test today" because a question was asked, and he had the answer to it. And while answering questions is often the correct response in a school setting, it wasn't a good choice in this situation. Answering a question that can lead to an unwanted outcome violates the social collective's desire to do less work. The rule to say nothing and preserve the illusion of not having classwork is an unwritten part of that unspoken neurotypical "code". Neurodivergent people are honest—perhaps to a fault! They're going to consistently violate rules like this unless those rules are made explicit to them. In this case, the "code" remained secret, and now all twenty-four kids glare at the gifted student because they must take the test, which means they're mad now, and they'll be expressing that feeling by making the gifted kid run for his live on the playground later.

Perhaps you're the Autistic person at work and your whole department has been sent to a conference. You pick your plenary and breakout sessions, and you attend them vigorously (after all, work is paying you to be there, and you're nothing if not a rule follower). You see some of your colleagues at—gasp!—the pool! Later, when your boss asks how everyone's conference has been, you mention that you haven't seen anyone in the breakout sessions (because they haven't been there, obviously) so they get in trouble for ditching work. Now people are angrily gossiping about you at the water cooler, and your boss is also a bit irked at you. You're not entirely sure why; he asked a question, and you answered it truthfully. Isn't that what you're supposed to do?

There's nothing inherently wrong with telling the truth. But when you have a social situation like these examples, being able to be socially aware is a vital life skill. There are times that the social capital one gains by engaging in a social lie (in these cases, withholding information to protect your peers) outweighs the gains for being forthright, because the cost in both cases is relatively negligible (you'll end up taking the test anyway, with more time to study; it isn't your responsibility that your coworkers are missing professional development opportunities). To know when to engage in group deception effectively, we must develop the ability to "read the room," which is part of the executive functioning suite of behaviors (Doyle, 2020). In the language of this book, reading the room is a key piece of understanding "the code;" some rules must be followed, some rules are guidelines, and some rules can be wholly ignored under the right circumstances. It takes a lot of practice to develop the social awareness to understand which rules are to be followed, which are to be ignored, and why (and to keep your mouth shut if you don't know).

This social awareness will also be helpful at parties, weddings, job interviews, riding the bus, playing Dungeons and Dragons, and whatever other various opportunities come our way, because to be in a community requires us to at least to try to comprehend its rules, even if we don't get them exactly. When we can understand what other people are doing, we can make the choice to model our behavior after theirs (if socially viable and consistent with our values) or stay out of the way. When we don't understand, we can have the skills to ask those questions (professional hint: it's often better to go along in the moment and find out why later, rather than asking during the interaction; asking what's happening can be a red herring to the bosses that something's afoot). In both situations, we increase our awareness of, and our ability to, navigate the world around us. And that's vital, because the world is where the people are, with all the positives and challenges they bring along, and we can't avoid them.

It is much easier to understand our own brains than it is to understand someone else's. We are easily stuck in our own heads; it's much more familiar ground. That's human nature. Evolutionarily speaking, understanding ourselves helped us understand our own needs, which helped us meet those needs and thus keep ourselves alive (Al-Shawaf & Lewis, 2020). The trick is expanding our own awareness to work with other peoples' views. Can we turn our curious minds to other people and connect with what they're doing, how they're feeling, and what they might be thinking? Other people exist, with their thoughts and opinions and quirks and values and feelings, and we cannot pretend they don't. Rather, we embrace the interpersonal chaos out there and try to pay attention to it all because it all contains information, even if we don't use it now (or ever). If you pay enough attention, sooner or later, you'll find *your* people who practice *your* particular brand of chaos.

Another piece of social awareness is understanding that all feelings have value and are appropriate in different situations. It's easy to want to be happy and want to be around other people who are happy, but real life just doesn't work that way. I often wish that it did. Honestly, if we could all just choose to be happy, I would have a different job (if not high school history teacher and theater director, I could open a brewery). I can't tell you how many times people come to therapy and say they want to be happy. Being happy is kind of like being nice. There are times it is appropriate and wonderful. Feeling happy feels pretty good.

But being happy isn't always the right solution, and it's not always possible. Happiness might feel better than some feelings (it's definitely better than a panic attack), but like all feelings, it eventually fades, which can paradoxically make us sadder because now we feel like we had something, and we've lost it.

If someone that you have a crush on comes up to you and asks you on a date, I want you to be able to respond appropriately to those moments. That's absolutely a great time to be happy! But what if you're *too* happy? (I wouldn't suggest throwing yourself a parade). Or, on the other side of things, what if someone that you *don't* have a crush on comes up to you and asks you on a date. You might not be happy about that; you might be curious, or ambivalent, or bemused. Those feelings are all valid, even feelings of disgust or anger that might feel socially inappropriate. But we need to know how to express ourselves *prosocially* to be successful. I want you to be able to navigate *that* situation with the appropriate skills and techniques. There is no "one size fits all" when it comes to interpersonal interactions, but being aware of the situation will help guide us in finding better solutions. When we can consider the needs of the other people involved in the situation, those data will absolutely guide us to a more effective social response (as *The Lonely Island* sang, "and I called my parents right after I was done [with sex]" which is a social and cultural no-no).

Let's consider another example involving feelings and social awareness. If you find yourself at a funeral, being giggly and happy and silly is probably not the right move. I'm not saying that you need to keen, or wail, or make the Tom Cruise "Goose just died in *Top Gun*" face, but there are definitely expected and unexpected emotional reactions in such a setting, with the former being more appropriate. If everyone else is being sad or quiet or reflective, then now is not the time to tell a silly joke. "So, this dead body walks into a bar...". Reading the room, like we talked about before, would indicate what the right solutions would be in those moments, and how to follow "the code." Being socially aware means remembering that other people matter, which ideally should remind us to read the room before we speak, especially if we'd like to keep our proverbial feet out of our mouths.

Neurodivergent people tend to be what psychologists call "context independent" in their actions, which means that their behavior is consistent, regardless of the situation (Sapey-Triomphe, Timmermans, & Wagemans, 2021). Sometimes that's a good thing, like being willing to pay your share of the bill at a dinner, and sometimes it's not, like ratting out your freshman year roommate for drinking underage in college "because the law says you have to be 21 to drink alcohol". Neurotypical people tend to be more context dependent, moving their behavior seamlessly from showing deference to the instructor in class to sending memes mocking them during breaktime (Liang, Runyan, & Fu, 2011). This inconsistency of behavior is often confusing and challenging to neurodivergent people; it's another aspect of the "code." You don't need to do exactly what they are doing to fit in, but finding a middle ground based on awareness of the broader social context isn't a bad idea either.

These examples might seem silly, and they are intentionally a bit hyperbolic to prove my point: the idea is that there are times when any feeling can be appropriate. And there are times when different communication strategies are better, based on the emotional setting that you find yourself in. No feelings are good or bad; they just are. It can be better to think of emotions and emotional situations as comfortable or uncomfortable. No one would blame you for wanting to be comfortable as much as possible. But the reality is, if you'd like to have relationships with people, then you must figure out how to navigate situations that are uncomfortable or challenging. To do so, we must manage our self-awareness and social awareness with prosocial relationship skills.

Relationship Skills

Perhaps because I'm a child of the 80's who grew up in the 90's, I sometimes have trouble taking the word skills'" seriously. Perhaps I've just seen it written as "Skillz" too many times. The word still implies an elevated ability, i.e., "I've got mad skills (z?)" or "No cap, I've got skills for days, FR, my dude." (Please excuse this poor attempt at contemporary slang from a verified Old).

While we all want (need, if you're a gifted kid) to have talent at things, I think that there's too much emphasis on elevated social skills at the expense of consistent, baseline competence. To use a sports metaphor (a risky proposition, given the likely audience for this book), baseball players who hit a lot of homeruns are incredibly valuable. Hitting homeruns is a skill that not many people have, and it is extremely helpful to the team. But homerun hitters also tend to strike out a lot, and tend to less meaningful less meaningful defensive positions, so their very real skill set is counter-balanced by related weakness. A good baseball team needs the other players as well, players who have mastered the basic skills of the game: getting on base (even if it isn't via homerun), catching and throwing the ball accurately, running fast, etc. Neither is better than the other; every skill has a place on the team!

From a social comparison perspective, it is far too easy to worship at the feet of the most socially skillful. For my generation, it was Zach Morris (Saved by the Bell) and Shawn Hunter (Boy Meets World); perhaps you're more of a Maddy Perez (Euphoria), Blair Waldorf (Gossip Girl), Barney Stinson (HIMYM), Don Draper (Mad Men), or Lauren Conrad (The Hills) fan. There are many great examples of social superstars from pop culture. But the archetype never changes: the social superstar navigates any situation with grace, poise, wit, and charm, and exits not only unscathed, but usually with some attractive person's contact information. Even if you're not a pop culture person (and this book is going be tricky for you if you aren't!), think of *that person* from your high school (You may go, Glen Coco, but it'll always be Regina George), the person who was the popular Alpha and set the social pace for the year. I guarantee you that a person's name and face immediately flashed into your brain. You may not have even participated in the social hierarchy (as my editor pointed out to me), and thus not necessarily wanted what that person had, but humans are social creatures, and we're wired to be on the lookout for social ease because those are people who tend to have enhanced value within their systems. Being around someone who is an Alpha means you're near the top of the food chain; you can feast on whatever That Person doesn't choose to eat, enhancing your chance of survival.

That Person is a strong avatar of interpersonal giftedness, one of the examples in Howard Gardner's Theory of Multiple Intelligences (2021). Interpersonal giftedness is a fine aspirational goal, but our focus will be on building the more basic, granular skills, which will allow us to develop the two keys to cracking "the code": confidence and competence. Having more competence in socializing allows us to make more friends, which gives us confidence. This confidence then leads us into situations that will organically call for us to develop higher-level skills (increased confidence) and give us many opportunities to practice. Like all skills, social skills are not a binary proposition; they exist on a continuum from very socially adept to…well, awkward: you know the low end when you see it (in my case, when I am inevitably seated next to an awkward person on a long flight).

What are basic relationship skills? There will be many detailed examples throughout the book, but I'm going to list the Core Four:

- Active Listening
- Asking Good Follow-up Questions
- Seeking Connection
- Metacommunication.

Active Listening

Boy did active listening get a bad rep in the 90s! It was mocked and satirized to death (if memes had existed then, it certainly would have been a popular topic). But at its core, active listening is a vital relationship skill. When you're listening to someone, it's so important to think about how you like to be listened to. Do you like a lot of non-verbal indicators of the other person paying attention to you? Or are you comfortable with someone staring at their phone, giving you the occasional "uh-huh" as you talk? Most of us would choose the former when we're talking, but easily default to the latter when we aren't the star of the show.

When you are listening, it is important to try to stay present. You may have thoughts about what you want to say next, or what is happening later, or what happened at work that morning; but you can make space for those thoughts by reminding yourself that your time will come to talk. Listening to what others say may even enhance the things that you want to say: conversation is a dialogue, not a monologue (I know, that's hard for many of us). Monologuing is frowned upon, even if few people come out and say that explicitly. The neurotypical social "code" dictates that everyone gets a turn in a group conversation, even if the frequency and duration of those turns feels capricious to you. And to make sure that everyone gets a turn, you can practice listening and waiting for your turn.

Asking Good Follow-up Questions (Nailed the transition!)

I've been doing improvisational acting (or improv, those games that they play on *Whose Line is it Anyway?*) for 30 years, and it's one of my favorite things to do (see Chapter 8). I've done a TEDx talk on how to live life through the rules of improv, using the #1 improv rule, which is always saying, "Yes, and…" when you're in an interpersonal situation. This mindset can be helpful for neurodivergent people in social situations because it moves us away from our natural stance of questioning "why" things are the way that they are towards a stance of accepting and responding, which makes for more prosocial interactions. It's easy to say "no" something that we don't like or don't understand, but negatives tend to grind conversations to a halt.

One of the best examples of this shift is the improv game called "Questions," where you can only communicate in questions. It's a fascinating social skills exercise, because you realize how much of your communication style defaults to *you talking*, rather than you *seeking a response* from the other person. When you play "Questions" you're forced to consider what you can do to keep the other person talking, and in that exploration, you'll find a vital social skill.

Good follow-up questions keep the conversation going. They encourage reflection, adding information and getting past the surface level. So, if you're a neurodivergent person who hates small talk because it always feels like it is too superficial, then this skill is for you. You can start small, with phrases like, "Can you tell me more?" or "What was that like for you?" or "Could you give an example to me?" These queries acknowledge the content that was shared and invite the conversational partner to add more information. There's an art to asking good follow-up questions, but mastery beyond these basics is unnecessary (unless you're in sales!). Instead, remember the following things:

○ People love to talk about themselves

○ People tend to respond fondly to people who show genuine interest in them

○ The more information you have, the easier it is to find those avenues towards deeper connection.

Seek Connection. *(I did it again!)*

Interpersonal connections drive meaningful relationships, but knowing how (and when) to make them is an art. How do you evolve from being a stranger to being an acquaintance? How do you move from classmates to dating? How do you get your boss to actually notice you, let alone give you that raise or promotion? It comes down to seeking connection, the shared interests and values that form the bedrock of a solid relationship. Because you're neurodivergent, you're going to seek an authentic connection: neurodivergent people are basically incapable of bullshit); hence the aforementioned dislike of small talk.

I've seen the entire gamut of connection seeking in my career. Most people try to wade into the pool with the classic Ralph Wiggum line from *The Simpsons*, "So…do you like…stuff?" (too broad!). I've also seen kids get into fights over which is the best form of Storm Troopers in the *Star Wars* universe, Death Troopers or Sith Troopers. (My friends, if you know enough about Star Wars to be able to debate at that level of detail, you absolutely have the depth and complexity you're seeking in a relationship, if you can focus on the 99.9% you have in common, not the minute fraction you disagree on.) The middle ground here is that everyone likes stuff, but it's the *specific* stuff that creates meaningful connection.

The coolest thing about meaningful connection is that you don't have to share the exact interest (though that certainly helps). It's the feelings around the interest that can draw us together. My favorite band of all time is Bruce Springsteen and the E Street Band. And while I love talking about Bruce with other people (or as we call him in Jersey, "Bruuuuuuuuuuuuuce"), I can absolutely map on to someone else who likes another band as much as I love "The Boss." My old boss, for example, loved Pearl Jam. I'm certainly appreciative of their music, but I wouldn't call myself a superfan; regardless, talking to my boss about her love of Eddie Vedder and the gang reminded me of talking about Bruce and the band. We bonded over the mutual acknowledgement of musical fandom—how we felt, thought, and communicated about music we loved most. It didn't matter that we didn't love the same band; we both loved a band in the same deep way. Think about the people you game with, or play D&D or LARP with: do you have everything in common, or do you rather share a deep passion around that activity?

Metacommunication

Metacommunication is one of the best relationship strategies that most people are unaware of (or unaware that they're doing it). Metacommunication is the skill of talking about talking—using words to frame and preface conversation in a way that enhances your message and limits negative outcomes. For example, we've all gotten the dreaded message from our boss, "Come see me, ASAP". Our brains need context to create meaning from content: without context we create our own narrative, which tends to be catastrophic in nature. In the absence of meaningful context, the boss message triggers all the alarm bells about being fired, transferred, sued, etc. But if your boss adds the simple phrase, "Not a big deal, just checking on something about the Sales Report," then you don't even need to know what that something *is*; your anxiety goes down because you have the necessary context.

You don't even need to be subtle with metacommunication for it to work! When I'm in session and I can't find an artful way to segue, sometimes I'll just name that process: "Hey, I know that we've been talking about Roblox for 40 minutes, but I need to redirect us to something more aligned with our therapy goals." Clunky? Yes. Effective? Also, yes. And it's more protective of the relationship than me just talking over my client or changing the subject like I just intercepted a pass in football. You can think of metacommunication as a preview of what's about to come; it helps us to say it, and it helps our audience to hear it, especially if we're about to have a difficult or surprising conversation. When you can name what is about to happen, or what you need to happen, then you've replaced anxiety-producing unknowns with meaningful context, which leads to far better outcomes. When you're doing any of the above skills, you may find that using metacommunication makes them all smoother.

There you have it! These four skills can form the foundation of any effective social person, from Zach Morris to Zach Galifianakis (at least the *Between 2 Ferns* version—it's on YouTube). As you can probably imagine, there's a lot more to successful relationship building and communication than these four topics, but it's a good overview.

Responsible Decision Making

For the last step in the CASEL model, we have the ideal of responsible decision making. A lot of us have bad associations with the word "responsible." It just feels *judgy*. to say "values-based" instead of "responsible." We covered values before, but if you're making decisions in social situations that are aligned with those core beliefs, the chances are pretty good that you're acting in a responsible manner anyway.

Responsible decision making has a lot to do with things we've already talked about. You might want to crack a joke at a funeral about Aunt Maude's new boyfriend, but you wait until you're on the car ride home where you're away from sensitive ears. You might want to check your phone during a boring lecture, but you excuse yourself and check your phone in the bathroom, so you don't show disrespect to the professor. You might try to keep from walking too close to someone on the sidewalk because it would make them uncomfortable, even though you wouldn't crowd them if they would just speed up!!

In all these scenarios, you could just act—and damn the consequences! *Acting* is a decision, but not necessarily a responsible one. A responsible decision acknowledges both the need dictated by the situation **and** the limits inherent in that situation. Responsibility, therefore, is both prosocial and context dependent (Liang, et al., 2011). The limits are real, even if we don't see them or agree with them. The problem is that the executive functioning weaknesses in the neurodivergent brain means that we are far more likely to go "Ready, Fire, Aim!" in these moments (Chapman, 2021), which means that we are all at increased risk of stepping on upturned rakes like Sideshow Bob from *The Simpsons*. That reality makes many of us want to avoid unknown or uncomfortable situations, which makes sense and can even protect us, but only in the short term. The fact is that we don't improve our behavior by avoiding the challenge of growth moments; we must learn how to handle them, and the only way to do that is by going through them. As I often say to my clients, when it comes to meaningful growth, the only way out is through.

But you don't have to do it alone or without a plan! Until we can identify those situational limits on our own and adapt our behavior to them, it is appropriate and encouraged to ask for help managing those moments, especially if they are new and/or outside of your comfort zone. Wanting to do well is one thing, but it pales in comparison to *knowing how* to do well. It's impossible to know how to do everything well, especially if you've tried before and failed: it is a perfectly natural anxiety. You're thinking that you shouldn't try what you've tried before, but you're not sure what the other options are, and there's only so much you can learn on Discord. This skill deficit is another area where our friend metacommunication comes in handy.

Putting pressure on yourself to get it all right (especially the first time) increases angst and makes us more aware of our faults and deficits. Think about how many stressful moments in life where you failed and got the feedback that you were *just supposed to know what to do.* (Can you imagine if society taught swimming that way?). How did that make you feel? Not great, I'd bet, because you are already aware of the fact that you failed but now you feel stupid for not knowing something that you didn't even know you were supposed to know! That "knowing" is, of course, part of the "code" that neurodivergent folks are locked out of by our neurotypical friends. Not knowing the "code" makes it harder to join in with broader social activities, which keeps us from developing the confidence and competence to be successful.

But you don't need to know it all, especially at first. You can find people who know more than you, what we call a More Knowledgeable Other (MKO) in the language of Vygotsky (Probine & Perry, 2021). As smart as you are about as many things as you're smart about, it's impossible to know everything. If you just dive in, assuming you know the rules or can just "figure it out," you're setting yourself up to make an unforced error. Asking for help requires a fair amount of humility, because it's hard to acknowledge when you don't know something, especially something that you feel like you "should" know. You also need to have access to a person who can serve as that MKO. (I think that this is why second- or third-children have a social advantage, because they've got an experienced person in-house). It may seem impossible to find that person, but you won't know until you ask.

For example, I remember the first time I got invited to a Sweet Sixteen birthday party—I was panicked! I didn't know how to dress (what the hell does dressy-casual mean!? Should I get my cummerbund pressed?). I didn't know what kind of gift was appropriate. I didn't know what expectations were at a Country Club. Instead of winging it (bad call) or not going (somehow a worse call), I called my best friend Allie and used metacommunication to express the situation I was in and how I was feeling about it. Allie, being a wise high school sophomore, was able to understand my plight and kindly laid out all the necessary details to me (she even colored in the female perspective, of which I was woefully ignorant). I don't remember exactly how the party went, but I do know that if it had been a disaster my brain would have been playing its lowlights on a loop for the last 25 years. So, it can't have been that bad! (And if it was, sorry Bridget!)

My point is metacommunication helps. Asking for help is good; using specific, prosocial language to communicate what help you need and why you need it is better. It's the difference between yelling, "Call 911!" and "My son got stung by a bee and he's going into anaphylactic shock, please bring an epi pen!" The more you practice giving more specific information, the more you create an environment that helps you. If you're going to be the most effective in asking for specific help, then adding in a specific person to ask (the MKO) is the last step.

When you are faced with a decision, regardless of the situation, you might feel like you have only two pathways: dig in or give in. You feel this way because having to decide is a stressful demand, and stress tends to activate our "fight or flight" response (Brown, et al., 2020). The first is to respond in the affirmative (the "give in" response), which is usually analogous to "flight." The second is to respond in the negative (the "dig in" response), which is usually analogous to "fight." When you feel like you have two options, you feel panicky and trapped; you tend to make worse decisions in these moments. Thankfully, there are always more responsible ways out of the situation.

I especially want to emphasize one piece of responsible decision making, what I like to call a *third door solution*. When our brains get stressed out, they tend to go to into all-or-nothing thinking, stuck in a faulty belief that there are only two options: A or B, give in or dig in. I like the idea of a "third door solution" because it reminds our brains that there is always another option. There's always a shade of gray between black and white. If you're deciding something and you're trying to be responsible, the third door between spontaneity and overthinking is taking a moment to consider the variables and options, in the context of your values, before deciding. It might feel like you can't take a moment to decide, but unless you're an ER doctor facing triage, you usually have more time than your anxiety is telling you. When you remove the (often) artificial constraint of time pressure, you'll find that you can think much more clearly.

You can get more information and use that information to find a meaningful and effective compromise between all parties involved, because part of making responsible decisions is knowing that we are accountable to far more than ourselves. We owe our friends, family, bosses, teachers, mentors, children, and clients effective and clear communication, not just to give us cover for our bad choices, but to provide context and understanding. Remember, in the absence of information, people make assumptions about things that happen, and those assumptions are often negative in nature; don't fall victim to the information vacuum. You can provide the context yourself and protect the relationship.

Let's say that someone invites you to a party, and you'd really like to go, but your extended family is visiting that weekend. That's a stressful situation to be in (seriously, why does this stuff always happen on the same weekend?!). You might feel like you must either spontaneously decide one or the other RIGHT NOW, or put off making the choice until you stress yourself into oblivion and have a panic attack. In psychology, when two decisions seem equally good and equally fraught, it is called ambivalence (Gary, Kiper, & Geist, 2022). Ambivalence will grind our decision-making to a halt because the pros and cons seem to cancel each other out until you can do nothing. So, it's helpful to change your relationship to the problem. This is a time to take a deep breath (use your square breathing!) and use responsible decision making to find a choice that is the best outcome for everyone.

Making the responsible decision in this scenario might seem complicated, but the decision-making process gives you a guide to do effectively. It doesn't mean that you can't go to the party, and it doesn't mean that you're going to blow off your grandparents (those are the "give in" and "dig in" responses, respectively). It means that you must take both pieces of information into account when deciding. You test how those data points align with your values when making a choice. And then you elevate the decision-making process with prosocial communication, self-management, interpersonal awareness, and self-awareness of when you know what to do and when you need to find an MKO (I'll see if Allie is still available for Helpline calls).

For example, if you're a student, you can ask an adult, "Hey, how long are we going to see grandma and grandpa, and can I go to this party when we're done?" Or you could say to your friend when they invite you, "You know what? I would love to go to the party, but my grandparents are visiting the weekend and that's important to me. But please invite me to the next one". If you're an adult, you can say, "As much as I'd like to go to this party, seeing my in-laws is really important to my partner. If I can swing by later, I'll be sure to text you."

These are not perfect responses. They all involve a certain amount of compromise, which means that we aren't getting exactly what we want. But their imperfect nature doesn't change the fact that they're good solutions from a prosocial perspective. You can get parts of what you want while still protecting your relationships, which are always necessary context. It's not an all-or-nothing decision, regardless of what our brains try to tell us! You were able to decide on a course of action and not stay frozen for eternity in ambivalence. But you must have the skills and awareness, and also practice them, so when the real-world challenges you to use these skills, you can rise to the occasion. As you keep reading, you'll learn more ways to rise.

CHAPTER 3

Being Neurodivergent in the Wild: The Neuropsychology of Neurodivergence

Now that we've defined our SEL skills and terms, let's make sure that we're moving forward with a shared definition of terms within the neurodivergent world. If you've bought this book (and thank you for that, by the way!) then you probably have at least a working understanding of the language of this field, but let's take a moment to clarify. We're also going to talk about your brain, because it's fun and informative. Most importantly, understanding brain differences offers a vital reframe of the reasons why our behaviors are different. It's not a choice for us to be the way that we are: our brains are quite literally different. We're going to unpack that in detail in this chapter.

But first, a story.

Once upon a time in the summer of 2006, I lived with my grandparents outside of Boston. My grandfather was a carpenter, and my grandmother is a retired schoolteacher. My grandmother is a beautiful, kind, patient woman, who also tends to be a very indirect communicator. If neurodivergent people are direct to a fault, then my grandmother is comfortably on the other side of the spectrum. While most of the time I'm able to crack her "code", there are times that I miss her intentions entirely. Here is one of those times!

> *It's Saturday morning and I'm sitting at the table drinking my coffee. My grandmother comes in and putters about the*

> *kitchen for a moment. Then she perks up and says, "Oh,*
> *it's supposed to rain later!"*
>
> *"Cool, nana." I say, somewhat nonplussed, and return to*
> *my newspaper.*
>
> *Shortly thereafter, I get a text from my mom. "Hey, nana's*
> *upset."*
>
> *Me: "Oh no! Why?" (via text)*
>
> *My mom: "Well, she said that she asked you to take in the*
> *laundry from the clothesline, but you didn't say anything."*
>
> *Me (desperately reviewing the day's events in my mind).*
> *"Uh, WTF. That didn't happen…" Then, a lightbulb*
> *moment: "Oh wait, I get it now."*

You see, when my grandmother said, "Oh, it's supposed to rain later!" what she was *actually* saying was, "Since it's going to rain later, I don't want the clean laundry on the clothesline outside to get wet, so would you mind taking that inside for me before it rains?" If she had said all that, I would have done it in a second!

But she didn't say it, so, I didn't do it. And I got to feel a big dose of "bad grandson" guilt for missing the implied message.

I tell this story because one of the biggest differences between neuro-divergent and neurotypical brains is in the way they communicate and interpret information. Logically, if I wanted you to take in the laundry, I would just ask you to do that. But not everyone commu-nicates that way! Remember that the "code" for prosocial behavior in the neurotypical community is generally indirect, protective communication (Salimova, 2021). Calling someone out (either telling them to do something or asking why they haven't done it) is seen as rude, so neurotypical people tend to tiptoe up to the point, hinting at it along the way. Neurodivergent folks tend to communicate more directly (some would say bluntly), preferring task efficiency to the vagueness of protecting feelings (Wittek & Bekkers, 2015). It's true that sometimes this approach ruffles feathers, but it also gets things done. What's the right answer? In true psychologist fashion, I'm going to say, "A little bit of both." (cue the groan from the audience). Hold on! There's science to help us!

One of the biggest changes in psychology over the last twenty years is the rise of the Neurodiversity Movement. The Neurodiversity Movement posits that since human diversity is a part of the species as a whole, why would diversity of human brains be any different (Ne'eman & Pellicano, 2022)? There are objective and quantifiable aspects of neurodivergence that make these brains different from neurotypical brains, whether we call it ADHD, Autism, giftedness, Dyslexia, Dysgraphia, OCD, Traumatic Brain Injury, or something else (see below) (Chapman, 2021). While not all neurodivergences co-occur, many do; in fact, having one neurodivergence strongly predicts others (Apperly, Lee, van der Kleij, & Devine, 2023). To choose just one example, being Autistic means that you have a 40% chance of having ADHD (Rong, Fan, Wu, Zang, & Zhou, 2022), as compared to an 8.7% chance in the general population (Reuben, 2024).

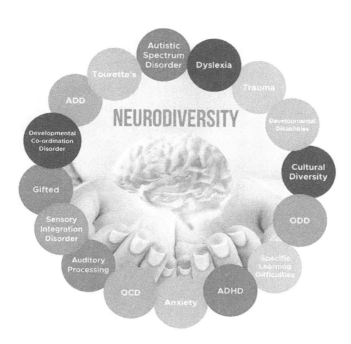

The neurotypical brain is one that operates largely within expected age and developmental norms (Armstrong, 2015). A neuro*divergent* brain is a brain that is quantifiably different in at least one way when compared to a neuro*typical* brain (Armstrong, 2015). The differences can be in form, function, fluency, morphology, electro-chemical function, and even amount of brain structures—from neurons to neurotransmitters. About 20% of people are neurodivergent in some way (CDC, 2023):

- ◯ Autism Spectrum Disorder is 1:36 in the population
- ◯ ADHD in 1:25 in the population
- ◯ Dyslexia is 1:10 in the population
- ◯ Giftedness, which is about 1:50 of the population

Whereas most neurodivergences are developmental in nature, PTSD is considered an *acquired* neurodivergence due to the changes that the brain undergoes after a traumatic event; it is similar to concussions, Traumatic Brain Injury, and even long COVID (Armstrong, 2015). We cannot yet do an MRI of the brain to determine brain differences, but that day is coming. And I'm excited for it!

Why am I excited, you ask? Other than being an excitable person by nature (I know, what a shock), I'm thrilled at the impact that this hard science is having on the broader societal perception of neurodivergences in schools, homes, and workplaces all over the world. We know that there are different brains out there that behave in different and unusual ways. There's nothing wrong with that! We just need to find ways for those brains to fit in, and that approach is more successful when it comes from shared understanding (in this case, of brain science). A fundamental tenet of the Neurodiversity Movement is "differences are not deficits," they are strengths consistent with the strengths-based approaches to intervention that have the best outcomes in education, parenting, mentorship, and mental health (Ne'eman & Pellicano, 2022).

Seeing the differences has never been the problem when it comes to neurodivergence, unfortunately. It's difficult to miss the ADHD kid running around the classroom, the Autistic adult info-dumping details about the construction of the Brooklyn Bridge, or the OCD professor counting paperclips before leaving her desk. In a world full of neurotypical people who created "the code" of appropriate behavior and thus maintain it, atypical behavior stands out. They get people noticed and ultimately diagnosed (especially in schools), but the entire process is more pathologized and deficit-based than necessary. Atypical people with atypical brains tend to act in atypical ways! For too long we haven't had the science to create the alternate narrative, that these different brains are not worse, and certainly are not the result of bad parenting, too much sugar, TikTok, Facebook, AIM (or whatever the technology-demon du jour is), "wokeness"(a false concept), or the decline of the nuclear family, etc.

Even though those narratives were never rooted in research (let alone actual science), you still hear people today that think ADHD is "just kids being bad" and just telling them to focus will be the cure. Recently, I saw a speech where a parenting "expert" (I wish I had a sarcasm font) claimed that "It's not Autism, it's Badism', implying that Autism isn't real, what we call Autism is just a word that we use to justify letting kids be "bad." Like that's even real! (Stop trying to make Badism happen, people. It's not gonna happen. Yes, that's another *Mean Girls* reference.) These ideas may be bunk "science" but they're out there and not going anywhere; people who seek such narratives will easily find a "mental illness isn't real" thread on social media to reinforce their beliefs.

People say that a lie gets halfway around the world before the truth gets a chance to put its pants on, and the same is true for psychological hypotheses, unfortunately. It is sadly a lot easier to spout nonsense on Twitter/X than it is to be responsible and make an informed, nuanced point that was informed by digging through dusty neuroscience journals to understand the neurodevelopmental role of the pre-frontal cortex. When people are allowed to create and propagate the narrative that a person's differences are some sort of character flaw, it explains why the rates of Anxiety and Major Depression Disorders in neurodivergent folks are significantly higher (27% and 20%, respectively) than in the neurotypical population (10% for each) (Karpinski, Kolb, Tetreault, & Borowski, 2018).

I would go so far as to say that the word "Disorder" in Attention-Deficit/Hyperactivity Disorder, Autism Spectrum Disorder, Specific Learning Disability in Reading (Dyslexia), Math (Dyscalculia), or Writing (Dysgraphia)—should officially be replaced with "Difference'. We should treat these *differences* as just different ways of navigating the world, rather than pathologizing them through a medical model that sees difference largely as a threat to a healthy system. If the medical and psychological fields moved towards understanding differences rather than judging them as deficits, then then more people would seek diagnosis and support. Can we please add "Neurodivergence" as a diagnostic code to the DSM-6? There's even evidence to support that neurodivergences are not mental illness, but in fact different ways of functioning that lead to mental illness *because of* the friction caused by forcing the neurotypical "code" onto neurodivergent brains (Chapman & Botha, 2023; Kelly, Martin, Taylor & Doherty, 2024).

Neurodivergence has long been treated as a kind of death sentence, caused by a societal fear that causes stigma against neurodivergence and mental illness, and a resistance to seeking diagnosis. I want to clarify that I'm not in the "neurodivergence is a superpower" camp because it drastically misses the point, tainting neurodivergence with a kind of toxic positivity. Your neurodivergence can most certainly be a strength, but no one with that difference is under the delusion that their differences are always perceived as positive. Diagnosis is not the end of the story, but rather the beginning; it should open doors to rooms that understand you and are equipped to support you properly. It is always better to know that you're a zebra, not a weird horse, even if you must change zoos to get the things you need. A zebra can do okay in a pen for horses, but it will do much better on the savannah.

All differences, including neurodivergence, can be seen in terms of strengths and weaknesses. Wolverine's adamantium claws and skeleton are a huge advantage in battle...unless he's fighting Magneto (the master of magnetism has a *slight* advantage over someone with literal metal bones—why do the X-Men keep sending him to those fights?!). My ADHD made me a better stand-up comic, but it absolutely makes being a parent harder sometimes. There is real psychological pain that can come with being neurodivergent, and that pain deserves diagnosis and treatment. But I will continue to argue that those neurodivergences are just different ways of interacting with the world, and when accommodated properly, can lead to profound successes. No one thinks that Mac users are pathological compared to PC users; it's just a different operating system. (Linux users on the other hand…yikes!! No, I'm kidding! Sorry, Garry!)

Our brains are complex and resist simple narratives of "good" or "bad," regardless of what other people think or say. Differences, once again, are not deficits, nor are they domination. Perhaps you know that your brain is different, and you bought this book to confirm the value of your differences and elevate your self-knowledge further. Perhaps you've always suspected that you have those differences, and now you're learning just how much there is to know. Perhaps your kid just got referred for a diagnosis at school and you're trying really hard not to freak out. Perhaps you're brand new to all this neurodiversity stuff and you're just now realizing that whatever made them call you "creepy loner" in high school is much better explained by acknowledging the very real social-emotional brain differences that come with Autism. Either way, welcome to the club. We are happy to have you.

Why is this all so challenging for us? Whether we're neurodivergent or neurotypical, we're all human, right? Why does it feel so strange to consider other peoples' emotions when communicating, even with people we know and (maybe) like? It all starts with brain science.

Let's explore the various brain differences between neurotypical and neurodivergent brains. I couldn't possibly characterize all the neuroscience that contributes to neurodivergence (if that interests you, please read "Insight into a Bright Mind" by my friend Dr. Nicole Tetreault) or this book would be much longer. Instead, I'm going to highlight a few relevant sections of the brain that we have consistently found to be different when comparing neurodivergent and neurotypical brains.

Remember, knowledge of brain differences helps establish a scientific counter-narrative to the "mental illness is simultaneously not real and all your fault" story that so many schools and workplaces use.

Mirror Neurons

Our brains are full of neurons, cells that fire messages to other neurons to make the brain and body function (Martin, et al., 2020). There are special neurons called "mirror neurons," which fire both when *we* act, and when we see another organism act (Waters, 2014). The mirror neuron not only tracks our own behavior, but it tracks the behavior of other relevant animals (like people, if you're of that persuasion). Mirror neurons are in the premotor cortex, the supplementary motor area, the primary somatosensory cortex, and the inferior parietal cortex (Molenberghs, Cunnington, & Mattingley, 2009). When another person does something socially or behaviorally relevant, our brains fire as if we're actually doing it ourselves, which can sometimes make us do it anyway (just as yawning can be contagious).

Why do these parts of the brain matter? They are all intimately related to tracking social behavior (Molenberghs, et al., 2009). We are social animals and are coded through evolution to observe and respond to what other people are doing. Think back to when we were hunters and gatherers. If someone in your tribe saw or heard something in the bushes and reacted to it, you reacting to their reaction might have saved your life. Such neuronal connections predicted survival and passed those genes on through generations, until now—when you just *know* when your kiddo is about to throw up, or your coworker is going to complain about the new overtime policy, or your teacher is going to catch your buddy cheating on a quiz.

For neurodivergent people, our mirror neurons fire at different wavelengths and at different rates, emphasizing different aspects of interpersonal behavior (Salimova, 2021). We have them, but they are dialed to a different frequency, not better or worse, but certainly unique. If you've ever been in a group of people and felt like they were all on a different wavelength than you, you actually weren't that far off, neurologically speaking. Different brains attend to and track different things. For a long time, neurotypical people thought that Autistic people didn't or couldn't attend to human behavior; but some really cool studies show us that their mirror neurons are looking at different things in social situations, namely goal-directed behavior (Chan & Han, 2020; Kelly, et al., 2024). It's not that Autistic people aren't understanding the other behavior: their brains are attending to different behaviors, triaging what feels most relevant to them to the top of the list.

Why does this matter? Your mirror neurons will be more adept at observing the patterns and values that come more naturally to you. For example, my grandfather always understood what my grandmother was talking about, regardless of the indirectness of her communication. Yes, some of that came from 50 years of marriage, but his brain also understood her brain, just as parents can always crack the "code" of their toddler's babbling ("Neen-yeah" is obviously peanut butter, what?), or how you could take any server from any restaurant in the world and plop them in another restaurant and they'd be OK once they figured out where the bathrooms and hostess station were (OK, Matt, "86" any more examples; they get it). Exposure helps us become more flexible and responsive to our environments. Mirror neurons are not the only thing that differentiates the neurotypical from the neurodivergent brain, but their impact on behavior and communication makes them an ideal example to begin with.

Ultimately, it is easier to take the style that you're more comfortable with (whether that is direct or indirect) and shift it a bit towards the other edge, taking its best parts with you. If you're an indirect communicator, you can try to say what you mean a little more often; if you're on the blunter side, you can say "please" or ask for help (that's meta-communication!). You don't have to wholly change, but if people are used to a particular style of communication from you (and probably are irritated by its shortcomings), then a little change goes a long way. It probably will feel weird at first, but the effort will be worth it when your conversations are flowing more easily, people are understanding you the first time you ask for something (and your grandmother's laundry is actually being taken in before the summer rainstorm!).

Sympathetic and Parasympathetic Nervous Systems

Bridging the gap between communication styles includes managing emotions (which we will explore more in Chapter 6), specifically, managing our anxiety. Our bodies work hard to protect us from pain and danger, sometimes overly so, and anxiety is our threat detection system (Martin, et al., 2020). It monitors our environment for dangers to ourselves and our self-esteem. Threats can (and often do) come from outside, but our anxiety additionally monitors our behavior to see if we're causing our own discomfort.

Anxiety can trigger the "fight, flight, freeze, or fawn" defense mechanisms regulated by the sympathetic nervous system (Brown, et al., 2020). You can think of the sympathetic nervous system as the "muscle" that chooses a coping strategy when a threat is detected. Do you run away—either physically or mentally—and hope to live another day? get ready to fight because your body feels backed into a corner and you might as well get some swings in if you're trapped? Or do you fawn, and emotionally attach or endear yourself to the threat because if you're in the pack you're less likely to be the Apex Predator's lunch? (Serious *Mean Girls: The Musical* vibes).

Not all discomfort is bad, of course, but our nervous system doesn't tend to see it that way. Our bodies like being happy but they will seek *safety*; they want to feel regulated and the best way to do that is to maintain emotional equilibrium (Al-Shawaf & Lewis, 2020). When we challenge social norms, our anxiety can spike because we are moving out of stasis into disruption. What we want from challenging a norm might be waiting for us on the other side of the anxiety we feel from challenging, but the threat presented by the anxiety may be too large to be easily overcome. Our brains tend to catastrophize anxious outcomes, telling us that if we try something new, a) it will be bad, b) that badness will be huge, and c) that huge badness will last forever. None of those things are true in the grand scheme of our lives, but our brains keep that a secret. When the catastrophic outcome doesn't arrive, your brain shrugged and said, "well, you stayed safe, and better safe than sorry!", without acknowledging the potentially positive experience you missed by staying safe.

People tend to describe their feelings as what I like to call "the eyebrows and mouths rule": emotions are most easily coded by how peoples' eyes and mouth move in response to a given feeling. Think of a time that you got anxious; you probably dropped your eyebrows and pulled your lips back, exposing some of your teeth (bonus points if you started chomping on your fingernails like they were an ear of corn). That's a classic anxiety response! Let's expand that picture: when you're anxious, how does your chest feel? Probably tight: your heart is racing. How about your forehead? Flop sweat (an actor's response to fear of "flopping" on stage) is a real thing. Do you hum or bounce your leg or twist your hair over your finger? (Hi, Katie!)

The point here is that the feeling of anxiety (like all emotions) predicates an entire body response. When your body tracks a threat, way more than just your eyebrows and mouth move; your heart rate increases, your pupils dilate, your lungs expand, your stomach inhibits production, your bladder relaxes, among many events that occur throughout your body (Ho, et al., 2020). All those physical behaviors give us clues to determine what emotion is impacting us in the moment; the more clues we get and understand, the better chance we have of identifying our feelings and proactively minimizing them.

When we have a powerful feeling, our sympathetic nervous system springs into action. If we can catch the response behavior before it accelerates, then we're keeping our brains and bodies in check. If we can't, then big behavior that comes from that big feeling. After that big feeling, our bodies want to return to baseline, because being emotionally activated takes a lot of energy (that our body would rather use for other things). I cannot tell you how many angry teen boys I've had to work with and physically redirect (sometimes for hours); but the one thing that they all have in common is when the emotional burst is over and the anger has run its course, they either a) burst into tears, b) fall asleep, or c) both. The body needs to recover after all that angst!

The part of the body responsible for re-regulating is the parasympathetic nervous system (Brown, et al., 2020). If the sympathetic nervous system is "fight, flight, freeze, or fawn," you could call its complimentary system the "rest, digest, destress, and recover" system. The parasympathetic nervous system wants our body to come back to baseline, so it can save energy for the next threat and response. It will eventually calm your body down on its own, but later we're going to discuss ways to speed that process along.

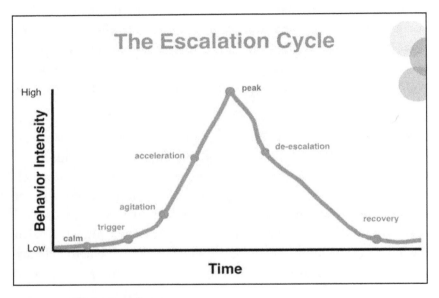

Prefrontal Cortex

Life presents us with an incredible amount of information every day, as much as 74GB (which is about 16 movies worth) of data to process (Levitin, 2015). The challenge is that when your brain moves as quickly as does a neurodivergent brain, you need a lot of control to manage that information appropriately. Unfortunately, being neurodivergent usually comes with a concurrent weakness in the prefrontal cortex, the part of the brain that regulates our behavior, especially organization and behavioral inhibition (Kolk & Rakic, 2022). When you combine brain speed with the lack of self-control, it's like trying to drive a 2024 Ferrari Testarossa with the brake system of a 1988 Dodge Dart—not a not a good combo! The prefrontal cortex is in the frontal lobe of the brain, the part of our cerebral cortex that really makes us *us*. It is responsible for executive functioning skills, which is a term I'm sure you've heard a million times if you're neurodivergent (usually weaponized against you, of course).

For those of you who don't have lingering trauma from common school interventions like "just use a planner" or "everyone has a tough time doing things that they don't like," let's quickly review the executive functioning suite of skills: time management, task switching, sustained attention, task initiation, task completion, organization, self-regulation, working memory, and behavioral inhibition (Zelazo, 2015). Behavioral inhibition is particularly important because we have increasing demands on our brains and attention, and we need the cognitive skills to be able to triage those requests to get things done (Kolk & Rakic, 2022). These are very important life skills! You absolutely need them for success at work and at school, as well as for parenting, friendship, dating, filing your taxes, making the sale, responding to that text, keeping plants alive, navigating the mall parking lot…you get my drift.

The problem is that a neurodivergent brain has weaker prefrontal cortex functioning in almost every situation, which results in more impulsivity, more disorganization, increased emotional dysregulation, and poorer decision-making (Zelazo, 2015). The prefrontal cortex is the slowest part of the brain to develop in neurotypical people, usually coming "fully online" sometime in the early twenties (Kolk & Rakic, 2022); since the prefrontal cortex helps us make good decisions, its delayed development can explain why you made those some of those "inspired" choices in college (no judgement! Everyone should do an Ice Luge at least once). In ADHD and gifted individuals, to pick two other neurotypes, the prefrontal cortex doesn't fully mature until the early to mid-thirties, essentially giving neurodivergent folks an extra decade of underdeveloped functioning (Kolk & Rakic, 2022). As a clarification, it's not that the prefrontal cortex flips from "off" to "on," but rather that it isn't as strong and consistent as it could be as it develops, causing moments of disorganization and dysregulating that can be draining to the person as they navigate the world. Thankfully, the prefrontal cortex like a muscle, in that the more we work it, the stronger it gets; we will discuss how to strengthen this part of the brain in Chapter Five.

Limbic System

I'm a psychologist, so talking about feelings is fundamental to my job. We all have feelings and can speak to their impact on us, from the highest highs to the lowest lows. But where do feelings come from? The limbic system is a complex series of structures in the brain that play a major role in regulating various aspects of human behavior, from memory and motivation to behavior and emotional regulation (Rolls, 2015). From a neuropsychological perspective, emotions are triggered by environmental stimuli that cause an electrochemical reaction in the limbic system. This neural system includes the amygdala, hippocampus, thalamus, hypothalamus, basal ganglia, cingulate gyrus, cerebrum, and the olfactory bulb, all working together to manage our emotional responses, especially those that are linked to broader survival instincts—fear, learning, social bonding, and memory consolidation. The limbic system is highly connected, through the thalamus, to our sympathetic and parasympathetic nervous systems, as its role is to both trigger the nervous response and help bring the system back to baseline when the threat is over (which is the job of the hypothalamus) (Ho, Pham, Miller, Kircanski, & Gotlib, 2020).

Of primary importance within the limbic system is the amygdala, a small, almond-shaped gland near the hippocampus, which is the brain's memory center (the reason you're so good at Pub Quiz, natch) (Chapman, 2021). The amygdala has the primary function of processing emotions, namely fear, anger, anxiety, and happiness. (It is also the part of the brain that my dad finds most fascinating.) Given its proximity to the hippocampus, the amygdala plays a major part in learning, especially through its role in creating emotional memories that we can respond to in the future (think about the first movie that really scared you, or the song that was playing during your first dance with someone who you had a crush on). In the neurotypical brain, the amygdala is about the size of an almond, or your thumbnail. In the neurodivergent brain (primarily in gifted brains), the amygdala can be up to twice as large! (Kuhn, et al., 2021). The larger the area of the brain dedicated to processing emotion, the more impactful the feeling can become.

Those emotions are processed in the cingulate gyrus, which regulates emotions and the behaviors associated with them (Rolls, 2015). This area of the brain is most indicated in monitoring the body's response to unpleasant experiences and learning from those to predict safer behavior in the future. Dysfunction in the cingulate gyrus can lead to an impaired sense of pain, unexpected emotions in terms of frequency, intensity, and duration (not to mention fit to environment, but we'll get to that), and inappropriate levels of fear. We see the most changes in the cingulate gyrus for people who are depressed, as well as the types of neurodivergence that one sees in OCD, Autistic, schizophrenic, and PTSD brains (Chan & Han, 2020).

Emotions don't just happen; they are the result of complex interplay between multiple brain structures and outside triggers. Emotions often lead to dramatic behaviors—both external (how many teen boys out there have punched a wall in anger and broken a knuckle?) and internal (seeming fine on the outside but screaming in panic inside when you're in a stalled elevator) — because our body communicates through behavior and behavior releases the emotion's energy (Ho, et al., 2020). Unfortunately, emotions are not logical and do not respond to many of the strategies we use to manage our thoughts and inner monologue. Has anyone ever told you to "calm down?" Probably yes. Did it work? Of course not! Feelings don't act rationally, so we cannot manage them rationally. They're not going to just go away; they need to be managed. It is best to think about managing our emotions through the lens of the "big three"—frequency, intensity, and duration—because we want less of all three and know it'll never get to zero.

Cerebral Cortex

The cerebral cortex is the outermost layer of the brain, comprised of six layers of nerve cells that contain somewhere around 15 billion neurons (Mzarik & Dombrowski, 2010). It's gray and folded in appearance, and both of those descriptions are important. The cerebral cortex is called gray matter because it is comprised of the dendrites of neurons, the sections of the nerve cells that receive chemical messages transmitted through the neuronal connections in the brain that are amplified by the fatty myelin sheath around the axon or neuron body. The "white matter" of the brain is internal, and the cerebral cortex's "grey matte'" is the outer layer. The folds of the brain are made up of grooves called sulci and raised areas called gyri (Damiani, Pereira, & Nascimento, 2017). These folds and grooves increase the brain's surface area, which enhances cognition and processing, as well as forming boundaries between parts of the brain.

The gyri and sulci help divide the cerebral cortex into the four lobes of the brain: frontal, parietal, temporal, and occipital (Prescott, Gavrilescu, Cunnington, O'Boyle, & Egan, 2010). This book will touch on the first three; although the occipital lobe (visual processing) is important (y'know, since seeing stuff is pretty necessary) it doesn't really factor into what we're discussing here. The frontal lobe involves many of the processes that make us functional beings: decision-making, consciousness, attention, emotional and behavioral control, personality, body movement, and intelligence. The parietal lobe provides us with sensory information (touch, pain, pressure, location, temperature), spatial awareness and manipulation (Carpenter, Baranek, Copeland, Compton, Zucker, Dawson, & Egger, 2019). The temporal lobe processes language, speech formation, hearing, nonverbal communication, sound to visual image conversion (think of a wee-ooo-wee-ooo coming from the behind you on the highway, what comes to mind?), and memory (Schulz & Stevenson, 2019). And with their powers combined...

...collectively, the cerebral cortex comprises the higher-order brain functions. It provides us with reasoning, emotion, memory, personality, learning, decision-making, and language (Prescott, et al, 2010). Specifically, for you gifted kids out there, we want to highlight the parietal-frontal integration area, which is where intelligence (and personality!) come from (Kuhn, et al., 2021). This unique intersection of the brain (right above your hairline, if you're thusly follicle-d) is comprised of many inter-related cortical networks that allow the brain to process information and communicate with other parts of the cortex, which gives us the cognition and processing we call intelligence (Haier & Jung, 2018). Interestingly, this area of the brain comes "online" a lot earlier in many gifted and twice-exceptional students, which provides credence to the precociousness often seen in young neurodivergent kids. Whenever I do a school observation, I can always find the gifted kid, not because they're necessarily doing complex calculus on the whiteboard (though that certainly does happen) but because their personalities read large and in-charge like Ferris Buehler.

That's a lot of brain science, and you probably didn't buy this book because you have more than a passing interest in neuroscience. (If you have more than passing interest, check out the Additional Resources section at the back of the book for some deep dives into brain science.) If we are going to talk about neurodivergence, we need to ground our conversations in brain science. The brain makes us who we are and defines how we feel and what we do. It is the reason that some of us get "the code", and others look around nonplussed for more context.

Growing up as a gifted kid in the 90's, I only knew that gifted meant "smart;" I didn't know that it meant having a brain with significant structural and functional differences. Knowledge, of course, is power; it's also vital context. In the absence of information, our brains tend to create their own narratives, and those narratives usually focus on ourselves as the main character of the story. Without another explanation, we tend to assume that we are the reason that something happened or didn't happen (cue Taylor Swift: "It's me. Hi. I'm the problem. It's me."). But if we see ourselves only as the catalyst, then ultimately our rationale (and that of the people around us) becomes focused on our personality, not our external context, and that can have very damaging downstream effects. In psychology, we call this tendency the Fundamental Attribution Error; we can excuse our own behaviors as the result of context, but since context is often invisible to everyone except for the person it impacts (Ross, 2018). For example, only you know that you're late to work today because you had a seven-minute meltdown this morning trying to get your bra to fit *just right,* but since other people don't have the context of what happened, they tend to falsely attribute our behaviors to our personality (i.e., you're irresponsible).

For example, gifted people are often considered to be emotionally intense, and that's true! But it's true because of brain structure, not because we're "soft" or "dramatic" or "spoiled millennials," or any such nonsense. The gifted brain processes emotions differently because of structural differences, whether that's a larger amygdala, a higher number of neuronal connections in the cerebral cortex, a weaker pre-frontal cortex, or higher reactivity in the sympathetic nervous system. Those brain differences don't provide us with excuses for behavior, but they do provide (to us and those around us) an explanation for why things are the way they are. If your thirteen-year-old is having an epic tantrum over not getting to watch more episodes of DBZ (Dragon Ball Z, a legendary anime), their behavior is stemming from the differences in their brain, not because they're a bad kid or you're a bad parent.

The brain differences are also helpful context for metacommunication. When I'm talking to neurotypical people, sometimes my brain jumps several steps ahead. I know that can come across as obnoxious or like a show-off (even writing this feels like a humble brag), but I cannot help it, it's just how my brain works! You would not believe how many times I've been accused of cheating at Trivial Pursuit, but I'm not surreptitiously Googling the answers; I just happen to know a lot of trivia and my brain moves fast! If I can explain my neuro-divergence, I can provide the necessary context around my unusual thoughts and actions that hopefully help people to understand me better. And if they can understand me better, it increases my chances of successfully interacting because they have a competing narrative that isn't "he's obnoxious."

This brings me back to helping my grandmother with the laundry. As soon as I processed my mom's text message, I rushed outside and started to help take the clothes down. Nana looked at me and said, "Oh no, you don't need to help; I've got this!", but of course at this point I was keyed into her indirect communication. I gently ignored her and kept helping, which she seemed satisfied with (neurotypicals! sheesh.) "Nana," I said, "I'm always happy to help you with this or any other chore around the house. I've just got a million thoughts bouncing around up here and sometimes I need you to be very direct with me about what you need me to do. I don't want you to think that I'm ignoring you! My brain just doesn't always pick up on those cues."

I think that this was a much deeper conversation than my grandmother had anticipated around bringing in the laundry, but she gamely stuck with me. She told me that she'd try, and that she supposed that she was used to talking "shorthand" with my grandpa, which made clear sense to me (that shorthand was their personal "code"). I promised her that we would meet in the middle and find a way to make things work. And the very next day, as I was eating breakfast, I heard a thwack of a notepad hitting the kitchen table. There, in my grandmother's beautiful penmanship, was a short list of things for me to do that day. She wanted me to run to the grocery store, take out the recycling, and move the davenport so she could dust behind it. Perfect!

Well, not totally perfect. "Nana!" I shouted. "Thank you for the list. I'll get right on it. But, um, what in the heck is a davenport?"

Fun Fact from my Editor: Captain Davenport commissioned the desk from a London furniture maker in the late 1800's. The davenport sofa was made by an unrelated Boston furniture maker called A.H.Davenport in the early 20th century.

My grandmother meant the desk. She was not (to the best of my knowledge) ever a sea captain.

CHAPTER 4
Asynchronous Development
The "Rule of Five" and How Asynchrony Impacts Us

I'd like to tell you a story. One of the kids I work with (I've changed some details here) is a great example of how the developmental pathways of neurodivergent people are very different, and how those differences have significant impacts. Jake is an eight-year-old boy from outside Baltimore, MD. His IQ is 162, and he's a second grader at a school for gifted students. Jake is extremely advanced in math, and when I say extremely, I want to be clear that I'm not exaggerating. Jake has been accelerated in math, which in this case means that Jake takes *graduate level courses* in calculus at the local university (which is one of the most prestigious universities in the country), in addition to his regular, accelerated education at the gifted school.

Jake is clearly brilliant. He understands math like some people understand how to breathe, and it's incredible to talk to him about it. He collects math facts like some kids collect baseball cards (or, considering the population that I work with, Pokémon cards). One of the best parts of working with gifted and other neurodivergent people is how awesome it is to see their brains work when they're engaged in what they're most passionate about, and Jake is a spectacular example of it. His passion is captivating and awe-inspiring to witness. Of course, while Jake's high IQ and incredible precocity in math are what helped his parents pick me as his therapist, that's not the reason why they brought him to me.

They sent Jake to me because Jake can't tie his shoes.

Let's back up for a moment. As I'm writing this book, I'm working with my six-year-old on tying her shoes, and it's tricky! The squirrel runs around the tree, through the hole, and comes out the other side… wait, is that right? Shoe tying is a complex psycho-motor process involving multiple areas of the brain. While we adults take tying our shoes for granted, there was a time that we all struggled to figure out just how the strings turned into a knot and how that knot stayed tied all day. At some point your brain matured enough so that you could get the steps down and do it on your own. Eventually, you did it so much that you could do it without thinking, by rote.

Not being able to tie one's shoes is not a reason to go to therapy (well, maybe Occupational Therapy). But Jake was having explosive meltdowns about it every morning *because he was struggling* to tie his shoes. You might think to yourself, what's the big deal? It's just shoes; get over it. But imagine this from Jake's perspective: you are an asynchronous person, and your brain is so advanced that you can do graduate level calculus at eight years old, but you can't tie your shoes, something that everyone else you know can do easily. You can imagine how painful that apparent failure might be. The disconnect is stark: Jake said he felt "…like they screwed up my parts when they were putting me together."

Certainly, we could teach Jake how to tie his shoes (and we did): that was not the whole story. To intervene with Jake in an effective way and set him up for success in the future, I had to help him understand how his brain was different—not "screwed up," and how those differences affect him in his everyday life. He had to understand that the very same developmental process that gave him such an advanced and remarkable brain also slowed his developmental maturation in other areas (fine motor skills and emotional regulation) when compared to his chronological peers. His development was asynchronous: he could catch up, but it would take some work.

We're here to talk about developmental asynchrony, a difference unique to neurodivergence (Silverman, 2017). It is one of the trickiest variables of being neurodivergent, especially considering that it is poorly understood and not often explained to families and professionals who work with the community. Understanding how your brain's development has been different than the norm, and how those differences manifest in your life, is vital to creating self-compassion and making connections that work for you.

What does this mean? The more gifted the child, the more asynchronous they are when compared to other kids their age; the more neurodivergent they are, the more asynchronous their development becomes internally (Silverman, 2017). Such an asynchronous system is under tremendous strain, because it's so far-flung: developmental systems are meant to hold closer together, and that's how most kids grow up (Kipping, Tuan, Fortier, & Qiu, 2017). When there's a broader spread of development levels across the different domains (i.e., a brilliant storyteller who doesn't have the fine motor skills to write her stories down), functionality is impacted because the system is working harder than it is designed to.

Let's look at a typical gifted kid in a regular education classroom. We'll call her Emily, she's nine years old, and in Mr. Sanchez's third grade. Emily may not look her chronological age, as most kids do, because physical maturity levels can vary wildly within neurodivergent people. In this case, she's surprisingly tall for a nine-year-old. Her emotional age is likely to lag behind her peers and her chronological age, which sets her up for conflict: adults unwittingly expect more from her because she often sounds so damn mature. When conflict does occur, Emily may not have the skills to manage it because of her relative social immaturity. Yes, the same child who sometimes speaks like a C-SPAN chyron just called you a "poopy mean-face." Meanwhile, Emily is cruising along at an intellectual capacity far beyond her peers and maybe some of her teachers. She's bored in class and acting out as a result; she needs appropriate intellectual stimulation and engagement, but we've got to remember that she's got relatively weak handwriting skills and may not be able to produce written output at the rate required for the next grade level. You've got to find a way to meet all her needs. Sounds fun, right?

We know that gifted children experience unusually fast brain development in the cerebral cortex. With six-month, 12-month and two-year checkups, we see that brain volume increases more in the second year of life than a neurotypical person (Solé-Casals, et al., 2019), and this happens more in the hippocampus and amygdala (which you hopefully remember from our previous discussion). Larger brain volumes exhibit more neural connections that are more robust; that increase persists in the gifted brain, unlike the Autistic brain, in which robust development tends to abate over time (Chan & Han, 2020).

When we're young, our brain overproduces neurons for redundancy's sake (there's safety in numbers) and over time the excess gets pruned (Thomas, 2016). The neuronal connections that remain are well-developed and stronger. With all these extra neurons, synaptic development becomes very important (Solé-Casals, et al., 2019). The denser our synaptic connections are, the more information can travel, which leads to a richer, deeper experience of the world. But the energy required to create all those connections and develop the cerebral cortex (the part of your brain that makes you *you*) is significant. It takes a lot of developmental energy to advance beyond the norms, so there's less energy left for other aspects of growth. This normally manifests in relative underdevelopment of fine-motor skills, social skills, emotional maturity, and executive functioning (Kipping, et al., 2017). In many neurodivergences, social and emotional development is limited because of enhanced neurocognitive development: essentially their brains are moving too fast to develop "emotional intelligence." This phenomenon can happen across the board (as in giftedness), in non-verbal intellectual areas (as in Autism or Dyslexia), or in kinesthetic areas (as with dancers and athletes) (Papandreou, Athinaiou, & Mavrogalou, 2023).

The metaphor I often use to explain this abstract concept is that the neurotypical brain has local roads and some highways, the gifted brain has those but also lots of superhighways. To further the metaphor, the interchanges with other superhighways are smooth and promote strong flow of "traffic," i.e., information. The problem is that the pre-frontal cortex, which would provide the stop signs on this network of roads, is under-developed and unable to offer the appropriate traffic signals, especially in times of high processing or stress. This mismatch between fast traffic and poor signage leads to car accidents, traffic congestion, and stress, which in turn leads to road rage in the driver (you).

The problem with the shoe-tying illustration is that the societal expectation around being able to tie one's shoes is based on neuro-typical behavior. The ages that we expect kids to be able to do certain things (riding bikes, tying shoes, driving cars, going to college, etc.) represents that neurotypical bias (I bet you've got an age number in mind for basically every example I just listed). Logically, that makes sense: about 80% of people are neurotypical so they represent some sort of majority (Doyle, 2020). Neurotypical people tend to develop synchronously, i.e., with cerebral coherence: the different devel-opmental areas—fine motor skills, emotional development, social development, and intellectual development—largely hang together.

Here's what development looks like for a neurotypical person, in this case a 12-year-old:

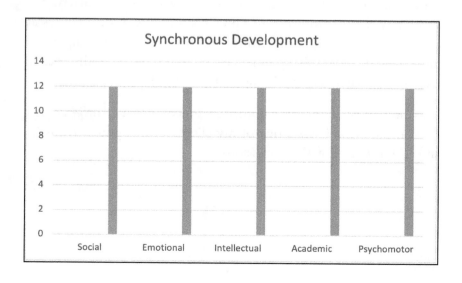

As you can see, this child is essentially twelve in every aspect of development. They "hold together" developmentally, which is what we expect in most kids. There's some variation of functionality, but it's all within an expected range. Such synchronicity allows us to coordinate and manage our understanding of that child.

Then there are the neurodivergent kids. One of the things that I heard growing up with ADHD was that ADHD kids' emotional maturity is really "their age in half and then add half of that back in," which my editor informs me is a complicated way to say ¾ of the person's age. A 12-year-old with ADHD has the emotional maturity of a nine-year-old. This rule of thumb is about is the developmental asynchrony common in ADHD kids: they tend to lag in emotional maturity (which almost certainly contributes to the emotional roller-coaster known as rejection sensitivity dysphoria). Now that we understand how things work, how do we do something about it?

The definition of asynchronous development is that the social, emotional, physical and creative aspects of a person develop in uneven trajectories outside of the norm (Silverman, 2017). Asynchrony implies a greater complexity, both in the person's mind, *and* in how they present externally. These people live life with qualitatively different experiences, and these differences occur in neurodivergent people of all cultures, ethnic groups and segments of society. We also know that neurodivergence predicts other neurodivergences at a much higher rate (just as getting one tattoo predicts getting many more—right, Allie? Julia? Jennie? Todd?), and more neurodivergence means more asynchrony (Kipping, et al., 2017).

Let's now look at the developmental process for a neuro*divergent* 12-year-old (in this case, one of my clients who is gifted, Autistic, and ADHD (used with permission):

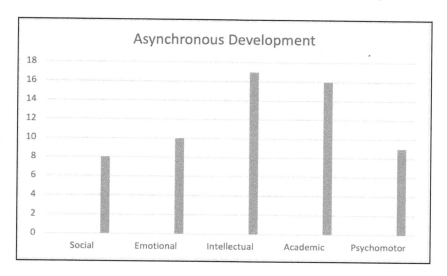

To intervene effectively with this kid, we need to create and implement interventions for *each* developmental level. There's a common assumption in my field, that every gifted kid is actually five kids in one, because of the different ways they develop across these five domains. It certainly feels that way when you work with them! This guideline was offered to me by my mentor, Dr. Jean Peterson, and I have henceforth referred to it as "The Rule of Five." It is asynchrony in action! (It makes the small classroom of seven gifted students seem like a much bigger undertaking!)

As we grow up and evolve into whole people, there are several areas of development. If you've raised kids (or even if you *are* a kid) then you know that growing up is not as simple as just getting older. If we are going to truly understand ourselves and crack our personal "code" (which will then allow us to better understand the neurotypical "code"), then we need to explore the different arenas of development in depth.

Social Development

One of the most visible changes in young life is how we develop as social creatures (Lee, Olszewski-Kubilius, & Thomson, 2012). We go from being very independent and alone, to making friends, to making good friends, to making best friends, to making groups of friends, to approaching romantic and sexual relationships, to having committed relationships, and maybe to getting married. Those social skills must develop *along with* our relationships, because it takes a very different suite of skills to get someone to pass the scissors in art class than to navigate a marriage opportunity. I often think of the fifth season of *Friends* (episode three, because I know you'll check) when Chandler (RIP Matthew Perry) and Monica are dating, and they have their first real fight as a couple.

> *"So I guess this is over."*
>
> *Monica: "What"*
>
> *Chandler: "Well, you and me. It had to end sometime."*
>
> *Monica: "Why, exactly?"*
>
> *Chandler: "Because of the weekend. We had a fight."*
>
> *Monica: "Chandler, that's crazy. If you give up every time you had a fight with someone, you'd never date anyone longer than…oh!"*
>
> *Chandler: "So, this isn't over?"*
>
> *Monica: "You're so cute! No. No. It was a fight. You deal with it, and you move on. It's nothing to freak out about."*
>
> *Chandler: "Really? OK."*
>
> *Monica: "Welcome to an adult relationship!"*

In the above scene, Chandler had never been in a relationship mature enough to have the partner survive a fight. But couples fight! And most of them survive those fights! Monica helps him see how conflict is a part of being in a relationship, and how they'll get through it because they want to stay together. She shows him how much he can grow, and how much he has grown. Chandler is one of my favorite TV characters ever (could he be any *more* of an influence on my sense of humor?); despite his social skills, he is a great example of how you can establish relationships with people and how those evolve over time as you grow and change and need different things. While Monica is an obvious example (the friends to lovers storyline is well-established here), we also get to see his relationships with Ross and Joey evolve throughout the show. Even his last interaction with Rachel shows his growth.

When Rachel is leaving (to go to Paris to start her new career, if you're one of the 17 people who never watched the show), Chandler says, "Let me just say something…Because once we get into this, I'm going to get all uncomfortable and probably make some stupid joke…I just want to say that I…I love you…And I'm going to miss you. And I'm so sad that you're leaving." Granted, he makes the stupid joke soon after, but the fact that he was able to tap into such sincerity, however briefly, shows his growth. Rachel had changed from the pretty girl in high school (yes, we've all seen the continuity problems in the flashback episodes, let's just move on, shall we?) to the pretty girl across the hall, to his pal, to his best friend's girlfriend, to his best friend's ex-girlfriend, to someone that he had his own deep relationship with. To use a more contemporary example, Dr. Sheldon Cooper (played by Jim Parsons) demonstrates remarkable interpersonal growth over the course of the *Big Bang Theory*, though I would argue that the TV series *Young Sheldon* (which depicts Sheldon Cooper in his youth, played by Iain Armitage) demonstrated that process more effectively and authentically.

Of course, real life isn't as clever or direct as on TV, but we can track relationships in real people, even if they don't have the benefit of writers. Let's look at the stages of typical relationship development and compare to how neurodivergent and gifted people would do. These stages are from the world of the late, great Marcia Gross (Gross, 2009).

Stage One is "The Play Partner"

In this earliest stage of friendship, the relationship is based on "play partnership," or the reciprocal sharing and exchanging of items and games during play. A person who engages another person in playing, whether consistently or intermittently, would meet this standard. This could be a person that you shoot hoops with at the YMCA or someone to play jump-rope with on the playground. It can even be the person you share a cubicle with or another parent in the pick-up line at school.

Stage Two is "People to Chat to"

In this stage relationships move beyond the activity you're playing into whether deeper shared interests exist that can be cultivated. People tend to choose friends with whom they share interests, especially outside of the activity (i.e., school or work) that brought them together. Though I went to graduate school with over 150 people, I was closest to those with whom I played recreational soccer (hi Al!).

Stage Three is "Help and Encouragement"

In this stage, a friend is seen as someone who will offer help, support, or encouragement with daily challenges. For a lot of people, however, the advantages of friendship tend to be unidirectional: the person does not necessarily see himself as having the obligation to provide help or support in return. You can think of someone who asks to copy your homework or someone who always does the coffee run at the office; there's a *delivery* of service, but not an exchange.

Stage Four is "Intimacy and Empathy"

In this stage, the person has come to realize that the best friendships are ones in which comfort and support flow both ways. For many people, the giving of affection and its reciprocation become fundamental to the relationship. Sharing of emotions and support lead to greater empathy and intimacy. You know that moment when your conversations move in depth and sincerity from "Hey, how about that local sports team?" to "Hey, do you think that I'm any good at this thing we do?"—that's this stage in action.

Stage Five is "The Sure Shelter"

In this stage, friendship is perceived as a deep and lasting relationship with trust, fidelity, and unconditional acceptance. This level of friendship promotes people dropping their "masks" and letting go of external "codes" of conduct; with this person, you can be yourself without pretense. These are the people that you can do anything with and feel joy, from being in each other's weddings to long rambling conversations.

Oftentimes gifted kids want to move their friendships right to stage four or five (Lee, et al., 2012). When I worked at a school for gifted kids, we would have a kid visit the school for a tour and assign them a student guide for the day. I cannot begin to tell you how many times those kids would end the day with the sincere pledge, "This person's my *best friend*"—even though they've known them for only three hours. You can see the neurodivergence at work here; there's the intensity about relationships, but also an obvious sense of relief: "I finally found someone who's on my wavelength! It's everything I've ever wanted". The problem is that most relationships that reach Stage Five do so *over time*; they evolve and mature organically (Lee, et al., 2012; Gross, 2009). If you cannonball in, you may find that there's not enough foundation to sustain the intensity. Once the initial charm wears off, you may find that the person wasn't your "BFF" after all. (Of course that doesn't make them your enemy!) The real takeaway here is that you cannot microwave a friendship; it's more like a good chili that you simmer over time.

One of the problems with social development is that people initially see everyone as a friend, and then see a conflicting duality, "friend or foe." That all-or-nothing thinking increases distress and can make us less willing to connect with others, which artificially decreases our potential for friendship (Cavilla, 2019). In actuality, life presents us with millions of social relationship styles—from teammate to "friends with benefits" to co-worker to vacation friend to arch nemesis. The more you're able to understand, identify, and appreciate different types of relationships, the more socially developed you become (Lee, et al., 2012).

Emotional Development

To manage social relationships, emotional skills must evolve apace. As relationships become more complex, we need to have not only the language for more advanced emotions, but the skills to identify and regulate them. Emotional stability is the ability to remain even-tempered, particularly in the face of challenges and threats (Ellis, Hoskin, & Ratnasingam, 2018). As with all emotional growth, becoming emotionally synchronous isn't about having fewer emotions, it's about being able to regulate them sooner and more effectively. Life's challenges don't stop, and they do get harder, so we must get stronger if we're going to keep up.

If you've had kids, you undoubtedly went through the phase where their crying could mean that they were hungry, scary, tired, hurt, bored, thirsty, lonely, overwhelmed, sick, or (as my wife was fond of saying during those days) "just being a toddler." So, what was causing the crying this time? Well, since the kid couldn't really tell us, we were often reduced to guessing the solution by trying multiple soothing techniques until the tears stopped. With or without kids, it's quite frustrating to face an emotional problem where the person cannot communicate with you.

Conversely, if you have occasion to be around teenagers (or, God help you, tweens) dating, you'll find yourself actively hoping for the rapid development of emotional maturity and honest communication (as opposed to my recent client's plan to "unfollow them on Instagram so they *know* I'm mad"). In terms of intellectual development, tweens and teens have most of the language that they'll develop in their lifetimes, and they're not shy about using it (or tweeting it, or texting it). But since their brains are still developing, they have an underdeveloped ability to regulate their feelings, which leads them to emotional highs lows and the occasional (or perhaps more frequent) verbal outburst.

As you get older, you start to seek more emotional stability, because the affective highs and lows of your teens and twenties start to feel childish (not to mention exhausting). I distinctly remember the sensation among our peer group, when gossiping about the drunken arguments between a couple at a party moved from "Oooh, spill the tea! I love drama!" to "I feel bad for them" to "They just need to grow up; this is exhausting (did I just reference Taylor Swift again?)." It just stopped feeling as vicariously satisfying, probably because we were getting our emotional satisfaction from different kinds of input: a career instead of a summer job; an apartment instead of a "room" behind a bookcase (Ben!); a beer after work instead of a bender. The meanings of these shifting stimuli represent developing maturity in the limbic system. The brain can derive more valuable dopamine from being regulated than from riding a dopamine burst of less regulated and probably more intense emotional shifts (Berger, et al., 2007).

It isn't an accident that you start seeking more relationship stability as you achieve more emotional stability. And we need to remember that not all relationships are romantic and/or sexual in nature. You seek mentorship rather than just managers; you get to know your parents as people; you find yourself spending less time with people stuck in "the good ol'" days' (except for bachelor (ette) parties and weddings, of course). The reinforcement patterns from our peers are also changing as we mature. Whereas opting out of a fun night out in college would have been a case for serious FOMO (Fear of Missing Out), those same friends who were drunk dialing you at 2am "rally for one more beer!" are now saying when you text cancelling tonight's plans, "Dude, I totally get it. Now I can go to bed early." These trends emphasize the importance of community in regulating asynchrony, which we will talk about more.

I'm sure you've all seen the meme that points out that "the punishments of my youth [going to bed early, staying in my room, not having plans on a Friday night] have become the rewards of my adulthood." The cost-benefit analysis of these events changes because our brains are learning to value events differently (Ellis, et al., 2018). Every age has problems, and all problems evoke emotional responses. Unfollowing someone on Instagram feels vital to a tween, just like trying not to bounce your rent check feels vital to a twentysomething. Let's not play the "misery Olympics" in comparing problems across the lifespan; things hurt when they hurt, and that hurt can only be experienced through the lens of that person's phase of life. The good news is that every challenge we overcome provides us with the skills and experience to better regulate problems in the future. If you live life long (and hard) enough, you'll find that one day you've somehow developed emotional maturity. And despite what your inner teen might shriek, you may actually welcome it.

Intellectual Development

One of the most gratifying things about working with people is to experience how they grow intellectually. Regardless of which neuro-divergence is under consideration, IQ as a score is relatively static throughout our lives. This is true for ADHD (Agnew-Blais, Polanczyk, Danese, Wertz, Moffitt, & Arseneault, 2020), giftedness (Bucaille, Jarry, Allard, Brochard, Peudenier, & Roy, 2022), Autism (Courchesne, et al., 2021), dyslexia (Toth & Siegel, 2020), and even twice-exceptional people (Goswami, Huss, Mead, & Fosker, 2021). What changes is how we are better able to use intellectual potential as we age. We don't get smarter, per se, but we do get more capable at working the systems that we are presented with (i.e., having a job, going to school, dating apps) We know more, we're able to tap into more areas of knowledge, both because we are exposed to more things, and because we learn things that are personally engaging and cause us to seek knowledge on our own. IQ is best understood as a measure of intellectual potential, and life experience helps us to better realize that potential.

Imagine you're a 6-year-old with an IQ of 144, you have the verbal capacity of an 11-year-old, and you've been assigned to do some writing in class. Most of your peers are neurotypical, and they'll likely be writing about what they did this weekend, or a TV show they saw, or their favorite dessert. And those are fine developmentally appropriate answers! But in your gifted brain you're contemplating an idea you had recently about a bear who has a magic cape that allows them to fly, and the bear uses its powers to stop villains in national parks. You're getting ready to that idea on paper, but you don't have the fine motor skills to write fast, and you might not have the time or enough paper to write out your idea. Maybe you don't know every word you need to know. Faced with these challenges, you have a meltdown instead of working on the assignment. You feel that if you don't finish the assignment, your teachers will never realize your intellectual ability.

The intellectual dynamic of *asynchrony* flares the most when there's a disconnect between your brilliant ideas and the skillset necessary to actualize those ideas. Many kids have beautiful unique ideas, but don't have the words, emotional regulation, or fine motor skills to get them out. That's why it is so important to let neurodivergent kids share their ideas in many ways. Give them a scribe—someone to write it down; let them use voice to text, or the chance to write or type it out. You can simply listen to people talk (not just kids!) and hear in their own words what they're capable of. You will find that they get more words out and feel better about what they're producing because you're allowing them to show their potential in ways that fit their developmental level and skills, rather than forcing them to play by a mismatched set of rules.

Academic Development

The most rewarding research I've done in my academic career has concerned the idea of the Performance Cliff. The Performance Cliff describes a phenomenon that occurs mainly in gifted and twice-exceptional students, where students perform at an advanced level academically for many years with minimal effort until they suddenly "fall off a cliff" *academically*, and begin performing poorly (Nicpon & Pfeiffer, 2011). This usually occurs between grades 7-10 (ages 13—16). The variables of this phenomenon are complex, but the basic idea is that eventually school demands diverge from the processes of their unique natural intelligence. They have not developed the resiliency and study skills of their neurotypical peers: they fall behind because they lack the fundamental academic scaffolding to support further success (Peterson, 2014).

Here's an excellent graphic about this phenomenon created by my super-talented wife, Dr. Julia Hodgson. She's way better at graphic design than I am.

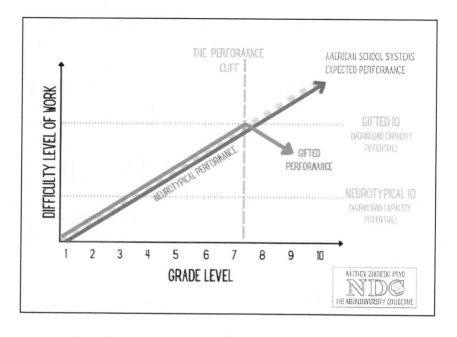

As one moves further into their education, workload and expectations get more demanding and complex. A person must develop the skills to maintain their academic performance and evolve to continue meeting those demands. Reading Tom Sawyer just to say you've read it is very different than reading it for the answers to questions—i.e., what town is Tom from? (St. Petersburg, Missouri, which is based on Hannibal, Missouri, where Mark Twain grew up). And reading for answers is different than reading for subjective and abstract concepts like themes, symbolism, and perspective. When I was in graduate school at Widener University, I often tried to warn the first-year students that grad school isn't just about amassment of knowledge: you wouldn't be in graduate school if you didn't know things. Graduate school is about *applying* knowledge. The students who adapted to that assessment (i.e., those who listened to me) did well; those who struggled to adapt and learn how to *apply* their knowledge often struggled.

Being gifted or neurodivergent does not predict doing well in school because intelligence and performance do not always align (Lovecky, 2014), especially if varieties of intelligence are not supported in the school environment, like kinesthetic intelligence (Gardner, 2021). When I do psycho-educational evaluations, I always get scores which reflect intellectual levels (IQ is an age-normed score) as well as academic levels (most achievement tests allow for both age- and grade-level comparisons). Both levels are important because we want to see a person's intellectual ability *and* how well school has captured that potential; their academic development should dovetail with intellectual ability (Bucaille, et al., 2021). You should also get repeated data sets (every three years is the standard) to show how well these measures align over time. When the data diverge, we see the risk of the Performance Cliff because the person's underlying skills are no longer keeping pace with their intellectual potential.

When we talk about academics and work, we must remind ourselves that there are atypical students and workers, and they will need atypical strategies. I say that at every school where I work, and I think it is fundamentally important. We must think outside the box, transcend academic rigidity, and meet the kids at *their current levels* of development, not where you think they are or should be. Allow your kid to soar where they're at a high level of challenge and enrichment, and provide support for any area of weakness. It can be difficult to find reading material for kids where content and challenge match an individual's needs, because more challenging books tend to have more mature themes. This is when we talk to librarians. What are other kids reading? What are the forgotten classics or indie darlings that might just thread this asynchronous needle.

And since life is about way more than just books, your kid might benefit from an alternative educational placement: acceleration, online learning, homeschooling, unschooling, or early college, just to name a few. It's not just guesswork, either. We can identify and teach the skills that a student might need to be successful in their current placement and begin preparing them for the skills they'll need for future academic challenges. When we do that skill-building with the best practices in gifted education, we better prepare students for their future (Lovecky, 2014). Thankfully, the Performance Cliff is one of the few phenomena in education and psychology that allows us to be proactive. We know the cliff is looming, and when it is likely to be precipitous, so we can front-load interventions and pedagogical strategies. This is perhaps the best argument for using gifted education practices in schools; the sooner we give kids of all abilities meaningful challenge (appropriate to their levels), the sooner they develop the supporting skills they need to be successful academically (Nicpon & Pfeiffer, 2011).

Psychomotor Development

Our psychomotor skills also develop as we age. When you watch a 2-year-old try to walk, you see the difference from a five-year-old walking, just like there's a difference between a 5-year-old and a 10-year-old and a 15-year-old riding their bikes. This is the area where Jake had problems; namely, he lagged development in fine motor skills.

Fine motor skills involve dexterity and the ability to manipulate objects (Brown, 2010). Painting, drawing, playing the recorder, hand-writing, using small tools—all these activities require your body to be able to achieve precise movement and manipulation. If your body is lagging in those skills—which is normal for the neurodivergent brain—you quickly become aware that few other people are experiencing those challenges. It can feel very isolating and stigmatizing to have such delays. If you look at any recess field across the country, most of the kids are playing some sort of ball game: sports enjoy elevated importance in American society. If your skills lag in that area, you feel immediately that you don't (or can't) fit in, which is tough.

In school or at work, the challenge of asynchronous fine motor skills may keep you from succeeding in "cooler" academic practices, like art or music. If you're academically inclined, you may find yourself struggling in arts classes due to these physical differences (those damn finger placements on the violin are brutal!). Many of my gifted STEM clients went to elite colleges and got perfect 4.0 GPAs in their core classes, and yet struggled to pass Introduction to Sculpture, Piano Basics, or Essentials of the Written Word. Your weaker handwriting may not matter as much in math class when you can use a calculator, but you will eventually have to write down answers somewhere, and those need to be legible. Regardless of your discipline, there are places where you cannot hide fine motor delays: filling pipettes, holding a surgical clamp, soldering, wiring, even using a screwdriver!

Research consistently shows that Autistic children can experience both gross and fine motor delays, as well as atypical motor patterns. A study by Johnson-Ecker and Parham (2000) showed that autistic children achieved lower scores in praxis tests (the ability to conceptualize, plan and co-ordinate movements to carry out a motor task) than their peers with typical development. Motor skill development depends on forming complex connections between different parts of the brain that link sensory information from the body with information from the environment, along with our innate motivation to plan and execute motor movements (Costa, Abelairas-Gomez, Arufe-Giráldez, Pazos-Couto, & Barcala-Furelos, 2015). The neurodivergent person may present with weaker balance, coordination, and proprioception (body awareness), all of which impede the ability to manage these skills.

As I said earlier, the more asynchronous a person's development, the more stress they are under. Psychomotor delays themselves are challenging, but when combined with any degree of social and emotional immaturity, you have a recipe for interpersonal conflict and poor self-esteem. Therefore, we need to set expectations for our kids about their motor skills because the lags in these skills are likely to be quite visible in their interactions with others. When they struggle, it's important to be able to zoom out to broader skill development: identify the things that come easily (ABC), the things one is great at (DEF), and the things that need help (XYZ). Needing help is not bad: skills are easily improved with the right interventions.

Chronological Development

Of course we must consider chronological age. With age come certain expectations—behavioral norms that are baked into our societies, that boil down to what we expect an 8-year-old, a 10-year-old, a 20-year-old, or a 30-year-old to be able to do or not do. For example, I expect a 30-year-old to have a job, and perhaps their own apartment. I don't expect them to pick their nose (at least in public): that's something we might expect from a 7-year-old. And a big part of working with asynchrony is understanding the role that our own expectations (implicit and explicit) might impose on how we interact with that person.

A lot of gifted kids get referred to me before we even know they're gifted kids, because their parents or teachers describe them as an "old soul." That's a well-worn chestnut in my field. Kids labeled in this way because they're thinking, acting, and talking in a manner that seems far beyond how they "should" be based on expectations related to their chronological age. This child isn't like the other semi-feral students in elementary school! This child is thoughtful, polite, and introspective. And while those traits are true, such behavioral highs can be seductive, as they can artificially shift our biases and expectations: we end up expecting the highest levels of behavior in all developmental areas, even though the child is asynchronous and logically has areas of delayed functionality in addition to their preternatural maturity. In doing so, we set our kids up to fail when they inevitably struggle at something.

When your kid has an emotional or behavioral outburst (yes, they're going to happen), it's vital to gather yourself before you respond. For example, you're trying to read this book, and you've actually got a minute of peace, but then your child choses THIS moment to recite a brand-new musical that they've written using a made-up language. That's frustrating! (And perhaps pulled from my experiences with my own children as I tried to find the time to write this book). Before you respond to your child's behavior and conclude that they are socially or emotionally immature, stop. Stop and remind yourself of the person's chronological age because that behavior might be totally in line with what's expected *for that age*. It's hard to do because gifted kids are very articulate and charismatic and passionate, and they create so much at a rate that is well beyond their years. With that amazing context, it's easy to forget they are only a ten-year-old, and that this behavior (however frustrating) is something ten-year-olds do. Your kid isn't bad; they're being a kid. It's not easy or fun to do these cognitive reframes, but their behavior is understandable, and identifying the overall context in such situations predicts better outcomes.

Once upon a time I was working with a very neurodivergent family in therapy. I was in a session with the mom, and she was expressing frustration with her daughter's inability to keep her room clean. Mom detailed the elaborate system she had devised for her daughter to organize her room, including baskets and labels and drawers and more. Mom was livid that her daughter wasn't following the plan. "She's so smart!" mom grumbled, "but she's also so lazy when it's something that she doesn't want to do." I waited a few moments and then asked mom to remind how old her daughter was.

"Nine," she said. She thought for a moment. "Is that...?"

"Way too young to do all that? Yup." I replied.

"But she can do so much sometimes!"

"Absolutely. And if we want her to reach that super-high level in other areas of her life, we need to understand that she's still nine. If we meet her where she's at chronologically, we can build her up to higher levels in other parts of her life."

We started with getting her to try and put her dirty clothes and towels in the hamper every day. Before the end of the summer, she had developed enough to be able to use two of the baskets. That was enough for us for now. "After all," mom said, "she's only nine!"

Connection

Managing asynchrony is ultimately in service of establishing connection, because the connections we establish may be as complex and multifaceted as we are. That's why it's vital that we talk about it with our students, our clients, our children, and ourselves. If we contain significant variability of interests, skills, strengths, weaknesses, motivations, and triggers, then we must have multitudes of interventions for all aspects of ourselves.

The intellectual level of a 6-year-old whose brain is like a 15-year-old will lead them to talk to older kids or people, because they can hang' with them intellectually. They can talk about more mature things, like the *New York Times* Crossword Puzzle (instead of the latest episode of *Miss Rachel*). One of the reasons that I'm successful working with neurodivergent kids is that I meet them where they are intellectually. I had a kid sidle up to me on the playground one day, give a world-weary sigh, plop down next to me and moan, "Can you believe what the Fed is doing? These Interest Rates are going to tank my investments!" And while it was hard (so hard!) not to laugh, I knew that this kid had an interest in finance that well-outstripped his other third grade peers (shocking, I know) and most adults in his life (including me, but he didn't need to know that). I asked to tell me more and we connected about the feelings that drove his interests in this area. As we've clarified several times in this book already, the whole point of understanding one's neurodivergence is to be able to find community and crack the world's "code" by establishing your own.

While there is significant benefit in establishing your own communities and "codes," a parallel struggle is the need for neurodivergent kids to connect with their same age peers at the same time, especially if the same age peers are neurotypical, because they represent the dominant paradigm. That doesn't mean that they need to be best friends, but you must be able to communicate effectively in different groups to successfully navigate the world.

Neurodivergent people can struggle to connect with others within their neurotype as well. When traveling for work, I encounter groups of neurodivergent folks navigating quite varied social scenarios. I've seen playgroups for gifted kids where they're all working together and creating wildly elaborate universes and games; and I've seen different gifted play groups consumed mostly with a lot of *parallel play*, where instead kids play in the same space but not together (Papacheck, Chai, & Green, 2016). That's not a bad thing! It's developmentally important to have your own activity to occupy you when you need the stability of emotional or intellectual refueling. When we are forced to do things outside of our comfort zone for too long, we increase social anxiety and feelings out burnout (Raymaker, et al., 2020). Those feelings are so unpleasant that the mere *possibility* of being stuck somewhere in the community with an empty social battery is enough to have neurodivergent people repeatedly opting out of social scenarios that they might genuinely like.

We also need neurodivergent people to experience coming together in successful interaction. When the neurodivergent people do come together effectively, WOW, it's a high-level conversation around things that lights everyone up. I once had a conversation with a group of gifted and twice-exceptional kids about which world leader from history (fictional and non-fictional) would have been most likely compete and win on *RuPaul's Drag Race*. (Gosh, I love my job sometimes). Each kid brought knowledge from their areas of expertise, and bounced ideas off each other until, ultimately, Eleanor Roosevelt was declared the winner (which, honestly, I understand).

At the end of the day, a gifted person has a great deal of shared understanding with another gifted person. The depth of interaction with another person, and the length of time that they can sustain those positive moments, can vary with their development and with the appropriateness of the others involved. But it's always worth trying to get people together who can connect. Even if my gifts are in writing and drawing and yours are in computer coding, the intellectual passion and intensity can go together.

We help the people in our lives understand the meaning of being neurodivergent, the strengths and weaknesses that come with that, and what asynchrony is. Knowing all of that can help set realistic expectations. Going back to Jake, I explained to him that his brain works differently. The same developmental pathway that sent him to graduate school at eight is also hurting him, if it's making it much harder to tie his shoes. Once I put that reality in context for him, the task was still hard, but he understood why. When our kids are struggling and don't know why, they are faster to melt down because they lose perspective (or maybe lacked it in the first place). Offering context helps kids explore strategies that help navigate being out of sync. The brain can adapt and change and learn new skills. We just need to be willing and invested to teach it.

Mindfulness is a good strategy for people to work on, because it involves bringing our awareness to what is happening right now and doing so without judgment: this is *really hard* for a neurodivergent person because of their intensities. Right now, take a moment and focus on your surroundings. What can you hear? What can you feel? The more you focus in the moment, the more we synch up with our environment and experience of things; it's almost like a superpower. As I'm writing this, I practiced this technique myself and was able to hear my neighbor listening to music (Counting Crows, good call!) three houses down. That music was playing the entire time, but I was so focused on my own stuff that I was "blind" to outer sensory experiences. Mind-body tools, like mindfulness, gets the brain and body flowing together; these techniques will help ground our kids, and help people feel more stable and secure, especially when those people have less experience in talking about feelings.

If mindfulness isn't for you (and it's certainly not for everyone), activities like yoga, martial arts, rock climbing, American Ninja Warrior, tai chi, Zumba, etc. are all things that help our kids get grounded in their own bodies, and thus more in control over them. You are likely going to need multiple peer groups to fit all the developmental areas of your child (who is like five kids in one!). One group might have a chronological fit, one might have a mental age match, one might share a deep interest, etc. I work with an 11-year-old who's really into astrophysics, and his best friend is a 45-year-old professor who lives in his neighborhood; they hang out two or three times a week, go on walks, talk about celestial bodies—it's adorable. We know most 11-year-olds don't have friends who are 45, but this is a cognitive and interest match. This same kid also goes to Boy Scouts with kids from his school who are his age, and that serves a very different need for him. He's encouraged to do both!

Another way to think about supporting asynchrony is in terms of riding bikes. If you were helping your kid learn how to ride a bike, you could stand at the end of the street with your arms crossed and say, "Okay, ride your bike to me." You might do this because you feel that your kid should know how to ride a bike at their age because you did, and other kids have as well. But your kid *hasn't* ridden a bike yet, which means that they're probably not ready to perform just because you need it. Your kid will probably learn how to do it eventually, but forcing it would cause a lot of scraped knees and banged heads and crying, and maybe a trip to the emergency room. Or you could choose to meet your kid where they are in their own development, rather than focusing on how to they compare to other kids. Stand right behind your kid and guide them along until they're ready to go on their own. You'll have to spend the time anyway, which might seem harder, but you can choose to enjoy the collaboration at your kids' pace and you both win. If the people in your life need that extra hand on the bike (or some training wheels), that's just where they are, that's not good or bad. If we're moving towards developing skills and independence, however slowly, it's a good thing to be right there with them and help them learn.

Dr. Linda Silverman (2017) said that asynchronous kids *feel* that conflict and *feel* more vulnerable because their asynchrony is atypical compared to the norm, to most people. We cannot magically "catch them up" in their domains of development, but we do know that people's developmental levels tend to regress to more expected, synchronous arrangements over time. Our job is to help them understand how they are different and support them in developing the skills to mitigate the differences, while also playing to their strengths. Asynchronous people may exist, as described in the "Rule of Five," but there's always a way to personalize their development so that they feel understood and seen as the person they are.

If you'd like to explore asynchrony further, look at the circle diagram below (no, I didn't steal it from Trivial Pursuit). It is a way to express our asynchronous levels externally! My therapy clients are very familiar with this exercise ☺.

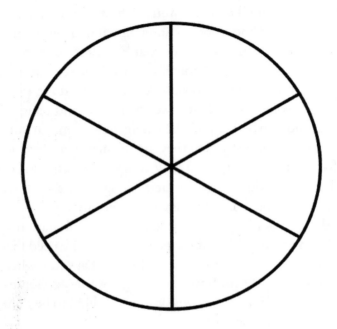

If the ring equals one's chronological age (I'm 40 at the time of writing this book, for example), you can use the pie pieces to see how you think your skill levels compare across the different domains of development: Social, Emotional, Psycho-Motor, Academic, Intellectual, and Special Interest/Occupation. I would be comparing myself to other 40-year-olds. It doesn't matter if they're psychologists, stay-at-home parents, CEOs, baristas, or gym teachers; how do I think I stack up? If you're at the norm for your age, you color in that entire wedge (pie piece) to the circle line; if you're below age norms, you make a mark somewhere inside the circle (75%? 10%?) and color that part of the wedge in. If you're living in your gifted era, and you're way beyond your average age-peer, then trace the lines outward beyond the circle until you get to the right level beyond your circle age. If you think you're 45% smarter than the average ten-year-old, and if you're a Davidson Young Scholar, you almost certainly are; you'd better go ahead and draw your intellectual line far out there.

It's an interesting exercise to do, and to have your loved ones do as well (especially your kids) to see how we each see ourselves and how other people see us as well. If someone has a much better view of you (especially if they think you're better than you think you are), it's a worthy conversation to have. Save each iteration and see how you grow over time!

CHAPTER 5
Executive Functioning and You: Why Focusing is Hard and How to Improve at it

Hooray, it's everyone's favorite topic! This chapter is going to be a real blast. Make sure that you top off the coffee, grab some strong peppermint gum, and maybe take a quick walk around the block. We've got to get our brains and bodies ready to talk about executive functioning. If you're listening to the audiobook, feel free to bump this up to 1.5x speed (which you've probably already done, if I know my population), but please don't go so fast that I sound like Alvin the Chipmunk! There's good stuff here, and I promise to make it more accessible and less shaming that the stuff you've probably been hearing about executive functioning your whole life.

OK, round of applause please, because I'm going to tell you a funny story about executive dysfunction.

I love doing trivia. I think that it's fun, engaging, feeds my competitive streak, and allows me to flex my ridiculous compendium of useless knowledge. Right after college I got a job working at the Harvard Psychophysiology Lab under the tutelage of Dr. Wendy Berry Mendes (there's no non-obnoxious way to say that you worked at Harvard, so I figure that at this point I might as well own it). As the summer progressed, I got to know several of the students well. One day they recruited me to their elite Pub Quiz team which participated in a hard-core, high-stakes underground league in greater Boston that faced off against teams from MIT, Tufts, Boston College, Boston University, Emerson College, among others. They needed me because of my encyclopedic knowledge of sports and broader pop culture; but more important, I was on the team! We finished 3-0 that summer and I was hooked for life.

Trivia has some significant therapeutic benefits, which I've incorporated into my clinical work. It teaches us self-regulation (waiting to answer), emotional regulation (being a good winner and a good loser), teamwork, frustration tolerance, and how to trust other people (Alamu, Adesina, & Awokola, 2021). Most importantly, trivia teaches us that life isn't just about being smart; it's also about getting lucky (Swain, Bogardus, & Lin, 2021). There is no way to know everything about everything. Sometimes you get questions that you know the answers to, and sometimes you don't. It's a vital experiential lesson for many of us who lean on our knowledge and over-prepare: sometimes there's no amount of preparation that can help you.

Several years ago, I was presenting my talk on therapeutic trivia at a conference, and we were playing my trivia game. I had divided the kids into ten groups of 4-6 kids each, so we could practice social skills in addition to showing how smart we are. We made the "code" of conduct clear so we could all do our best to follow it. I break my trivia questions into categories: Science, ELA, Grab Bag, Pop Culture, Math, History, and The Bridge of Destiny. In this story, I was asking a science question: What is the atomic weight of Uranium? While everybody was scratching their heads, trying to remember the atomic weight of Uranium, I didn't realize one of the kids was in the adjacent bathroom. I'll call him Bryan. Bryan had introduced himself to me earlier and told me that he was from Texas, that he could recite Pi to over 167 places, and that he was a big fan of science, especially chemistry. He was finishing up in the bathroom when I asked the question. He heard the word Uranium through the door, realized that he knew the answer and wanted to quickly come help his team. Which he did! Except he forgot one thing: to pull up his pants.

Suddenly, we have this kid come tearing out of the bathroom with his pants around his ankles to sprint (OK, waddle) into the middle of the classroom and yell, before God and country, "the atomic weight of Uranium is 238.02891 Atomic Units!" which was of course the right answer and highly specific. First, he was very proud of himself. Second, he had violated one of the rules of the game: each group was supposed to write down their answers and bring them up to me. And lastly, his pants were around his ankles. The room cracked up laughing, and once he realized the situation, he was a good sport about it. We moved on with the game and Bryan's team ended up winning! As we were wrapping up, I remember thinking to myself, "that's *exactly* that I mean when I talk about executive functioning deficits in gifted kids; Bryan's brain just couldn't wait and follow the rules." And then I ran after Bryan's family to ask if I could tell this story in the future. (Thanks, guys!)

Sometimes, despite our best efforts and high levels of intelligence, our impulses overwhelm our best intentions, and we have executive dysfunction. Executive dysfunction is when the cognitive processes that regulate other cognitive processes are disrupted and errors occur (Lambek, Tannock, Dalsgaard, Trillingsgaard, Damm, & Thomsen, 2011). In school, that can be "I forgot my homework," or "I didn't know we had a test today!" At work, that could mean, "What's a W2 and why do you need that form?" or "My ID badge is around here somewhere…" Sometimes executive dysfunction means you get so overwhelmed by what's going on that you sprint out of the bathroom with your pants around your ankles to answer a trivia question out loud for everyone to hear. (We made Bryan go back and wash his hands, for the record.)

When we talk about the executive function, we must talk about my favorite part of the brain, the prefrontal cortex! It's right there in the front of your head (I'm pointing at it, not that you can see me). The prefrontal cortex (PFC) concerns executive functioning skills, which include planning, follow-through, task initiation, task completion, self-regulation, time management, attention, and organization (Kolk & Rakic, 2022). Most importantly, executive functioning involves the idea of behavioral inhibition. You want to do a thing, and you have to make sure the time and place is right for you to do the thing. To go back to the child from the classroom trivia story: Bryan knew the answer, which meets the responsibility of the game, but it was clearly the wrong time and place for him to answer the question...at least until he pulled his shorts up, right? We need to be able to stop and think before we respond, which is challenging enough for people, and even more challenging when you're neurodivergent.

One of my favorite exercises during my talks serves to normalize how difficult behavioral inhibition can be. I ask a room full of adults (often teachers and other educational professionals) what their state capital is. Inevitably, they all shout out the answer like the scene in *Hamilton* where they're trying to decide where to put the nation's capital (it isn't pretty) or, if you're not a theatre kid, like asking a room of sixth graders what movie we should watch in class today. Chaos! None of the teachers ever raise their hands to answer, even though they are professionals who expect that from their students. Why don't they raise their hands? "Because it's obvious!" they say. I agree with them! So, now, imagine being a gifted kid in a regular education class and feeling that way about every question.

What happens, specifically in the gifted brain, is superhighways of neural connections—lots of information whipping through the brain. The job of the prefrontal cortex is to sort all that information and determine when to respond, how to respond, how much to respond and when to stop responding (Kircher-Morris, 2022). With all those things are happening, the brain gets bogged down, like a bunch of cars trying to get off at the same exit in a messy traffic jam: it's a structural bottleneck. Bottlenecks are high stress situations, and higher stress leads to more errors and accidents. Unfortunately, the prefrontal cortex often acts as a neuropsychological bottleneck and can create that same stressful crunch when there's too much information to sort and not the time or space to sort it effectively. That's how our brains are made, and that's nobody's fault. We need to understand what's happening from a neuropsychological perspective, as we seek to intervene with those who have executive functioning deficits.

Asynchronous development often shows up as lagging executive functioning skills, particularly insufficient attention and organization. Your kid may need additional support and skills training in this area because of how their brain has grown. To paraphrase the Genie from *Aladdin*, "Phenomenal mental powers!!! Itty bitty focus space." I've always suspected that this brain difference this is where the idea of the "absent-minded professor" comes from. The professor is clearly intelligent; they were hired to teach the class, after all. But teaching the class is far more interesting than doing the things (i.e., making copies, grading papers) that running that same class entails. A lot of smart people don't do so well with remembering or organizing things which seem less important than the big ideas of finishing the project or getting the kids to soccer practice. They are smart enough to get into the spaces where they can flex their brains; our job is to help them stay focused there by helping them develop executive functioning skills.

Cognitive controls like executive function take a lot of energy (Ott & Nieder, 2019). If you need to gain information you must pay attention, which can be challenging depending on the type and format of that information. To retain the information, you must encode it in the brain, first in working memory, and eventually in long-term storage. Then you must use your skills to retrieve and then communicate that information. People cannot take our knowledge at our word: we must be able to demonstrate it, or they may not believe it. The cognitive-informational loop cannot be closed until we learn the information, store it, and ultimately communicate it in some way to an audience (Landry, 2021) verbally, in writing, through nonverbal communication, texting, tweeting—heck, it could be an interpretive dance if you're in that mood, right?

The brain supplies the energy for this process using dopamine, which is an excitatory neurotransmitter (Landry, 2021). The brain says, "ooh, I like this!" (very scientific, you know) and energizes the body so it can be ready to go out and get more. To get the thing that you want, it takes some dopamine to make it happen, but you get more dopamine for completing the task, so you end up with a slight net positive (Ott & Nieder, 2019). It's a what we call a micro-circuit.

You need dopamine to get those tasks done, but you gain dopamine for completing them, like when you go to the gym and work out but somehow end up with more energy than when you started. The problem is with people who are running low on dopamine and don't have the energy to regulate themselves: they are not going to be able to work the microcircuit and gain more dopamine from completing the task (Landry, 2021; Ott & Nieder, 2019). They fall further and further into dopamine deficit until they get in trouble for being off task or whatever "the code" is asking them to do. To survive this deficit, they will attempt to "borrow" dopamine from tomorrow's load, which puts us down the spiral into burnout (Raymaker, et al., 2020).

It's important to note that part of the neurotypical "code" is self-discipline. Self-discipline, along with respect, are good ideas that have been bastardized to become a tool of the ill-informed to move the goal post so they can judge people they see as breaking "the code". Discipline *is* important, and there's value in learning it for yourself. But for neurotypicals, the bar to clear for managing self-discipline is much lower than it is in the neurodivergent brain! (Landry, 2021). Our brain's ability to use dopamine to start, sustain, and stop tasks is vital to developing and maintaining self-discipline (Berger, et al., 2007). When it comes to task completion, poor use of dopamine in the neurodivergent brain isn't the brain saying, "I don't want to"; the brain is saying, "I can't". That's a huge difference. The skill isn't just weak, it's not there.

What this all means for one's child on the playground, my teen in school, or your partner at work, is that their brain has these differences (which are not deficits!). There are natural differences in the gifted brain, the Autistic brain, the ADHD brain, the Dyslexic brain, etc. Many of such structural and functional differences come from the prefrontal cortex, which of course is the primary source of executive functioning skills (Kolk & Rakic, 2022). But the prefrontal cortex also regulates personality, moral judgment, self-monitoring, as well as behavior, emotions, and awareness of other people. If that part of the brain comes "online" later, it's more likely to make mistakes, to struggle with organization, self-monitoring and impulse control.

When we think about how that shows up in our kids—yelling out in class, reactive behavior, abandoning a project to start a new project, giving up when things get hard—it shows you just how many parts of life these skills impact. If we don't understand the role of the brain in these behaviors, then the neurodivergent *person* gets the blame because of the Fundamental Attribution Error. I can see all of you nodding along out there in the universe.

That's because that part of the brain is coming "online" later. In neurotypical kids, the prefrontal cortex doesn't fully mature until their twenties, which explains a lot of the impulsive, scattered, and dysregulated behavior that is seen in *all* young people as they mature. In neurodivergent kids, however, that development might not finish until their late twenties to early thirties. So, we have to offer those kids more scaffolding, more structural support to help them get to a functional level. Those supports could be mentorship, therapy, apps, medication, exercise, or yoga. But we know with certainty that "just work harder" is not going to cut it.

As we reflect on this, think about your kids, *but also about yourself.* If neurodivergence is a family affair, did these behaviors happen to you? Did executive dysfunction negatively impact your partner? It probably did, based on what we know about the heritability of neurodivergence. But now you're a functional adult! You made it! So, if these issues are things that you dealt with in your life, take a moment to reflect on what things worked for you and what things pissed you off. It's a great starting point to learn how to talk to the next generation.

Speaking of that next generation, it's amazing to me when I talk to families in my role as a child psychologist, how often they'll say something like, "Oh yeah, this was totally me as a kid. And I wish someone had understood me. I wish someone had supported me, but anyway, I wish *my* kid could get it together." (This happens enough that we usually call it "Apple-Tree Syndrome.") I point out to that adult, "You just said that your kid was you 30 years ago, and you didn't get what you needed. Don't make the same mistakes that your parents made with you. This issue that you're navigating with your family is an opportunity to correct those past behaviors and possibly heal yourself in the process." Shame doesn't promote healing; understanding does.

Most people know executive dysfunction in terms of *attention deficit hyperactivity disorder* (ADHD), to the point where many use the terms interchangeably (which is not accurate). ADHD is a neurodevelopmental pattern of dysfunction and underperformance in the prefrontal cortex (Kolk & Rakic, 2022). There are three types of ADHD: the inattentive type, the hyperactive type, and the combined type.

- ○ Inattentive ADHD manifests as being lost in your thoughts—your head is in the clouds; you act like the traditional absent-minded professor: "I got all the way to class, and I forgot my backpack"—that sort of thing.

- ○ Hyperactive ADHD is what a lot of people understand ADHD to be; it's the act of your running out of your seat in the classroom, flipping pencils across the room to your friends, you can't sit still, shouting out, "Squirrel!", and the clichés we see on TV.

- ○ Combined type is where you have a little bit of column A and little bit of column B (that's me!).

It is worth noting that ADHD comes with strengths, like high processing speed, creativity and an ability to think outside the box (Tisterelli, Fagnani, Troianiello, Stazi, & Adriani, 2020; (Hai & Climie, 2022). Interpersonally, ADHD people tend to be high in charisma and easily connect with peers, at least in the short term. When ADHD people hyperfocus on something, they can work for hours and produce an incredible quantity and quality of work; during a hyperfocus state, that dopamine circuit is running wide open like a waterwheel during a heavy rainstorm. But ADHD is *not* a superpower. It comes with some significant weaknesses, including poor organization, lack of follow through, and dysregulation.

Like all neurodivergent folks, playing to an ADHDer's strengths brings out the best in them, and their bests can be spectacular. For example, you want somebody with ADHD to be your date to a wedding, because they're fun! They'll be on the dance floor all night, they tend to be good at navigating those inevitable awkward wedding ceremony moments, they love highly stimulating environments (my wife says that I look like a meerkat at weddings, constantly whipping my head about at new stimuli), and they'll make lots of friends, because nobody rides the dopamine high of a wedding like someone with ADHD (Hai & Climie, 2022).

On the flip side, you don't necessarily want to bring that same ADHD person to a formal dinner at your boss's house, sitting at length with spoken and unspoken rules to follow. They will work hard to self-regulate, which will make them more distracted, tense, and likely to melt down later. When it's hard to stay focused, the use of energy paradoxically makes you less attentive and engaged. It's not to say someone with ADHD can't ever survive at formal events. It's just not an environment that naturally fits their skill set.

You might be wondering about these examples because they both reference adults, and there's a societal myth that kids "outgrow" their ADHD (Tisterelli, et al., 2020). While neurodevelopment does occur in the prefrontal cortex, ADHD doesn't magically disappear after you turn 18 (nor does Autism, which is a separate but related problem). You gain more control over your life as you move into college and work, and having more control can give the illusion that you've "gotten better." But many of the underlying neuropsychological differences are still in play, such as emotional dysregulation, weak sustained focus, and poor organization skills. In fact, without the scaffolding support that school and college provide, many ADHD people will report that their symptoms get worse because now they're wholly responsible for creating and maintaining their own structure (Hai & Climie, 2022).

Think about what ADHD looks like in kids at school: it can take them a long time to complete assignments, especially if it's not something they want to do. They might have trouble staying on task. They might be disorganized, have poor time management, and have difficulty sitting still. They may zone out in conversations, even with superiors, and then miss the vital content and messages. Did you ever notice that teachers are most likely to write the homework on the board at the beginning or end of class, which are the two times that students are most dysregulated? It is important for us to realize how similar many of the skills that predict effective school behavior are to what one needs to be successful at a job. Writing a ten-page book report on Sacajawea for your history teacher may not look the same as compiling a ten-page report of outstanding client balances for your boss, but neuropsychologically they are the same dynamic.

None of the behaviors that I mentioned above are like the stereo-typical "sprinting around the classroom and throwing pencils across the room" that a lot of people associate with ADHD. Many neuro-divergent people present with subtler forms of executive dysfunction, which means that these symptoms might get missed or misdiagnosed. I cannot tell you how many people I've assessed over the years who have said, "I can't have ADHD, I never yelled out in class or randomly pulled the fire alarm." But you *can* have had ADHD if you were lost in your own thoughts, constantly scrambling to keep up with your work, and never feeling quite like you knew what was going on around you. Everyone struggles with these behaviors to an extent, but with ADHD the struggles are more intense, more frequent, and longer lasting (psychologists call this The Big Three; the more intense behaviors are on these three scales indicates a higher likelihood of having challenges). For example, everybody gets bored, but do you get so bored at work that you desperately seek a dopamine hit to self-regulate, and end up diving down Wikipedia rabbit holes in a sort of dissociative hyper-focus and "wake up" three hours later with your boss glaring at you? Probably not, but it does happen to people with ADHD.

Considering executive functioning skills: life provides us with many challenges which activate our executive dysfunction, from work to school to friends to hobbies. But it's also true that pretty much everything in life also organically provides us with opportunities to practice executive functioning skills. The trick is to become aware of these opportunities and approach them with intention. The homework is on the board, and you must write down the homework in your homework book. When you get home, you can look at the homework in your homework book, and then take the papers out and find your pens. Then you do the work. Then you put the homework back in its folder and put the folder in the backpack so you can bring it to school the next day. All of that is executive functioning! If you see how many steps must be remembered in that process, steps that come automatically to neurotypical people, then you can understand just how hard functioning in life can be for someone with executive dysfunction.

If those skills don't come easily for you, asking you to practice them doesn't feel good. It's a bit of a "chicken or egg" problem: if you were more engaged, you'd be able to focus, but since you're less engaged, you must practice harder, which requires you stay plugged in to an environment that is draining for you. To continue our conversation about building executive functioning skills, let's establish that there are three levels to executive functioning: starting a task, sustaining a task, and stopping a task. You can have problems *starting* the task because you don't want to because it feels difficult. Most ADHD problems revolve around *sustaining* attention during the task despite distractions—thoughts of things you'd rather be doing. Lastly, many ADHDers struggle with *stopping* a task (finishing and moving on—what we call task switching). Once you get locked into doing something, it's hard to pivot, especially if what we're doing is a preferred task.

Let's demonstrate the three levels of challenge right now. With people around I'd grab a volunteer from the audience to illustrate this point, but since we're not together, do this on your own. Look at my thumb (here's a picture of a thumb). Start when I say "go", and then time yourself as you stare to see how long it took you to get bored and stop looking at the thumb. "GO!" Tick...tick...tick... If any of you made it past ten seconds, I'm impressed, because this is not an exciting task.

Check in with yourself now that it's over. What was hardest for you? *Starting* to look at the thumb? *Sustaining* that engagement? Or *stopping*? (If you're still staring you can stop now). It's a great way to demonstrate that many tasks we ask people to do are boring and arbitrary, and can trigger challenges in any of the three levels of executive dysfunction.

I mentioned before that not all executive dysfunction comes from ADHD, even though they're commonly linked. Executive dysfunction can be a part of almost every mental health condition (Rabinovici, Stephens, & Possin, 2015). Executive dysfunction can come from a brain injury, a concussion, or a migraine; anxiety makes it harder to sustain focus because there are a million things competing for your attention, and they all feel like threats; depression saps your energy, making it harder to get the dopamine microcircuit started because your brain is drained of energy. Trauma (which is unfortunately common for the neurodivergent) also impacts the ability to self-regulate and sustain focus, in a classroom for example. So, the presence of executive functioning deficits doesn't necessarily indicate ADHD.

Executive Functioning Strategies

Overview

Executive dysfunction comes from a variety of mental illnesses and neurodivergences, so what do we do about it? The first thing is to educate ourselves about how the brain works, especially the prefrontal cortex (hey, you've already done that part!). Next, we set realistic expectations. Nobody pays attention all the time, so expecting someone to do so sets them up to fail (even if they're neurotypical). Third, we focus on skill development, with an emphasis on repeatable, concrete tasks. Developing executive functioning skills requires help from the adults, the teachers, the aides, the principals, school counselors, the bosses, the managers, HR…everybody's got to be pulling in the same direction. How can we support a person through that skill development? A lot of positive reinforcement (rewards are our friend), a lot of structure, ample systems for double checking and as safety nets, and open and honest conversations about how, when, and why we struggle.

It is also important to avoid blame and shame. Ross Greene says kids do as well as they can (Greene & Albon, 2005), which is 1000% true in my experience as a clinician, a parent, a partner, and a person who has struggled with these issues my whole life. No one wants to struggle or melt down! Who would choose to be that upset over being picked last in kickball? Feeling blamed or shamed is uncomfortable, embarrassing, and unwelcome; it's very dysregulating to our bodies. Let's assume our kids don't want to feel blamed or shamed, because it feels bad, and they don't want to be upset and struggle as a result. This should empower us to help them get out of those feelings. We want to collaborate with a positive solution. Remind neurodivergent people that they don't have to be perfect –perfect is impossible. We acknowledge that mistakes have been made, they will likely be made in the future, and all we can do is try to fix them—hopefully together!

Organization

I get a lot of opportunities to work on forgetting things with my clients. Every time I work with a neurodivergent person, I'm always saying, "All right, what'd they leave in my office this time?" Shoes, hats, coats. An inhaler. A Chromebook. A prom dress. I could clothe an army with the stuff that's been left in my office over the years. One time, I found a kid's walking boot in my office, for his broken foot! How do you leave without that?! Kids will need constant support and skills training to remember their stuff consistently. That's just a reality based on neuropsychological development. If we approach this skill deficit with humor and intention, you can make their version of "spectacles, testicles, wallet, and watch" (which started as a secular aping of the sign of the cross but has evolved into "do I have my stuff?" mantra) natural and repeatable. Perhaps we could use: "I've got my smart phone, my bag, and my shoes, but do I need any more clues?" Let's keep workshopping it.

We teach self-regulatory skills to provide the ability to self-regulate and manage environmental stressors and unexpected events (Gilbert & Burgess, 2008). While it is impossible in any environment to fully control unexpected events, it is best for neurodivergent people to make the "codes" of conduct explicit, understandable, achievable, predictable, and flexible as needed. Understanding the environment *must* be a part of the intervention! The single biggest predictor of a child having major executive dysfunction is lack of fit with their environment (Kircher-Morris, 2022; Hai & Climie, 2022). You can have a brain that doesn't want to follow typical rules, but if you're in a supportive environment that clarifies what matters and offers support in getting stuff done, then you can do quite well.

For example, I've done work with an amazing school for the gifted in Ontario, Canada called Revel Academy. Their whole building is a giant workspace. If you're walking by the art room you're reminded, "Oh yeah, I need to work on my art project!", and you can dip in there for a little while to do your art. Then you can move on to the next academic task or project when your brain and body is ready. This kind of organizational structure supports executive functioning in a way that's organic and natural. If you put that kid in a traditional school system, where Johnny has to do art when the school says it's time to do art, the disparity of organization and readiness will cause conflict.

Sustaining Attention

Another way to support people with executive dysfunction is to first get their attention, figure out how to keep it while it's needed, and *release it when it's no longer needed*. When we trigger attention, it is often fleeting. If I clap loudly, you're probably going to look at my hands, but you're not going to keep looking because my hand isn't doing anything anymore. We need to change or challenge the current understanding to gain the students attention. When we do something surprising, complex and novel, it engages the neurodivergent brain because novel things release a lot of dopamine, and extra dopamine can fuel future positive behaviors (Chan & Han, 2020). These novel instructions and activities can be in academics, in the arts, in sports, at work—in basically any task that can become boring to the active neurodivergent mind.

In terms of sustaining attention, a good place to start is always somewhere connected to the kid's interest. One of the biggest mistakes we make as academic and mental health professionals is to ask kids to build executive functioning skills in areas or classes that they don't like. As you know, I have ADHD, and I was a kid who struggled with math. And yet in every math class, the teachers would be "on me," saying "You've really got to focus! Really dial in! Because you want to meet your potential, right?"

As a student I didn't want to focus on math, because math was hard. I didn't like it, and I wanted to be out of there as soon as I could (mentally *and* physically—lots of daydreaming for me in those classes!). Math is an important skill, even if a big challenge for some. We can increase the chances of developing that skill by building it in areas where kids are really focused. I was always able to pay attention in art, because I was good at it, and I found it to be an engaging, interesting, and immersive experience. I was able to build more executive functioning skills in that class, which opened the door to success in other subjects. How do we apply the things that work in art to math? How can we make math class more like art class? We're making it a fun game, we're putting in novelty. A kid who doesn't want to do a page of math word problems might prefer to do a design based on fractals, so we allow the artistic approach, in which they'll be more successful because they're personally engaged.

We develop their interests through situations. We focus the content to get them more engaged. We turn the content that we're giving them into content that they feel some ownership of based on their individual interest. If your student gets interested in World War II because their grandfather served, then chase that interest! We can send other academic content through the lens of that interest with activities like writing stories in ELA, doing science experiments about explosions, painting battlefields, etc. The executive functioning skills that we build in areas of interest not only concretize faster in our brains, but they are also more generalizable to other areas of our lives (Cavilla, 2019; Chapman, 2021; Böckler, Knoblich, & Sebanz, 2010).

Differentiated Instruction

Success in connecting to people with executive dysfunction boils down to differentiation of instruction, which we learn from Carol Ann Tomlinson's work (Tomlinson & Jarvis, 2023). Teachers and bosses can differentiate the content (what's being taught), the process (how it's being taught), and the product (how we're asking for them to offer demonstrations of knowledge), according to the person's readiness to learn it, interest in learning it, and their learning profile. Educational platforms have traditionally been monolithic in how they present and deliver information: the instructor says the content, the students write it down, and then at some point there's a test. This model has been the dominant paradigm in education for years and unfortunately, I don't think that it's going anywhere.

People like to have choices in how they're taught, what they're taught, and how they are assessed. When I give talks on this subject, I'll say that we're going to learn about something arbitrary, like the War of 1812. The standard measure of learning for this subject would be a Chapter Test, and I'll ask who likes taking tests. People grumble but usually indicate that they might not *like* taking a test, but they're willing to do so. Then I'll ask the room if, instead of taking a test, they'd rather do a presentation on the War of 1812 or write a paper. Suddenly, people are engaged; the extroverts are already planning their presentations ("Can I hire reenactors?") and the deep thinkers are plotting out their papers. Those who want to take the test can do so; those who would benefit from showing their knowledge in another way can move from surviving to thriving.

Every single person in a position of authority who needs to instruct others can use these strategies. If your kid isn't responding to the classic "drill'em and kill'em" math worksheets, then you officially have my permission to change it up. Go to the dollar store, buy a big bag of M&Ms and dump them out on the table. Let the kid do the math as a manipulative exercise—whether it's counting, probability, statistics or geometry. And then let the kid eat the candy! If your employee is having trouble learning by watching sales training videos, send them to a professional development workshop so they can learn in person and experience it properly. Anyone can make these changes and, when we do, we all win.

Communication

It is vital to utilize concrete communication with neurodivergent people, especially those with executive dysfunction. It's easy to say, "You know what I mean!" but that is often *not true*. It is our job to clearly and concretely state what we need, how we need it done, why it has to happen, and what the time frame is. All those points are helpful, but the time frame part is particularly important when working gifted and ADHD people. They are the masters of visiting what I like to call "The Magical Land of Later." Go to the gym? Pay those outstanding bills? Text that boy? I'll just do it later! Conflict arises because you know it needs to be done now—when there's actually time to do it, and not later—when your person is going to be tired, distracted, and motivated to put it off (again). The best time to start was five hours ago; the second-best time to start is right now.

It is important to note that when neurodivergent people say they know they must do the thing but they're just going to do it later, they're not lying to you. They genuinely want to remember to do it! They think they can remember because sometimes they do (they will clearly and vocally remind you of when they did remember!). But in general, that's not how their brains work. They might hate the structure, but the structure will help them get it done within reasonable limits. Give them a list. Back up the files. Set a timer. Executive dysfunction isn't a choice, so their struggles aren't their fault. If they want their life to get better, then those struggles are something that they need to take ownership of to help their brains do better.

The best way to give instructions to people with ADHD or executive functioning deficits is what we call the SCOOPER technique. SCOOPER is a way to structure your messaging with content and context to ensure that there are no miscommunications. I'll walk through the steps with a theoretical client named Marcela. I need Marcela to go get my presentation files from my work computer because I'm stuck on a conference call.

S	Same Place	Instead of yelling the instructions down the hall, I put the call on mute for a moment, then go to Marcela's desk or ask her to come to mine, so we are in the same place and can make a solid connection.
C	Clear Instructions	I know what I want her to do before I ask her, so I rehearse my request and troubleshoot any problems. Be sure to say what you mean.
O	On Time	I give Marcela a very clear timeline of when I need this done. Is it within five minutes? Is it by the end of the day?
O	One More Time	I ask Marcela to repeat the instructions (including timeframe)so I know she understood them.
P	Perform	Marcela performs the task.
E	Evaluate	I evaluate how Marcela did on the task. If she was successful, we move to the last step. If she missed something, we do steps O-P-E again until it's accurate.
R	Reward	You deserve to have a preferred object as a reward afterwards, right? We always close the loop with a reward, because that's what makes the dopamine circuit in the brain work.

As you use this technique, you may find that you don't need to use all seven steps every time. That's great! But if you are having a bad executive functioning day, it's a good place to start.

Structure and Routine

Routine is key to how ADHD people manage: they need routine, but they will almost certainly hate it. It takes a lot of mental energy to opt into something; making the choice to act is hard. There are two ways to create routine that will be more effective at helping our people get things done. The first is tying a non-preferred but necessary activity to something that is already happening. For example, I hate going to the gym, but I know that I have to go! So, I always go on my way home from dropping my kids off at school. It's on my way and I can stop, do my treadmill, and then go home to shower and start my day. If I miss that window, I will certainly intend to go to the gym later, but realistically there's no way that's going to happen. Tying it to something established in my schedule makes me do the thing far more consistently.

Another strategy I use to develop structure with a lot of my clients is an adaptation of the Pomodoro technique of time management. Nobody can work constantly without breaks, but the neurodivergent brain tends to think in extremes: you MUST work on this and NO you can't do anything else. But you need a break, need to do other things, so you waste brain time arguing with yourself about if and when you can take a break. Instead, build in the breaks! You don't have to earn the break if the break is built in. For every hour, we plan a 15-minute break. I set two timers, one for 45 minutes, and one for 15 minutes. When 45 minutes is up, you start the 15-minute timer. When 15 minutes have passed, you repeat the cycle, which becomes a predictable rhythm, which helps the ADHD brain build constructive habits. (You can adjust the times individually—a 5-minute break every 15 minutes, or a 10-minute break every 30 minutes—to suit each person best.) The person gets an automatic break without fretting about it. Their brain is calmed by the routine, and there is more energy for the project.

Speaking of energy, it is also vital to move your body. Take breaks, dance, wiggle, play sports, listen to music at your desk (with headphones, of course)—whatever gets your body moving. Research shows that we don't let people move enough, we expect them to sit still too much, especially at work and school (Olive, et al., 2020). Kids in particular are not built to sit still, but neither are adults! How often do you walk around the office when you don't really have much to do, but you get a cup of coffee and rustle some papers, just to get some energy out. There's nothing wrong with that. We know that people who are allowed to move their bodies learn more, remember it longer, and are more engaged (Keeley & Fox, 2009). But daily school and work expectations are so demanding that very few people give themselves time to get up and move around (Barenberg, Burse & Dutke, 2011). Give yourself, your kids, and your employees time and space to move around and you'll be amazed at how much more productive they become. Schedule a few "brain breaks" in the day so people don't have tired brains and stiff bodies by mid-afternoon. Much of managing executive dysfunction is creating constructive off-task time so we can re-regulate and get much more done afterwards (Zelazo, 2015; Costa, et al., 2015).

I often feel like having an ADHD brain is like having 10% extra energy, so you're running at 110% capacity. Letting a person burn off that extra energy has huge benefit. Studies show that letting people doodle while they're taking notes helps them to retain more information (Andrade, 2010; Barenberg, et al., 2011). Have fidget toys available for everyone with clear rules about their use. People are less likely to distract the group with their fidgets if they've been instructed on when and how to use them. One of my favorite strategies regarding fidgets is to have a person create their own "bored box." I have them bring to class their preferred fidgets—quiet activities for when they finish work early or are struggling to get started—things like a Rubik's Cube, Sudoku books, and word searches (not iPods or Nintendo Switch). When the kid finishes their work early or they're stuck, they can reach into their "bored box" for a distraction to help get their brain unstuck.

Additionally, any rote activity can be helpful to burn off extra energy before engaging in something challenging. Doing laundry, washing dishes, putting things away, etc. allows you to put your brain on cruise control and focus on the task you need to do because your hands are busy. You can listen to music while you're working (but no music videos—it is too stimulating to have auditory and visual input at the same time). Visual stimuli increase neuropsychological stimulation so they're less helpful in redirecting energy to task completion (Carpenter, et al., 2019; Reuben, 2024). If you walk into your kid's kindergarten class or the break room at work and there's a gazillion posters on the wall, it is worth considering taking some of those down to reduce mental distractions.

What if you're one of those ADHD people who have trouble getting tasks started? You might try body-doubling. Body-doubling is the process of getting someone to be an accountability partner while you get things done (Eagle, Baltaxe-Admony, & Ringland, 2023). It works by activating the mirror neurons that we discussed earlier: when someone around us is working, our brains become aware of the fact that work is getting done, and that awareness makes it easier for us to get unstuck. The cool thing about body-doubling is that you're probably already using it. You put off going to the grocery store until your friend can come with you; you clean your entire apartment while on the phone with your mom. The presence of another person gives us just enough external "gravity" to get us moving in a positive direction. And the other person doesn't need to be doing the same thing, they just need to be doing something. For my college-aged clients, I cannot tell you how many times I've used body doubling to get them to do a load of laundry, or complete their résumé, or clean their dorm room. When you really need to get something done, schedule someone to be there with you, even virtually. You'll be glad you did.

Mindset

Finally, let's discuss the idea that the people in your life with executive dysfunction are not lazy. In my opinion, lazy doesn't exist. Most people would rather get things done than not, but it can be quite challenging to just do things. When we don't do things, we get called lazy. But what looks like laziness is an outward expression of the brain being overwhelmed, and when it's overwhelmed, it taps out. It says, "I just can't do this." And we get overwhelmed because while the task seems simple on the surface (for example, go mow the lawn), the neurodivergent brain immediately starts thinking about all the things that need to happen in order to mow the lawn. To paraphrase one of my clients, in order to mow the lawn, he had to 1) put on his gardening clothes, which meant that he had to 2) go check the laundry to see if they were clean, which they weren't, so he 3) decided to go fill up the gas tank for the mower while he was waiting, so he 4) put on other clothes so he could 5) go to the gas station. But his mom saw him leaving the house and yelled at him for not mowing the lawn.

When you see all theoretical options at the same time and get bogged down by the sheer number of possibilities, I call it "galaxy brain". It's common in neurodivergent people, and it's probably the reason you're getting stuck. Every decision we make is a thread on a broader tapestry of life; when you pull one, the entire image is impacted. Many neurotypical people can just do the thing that they're presented with; they don't (or don't have to) see it in its broader context. But that's just how the neurodivergent brain works! We drown in context. The problem is that we are fighting these powerful battles internally. From the outside, we just look like we're scrolling through TikTok or Reddit. Knowing that the brain is actually *overworking* and not being lazy can help us change our approach. We ask, "what's getting in your way?" because we want to be supportive and curious, not critical.

That shift is hugely beneficial to these people because it is so easy to say, "Well, look at them! They're playing Minecraft and not doing their homework! They should be doing their homework." Of course they should. Doing the task that you've been assigned is a part of the "code" of human behavior. But, since they know they should be doing their homework and they're not, the better question is, "what's getting in their way?" If we assume that there's an environmental factor that's keeping them from doing the homework, we opt out of the Fundamental Attribution Error (blaming the person rather than the context) and seek a better explanation. Their reason might be "Mom, I don't know where my textbook is." Or it might be "Boss, honestly, I can't even figure out how to get started". Or "Oh my gosh, I forgot I have to work tonight! Thanks, grandma". Or "AHH! Galaxy Brain"! Those reasons explain distracted behavior far better than calling someone lazy. Calling someone lazy tends to hurt their feelings, and a person with hurt feelings has a harder time getting things done.

We want to set expectations. Overcoming executive functioning challenges is hard to do. It's hard for kids as well as adults. If you've ever lost your glasses, you recognize the indignity of trying to find the thing you need without the thing which you need to find it; if you don't have enough dopamine in reserve, you've got nothing to draw from to help you complete a non-preferred task. Please share this fact with your teachers, with your coworkers, with your family, whatever, whoever needs to know. Nobody *chooses* to act this way. Watch a person with executive functioning deficits try to find something important that they've lost (like their keys) and just look at them: who would choose to feel this way? Nobody. Help them navigate the situation and build in sustainable strategies to prevent these moments from happening again. However and whenever you come out of the situation, make sure that you reward yourself. Dopamine is your friend! Using lots of rewards and positive reinforcement strengthens the dopamine circuit so we get more capable of doing more things... even if we don't want to.

You did it! You've survived reading an entire chapter on Executive Functioning. Go get yourself a treat and move your body. The next chapter can start whenever you're ready.

CHAPTER 6
Riding Out the Storm: What are Emotions and Where Do They Come From. The Challenge of Feelings!

UGH, Feelings.

Fundamentally, feelings are my job. I spent a lot of time working with people to better understand their feelings, to process where they come from, and develop strategies around managing them; because feelings can and will take over. When those moments arise, you've probably tried dozens of strategies—from bargaining to pleading to ignoring—to ride out those emotional bursts. One of the messy parts of being neurodivergent in a neurotypical world is that there are a lot of unspoken and unwritten "codes" around emotions: who can show what emotions in what situations. Since neurodivergent people tend to be emotionally intense, we often violate those "codes" which can bring shame and embarrassment and potentially increase our emotional volatility in the future.

In this chapter, we're going to learn how to better manage emotional outbursts. We've already covered where big feelings come from in the neurodivergent brain (our friend the limbic system, with a helping hand from our relatively underdeveloped prefrontal cortex), so we'll use this chapter to develop the language to communicate about emotions, and strategies to help regulate people. We're not going to teach our people to not have feelings, and we're not going to give up on our ability to help them manage their feelings. It's very tempting to wish that the people in our lives either had no emotions or had only positive ones, but part of being an authentic friend is accepting all aspects of someone, even if we don't like the messy parts. For example, I'm an ugly crier and my wife loves me anyway. I cannot offer a foolproof solution to make all emotions easily controllable, but I can provide information and strategies that will increase your awareness of emotions and help you survive the behaviors that come with them.

If you're neurodivergent, you experience emotions differently than neurotypical people (Damiani, et al., 2017). This has three major facets: the triggers of the emotions, the intensity of the emotions, and the form of the emotional expression. Something that makes neurotypical people emotional might not affect you as a neurodivergent person, or it might make you have an entirely different emotion. I remember seeing the play *The Laramie Project* in college with two friends, one of whom was profoundly gifted and Autistic; while the rest of the audience was sobbing openly, she was visibly frustrated that they were using a type of wood in the staging that was not native to Wyoming, where the play takes place. You might express emotions differently than expected, either with more intensity (gifted people don't get sad, they get despondent) or with less inhibition (ADHD makes my feelings very strong and active).

A lot of people seek my therapy for help with their emotions. Specifically, they want their unpleasant emotions GONE. "Dr. Matt," they'll say, "I don't want to be angry anymore. Or anxious. Or depressed." Well, welcome to the club. Every time I smack my head on something (like a car door or a tree branch), I get irrationally furious. I hate feeling that way! But I know that the reaction isn't in my control; my response to the reaction can be.

From a human perspective, the goal of wanting to rid ourselves of uncomfortable emotions makes a lot of sense. Who likes to be angry or depressed or anxious? Those feelings are super unpleasant. But the reality is that emotions serve a vital need for us, no matter how much we might dread them. Emotions are neither good nor bad, they just are. And every emotion has a place! If you wanted to never be sad again, that would make sense...until you got invited to a funeral, or lost your job, or finished in last place in your Fantasy Football League (not that I have any personal experience with that happening...).

I'm going to let you in on a secret: the goal of life is *not* to be happy—happiness is fleeting! The goal of life is to be *regulated*. That means that your emotions don't get too high or too low, and crucially, they match or can be made to match the emotional energy of the environment you find yourself in (Bierman & Sanders, 2021). Sitting at your desk, whether that desk is at work or school, requires a different kind of emotional regulation than when you're at a pep rally or a concert. Self-regulation is a set of skills that give us awareness and control over our emotions. When we are in more control of our emotions, we become better employees, students, partners, parents, friends, and human beings. Any person can learn to become more emotionally aware and thus more emotionally regulated, and when that happens, their skills and presence can positively impact their systems.

Before I tell you the key to getting those skills, I want to acknowledge that this development is really hard to do. The process is super frustrating. I guarantee that at some point you're going to feel overwhelmed by what you're trying to do, you're going to have rough days, you're going to think that you're not accomplishing anything, and therefore therapy is a waste of time and money. Those feelings are all normal. It doesn't make you a bad parent or educator or mental health professional when your frustrated person feels that way. The frustration will not just go away, skill building will help, therapy is not actually a waste of time. If you don't want to stay frustrated and emotionally out of balance (and you wouldn't be talking to a therapist or reading this book if you did), then you must change the way you interact with your feelings to change their impact on you.

Instead of fighting off feelings, we try to embrace them. Feelings cannot be made to go away, and they don't always play fair. The harder you try to fight them, the more they stick around, but if you leave them alone, you can make space for moving around them. Think of dealing with your feelings as trying to hold a heavy chair above your head. You don't want to have the hurt (i.e., the big feelings) crash down on you, so you work hard to hold the chair up. The problem is that sooner or later, your arms are going to get tired, and the chair will fall. You'll be upset that you failed and beset by the feelings that you're trying to avoid (as they crash onto your head). In these moments, it is smarter to put the chair (and the feelings it represents) down and move away. It's still there, and you don't have to be happy about that, but now you're not spending all your energy keeping it suspended. You gain the freedom to navigate around your feelings more constructively!

The goal here is not to eliminate feelings, but to reduce their overwhelming force on a decreasing scale of what I like to call "the big three": frequency, intensity, and duration. If you're an angry person, the goal is to have less intense anger, for example, being frustrated rather than rageful. You want to feel anger less often, and with less duration, which means working on your self-regulation and avoiding triggers. Trying to rush through our experience of emotions can prolong them because our focus on them is more intense. Instead, use regulation skills and monitor duration of emotional intensity *post-facto:* how long did it take me to move through that anger? Cool, it was only fifteen minutes—I used to be mad *all day!*

To shift our thinking around our emotions in this way, it can be helpful to use an overarching simile. Emotional experiences can be like thunderstorms: scary, intense, seem to come from nowhere, and can ruin your day in a hurry; they can also be dangerous. When a thunderstorm arrives, you're allowed to be upset, frustrated, overwhelmed, even scared! But it is not helpful to get mad at the thunderstorm; it's an act of nature and not "out to get us." If you follow your instinct to be mad at a thunderstorm, you might run outside to yell at it, which puts you in more danger. Instead, when the storm arrives, alter your plans and get somewhere safe. You feel overwhelmed when the storm arises—"of COURSE this is happening to me!" But you can learn to "weather the storm" before you let the emotional lightning strike. Giving in to an emotional storm can increase feelings of frustration and resentment, and makes recovery more difficult. Managing your response with appropriate skills is a better approach.

According to the National Weather Service, the average thunderstorm lasts 30 minutes (Hayward, Whitworth, Pepin, & Dorling, 2020). (Stick with me, because this is when the metaphor kicks into high gear.) That may seem like a long time (especially if you're in it!), but as Maya Angelou said, "all storms run out of rain eventually". When it's over, you survey the damage and get back to what you were doing. When the time is right, you think about what you learned from this storm and what you can do differently next time. Each storm contains a lesson, even if the lesson is "I hate storms". Getting your feelings validated is an important part of the process, especially when you connect your feelings to the coping strategies you can use to manage them (i.e., "I hate storms, so I hide in the basement"). It can be helpful to involve anyone else impacted by the storm, so you can share your varied experiences and perspectives to build more better coping skills—because a storm *will* come again. You might as well accept that fact, even if you don't like it, and learn from the experience.

Naming Your Feelings

That desire to learn lends itself to our first skill. Neuroscience tells us that our brains and bodies are intimately connected, and one way to use that connection to our advantage is to name what we are feeling (Weissman & Mendes, 2021). I'm not going to tell you "Just calm down", because that strategy never works. Instead, naming the challenging feeling causes our nervous system to unlock regulation strategies specific to that feeling, rather than just chaotically trying to calm down (Ho, et al., 2020). You can shout it, write it down, whisper it to yourself, text it to a friend (or yourself), or skywrite it, but when you articulate what's happening to you, you move your mind from *"something* is happening!" to *"that feeling* is happening!", which helps you get under control faster. It doesn't happen right away, but you can use this strategy to lower the intensity and duration of challenging feelings, which is always a good thing.

Why do I know that this works? Because I use it myself. Not just in therapy, though it's certainly very helpful there. As an emotional person, I often feel the need to wrangle my own motions, and this skill is what I use. The first time I used it was in a hotel room in Chicago in July 2017. My wife and I had flown out of Philadelphia very early that morning, and it was after 1pm by the time that we got to our hotel room for the Supporting the Emotional Needs of the Gifted (SENG) conference. I was tired, impatient, nervous and excited in some amalgamation, which is a bad combination at any point, but especially when you haven't eaten since half an Egg bagel at the Philadelphia Airport at 6:30am.

Once we got to the hotel room, my wife went to freshen up. I wanted to watch five minutes of ESPN while I was waiting for her, but I couldn't get the TV to go on. I kept trying, nothing was happening, and I was getting madder and madder and madder. When my wife came out of the bathroom, I was stomping around the room like a lion in a cage, red-faced and sweaty. She looked at me and said simply, "What's going on?" I proceeded to rant and rave about how unfair the universe was and all I wanted to do was watch some SportsCenter and I hate everything. After a minute, she replied, "OK, so how do you feel?"

"WHAT?!" I barked, still seeing red.

"How do you feel?"

"How do I feel? How do I FEEL!? I FEEL PISSED OFF!!!" I snarled. And then, as I said my feeling aloud, suddenly it was like a wave of peace came over me. I felt the anger draining out of my body. "Oh," was all I could say. Once I had calmed down, I realized that there was a little slot right by the light switch, just the size of my room key card. I inserted it, the lights immediately flipped on, and I got what I wanted. I sheepishly watched my five minutes of ESPN and then we went out and got sandwiches. I've told this story dozens of times in therapy and in talks all over the country because this "naming the emotion" strategy works. It might not always work so fast, but the psychophysiology behind it is sound, and we can use it to our advantage.

I still use it! I was driving over the Chesapeake Bay Bridge recently, on the way back from a family vacation in Washington, D.C. If you've never been over that bridge, DON'T. It's really scary! The winds were high, and driving was difficult. I found myself getting panicky, but I quickly identified the feeling and articulated it to my wife. Naming the feeling lowered my anxiety and made more receptive to help. She was able to support me, and my anxiety stayed low enough to get us safely across the bridge. It helps that my wife is a psychologist, but naming feelings (and being prompted to name them) is a skill anyone can take advantage of.

Now that I've shown you that it works, let me explain why. It's a bit of an over-simplification but think of the brain in two parts: the cerebral cortex (the thinking, or "wizard"brain) and the cerebellum (the survival, or "lizard" brain). Everything that makes us who we are is in the "wizard" brain, including our personality, coping skills, and communicative abilities. The basic "lizard" brain focuses on keeping us alive, managing breathing, heart rate, and sleep, etc. When the sympathetic nervous system is triggered, the "lizard" brain leaps into action to keep us alive, which it's really good at! But this means that our more complex thinking brain, the top part where all our skills are, is going "offline." We don't need to be thinking complex thoughts when we're running for our lives from a swarm of killer bees. Our overall energy needs to be focused on escaping.

What this means for us is that when our loved ones are upset, our go-to move is to say, "Hey, calm down!" or "Use your words," or "Tell me what happened." Unwittingly, to a stressed-out emotional person, these questions come across as demands. (Picture Jack Bauer yelling at you, "TELL ME WHAT'S WRONG!!!" in an interrogation room at the CTU). Our people may not be able to respond to such a simple request because the thinking part of your brain essentially goes offline when there's a perceived threat. Think about the eyes of the last really upset person you saw; did it look like they were "themselves?" Probably not. So, we can't use our normal coping strategies with a very emotionally dysregulated person.

While they're so dysregulated and the "lizard brain" is running the show, all we can do is try to keep them safe. We figuratively ride out the storm. The screaming, wailing, kicking, cursing person is not the ideal figure for an emotional intervention; if they aren't a threat to themselves or others, we can let the emotions run themselves out. When we can get peoples' bodies back under control, then they come back into themselves and become much more receptive to our strategies. When a person can ground themselves after an emotional outburst, they are showing their autonomy and their ability to seize meaningful control of their own life. Getting them more regulated can start a virtuous cycle: the thinking brain is more "online," and more able to use words and abstract thought to communicate the situation and needs. When a person can communicate their needs, people can help them more easily and readily.

I mentioned that you might need to be the person who must calm someone down. Regardless of our station in life (CEO, parent, teacher, friend, bus driver—whatever), if we interact with people in any capacity, the opportunity will surely arise in which you must help someone else regulate their feelings and behavior. And there's a lot of information out there suggesting that *you* have to be calm in order to calm someone else down. But that's not always helpful or possible; frankly, it's not true! Trying to calm down is a demand that you put on yourself and thus is counter-indicated to calming down. So, if you can be calm, great! Use it! And if you can't be calm, then you can use co-regulation.

Co-regulation

Co-regulation is when two or more people come together to help each other navigate their feelings, creating a supportive environment in which they collaborate to help regulate those emotions (Butler & Randall, 2013). By sharing support and understanding, each person in the situation is better able to self-regulate. Most of the time, one person will be more upset than the other. The best way to think about co-regulation is, when our shared calmness confronts a storm, the seas become easier to navigate. It's not our job to smooth things completely, but the more regulation we can share through our words, presence, and actions, the more we facilitate the other person calming down.

So how do we coregulate? The first thing is that you notice how the other person is feeling. This is a simple step, but it is so often missed. You might say, "You look really upset right now". You could also offer some metacommunication so your statement isn't quite as blunt. You might open with, "Hey can check in with you for a minute?" or "We haven't talked in a while, and I'm wondering what's new with you". We want to ask question about their emotions to create a space where they can share their feelings.

The second step is to note how *you* are feeling about *their* feeling. Remember, you don't have to be calm, or chill, or zen about it. You might say, "Seeing you that way bums me out; I'm sorry for whatever is happening to you". In therapy I'll express that I'm scared for a client, or angry on their behalf, and even disappointed (if it's warranted; I try to be authentic). It's important to note, however, that you are saying how you feel, not assessing fault. Expressing blame will make people defensive and shut down. Neutrally sharing your feeling has the dual effect of calming you down (because you named your feeling) and establishing an emotionally open line of communication. Your openness allows the other person to be open. Your openness is a way of modeling vulnerability, which makes it easier for the other person to be vulnerable as well.

The third step is to have an open conversation about what happened, and how everyone feels about it. Once you've gotten them to share, you've got to be willing to ride out the storm with them. You don't need to fix it—in fact, it would almost certainly be better if you didn't. We all have a human tendency to problem-solve. Being upset ourselves is uncomfortable enough, but when other people are upset, it can be more intense. Our brains want that thing to go immediately, so we stop listening and jump in with solutions. The problem with this move, no matter how well-intentioned, is that we risk minimizing the other person's emotions and not hearing their whole story. Sometimes a person just needs to vent. In a situation where an upset person is telling their story, it can be helpful to use metacommunication and ask, "Do you want advice or are you just looking to vent?" Their answer helps you organize what you need to do; if the person just needs a listening ear, you can sit back and let the storm pass. The neurotypical social "code" where one is supposed to "just know" what to do in these situations does not work well for neurodivergent people. I would much rather ask and get more information that will make me more helpful.

This listening skill might be way outside your comfort zone—I get it! Co-regulation violates a lot of the unspoken "code" about managing emotions, namely, that we shouldn't do it at all in public and just need to take care of ourselves on our own. But that way of thinking and acting is going the way of the dodo, i.e., inept and foolish. Emotionally aware schools and workplaces are the new norm, and we all need to get on board if we're going to meet the needs of our contemporaries. Remember that the "code" would dictate that you meet someone's feelings with judgment and negativity; though the upset person might expect that response, imagine how much more powerful it would be to give them the opposite, and lead with love and support.

Despite the importance of offering emotional support rather than judgement, that doesn't make it any easier to do. This is literally my job, and sometimes I still find it hard to do. But when I'm struggling to connect with my own feelings so I can connect with other people, I remember a simple mantra: *be curious, not furious.* If Jill in your office is crying softly at her desk, your first thought might be how that is frustrating because you're trying to get some work done. That's a critical thought. But if you think about who Jill really is, and how she rarely acts like that, you become curious, which allows you to be far more receptive and helpful. When I am curious about someone's behavior, I am reminded of their humanity, which gives me perspective and empathy. A good way to think about this shift is to move from an "us versus others" mindset to thinking of the situation as "all of us versus the problem." Curiosity helps us get there.

Emotions, Behaviors, and Theory of Mind

Another important thing to understand about feelings is that they **cannot** be wrong. I am a grown man with a doctorate, and I hate yellow mustard. And I know that at least some of you out there are nodding vigorously at this statement because yellow mustard is THE WORST. My dislike of yellow mustard might not make any sense to you. But that doesn't make me wrong, any more than your preferences concerning your favorite food or least favorite movie, or favorite board game make you wrong. I lead with this example because even well-intentioned people tend to argue with me when they hear this opinion: "Oh, but I love yellow mustard!" "Have you tried this other brand?" "Who hates a condiment that much?" My feelings are my feelings; the sooner we all accept their existence, the faster we can all move forward.

Neurodivergent people tend to hold their opinions close and intensely (Brown, et al., 2022). You may struggle to have perspective of why someone else feels differently than you do about something. In psychology we call this phenomenon the Theory of Mind, which is the ability to understand that other people exist outside of you and have their own experience and opinions of the world (Carlson, Koenig, & Harms, 2013). If you don't believe me, post on Reddit about your favorite Star Wars movie and defend your choice in the comments. Then watch the sparks fly! (Personally, I think it's *Empire Strikes Back*, but I would listen to other choices). You'll see many arguments that boil down to, "How could you possibly think that?!" And that's the problem—they've made no attempt to understand your point of view! One of the biggest mistakes that we make as humans is arguing with others about the "accuracy" of their feelings, because we are all so different. Not agreeing is fine! You don't have to agree with someone's feelings to be able to help them, but just arguing doesn't help.

Feelings lead directly to behaviors (Carpenter, et al., 2019), which can create a different disconnect around Theory of Mind (Carlson, et al., 2013). I'm someone who tends to express my emotions through outward behavior; I stomp my foot, grit my teeth, etc., because those behaviors make sense to me. I'm an extrovert neurotype, so those behaviors make sense to me. If you're wired differently, you might internalize your emotions, showing no external change in behavior, but meanwhile your internal systems are charging up and getting ready to burst. When you inevitably explode from trying to hold all these feelings in, someone might say, "Well, why didn't you just tell me you were feeling that way?" And you can reasonably respond, "Why should I have to tell you? Doesn't my behavior communicate my needs?"

"Wait, hold on a second," you say. "Are you trying to tell me that my employee can dump out all the coffee in the break room because he's a bad day??" Absolutely not. (Seriously, you don't mess with coffee). Whatever reason that your employee has for having a bad day is their own, and they have the right to feel that way. But the second, linked truth about feelings is that we are responsible for the choices that we make when we are emotionally activated. This axiom is so important that it is one of my bedrock rules as a therapist. You are allowed to feel however you feel about whatever happens to you, but it's **what you do with those feelings** that matters most.

Intention vs. Impact

For example, last year I was asked to consult on a case at a local high school. A student (we'll call her Kelly) had auditioned for the spring musical *Fiddler on the Roof* (also fictionalized for confidentiality), hoping for the lead (Golde, Tevye's wife), or at least Tzeitel (the eldest daughter). Instead, she was cast as Chava, the youngest daughter. Kelly was devasted, and she had a right to be! She felt that she had given her best audition and couldn't believe that she didn't get a part she wanted.

What happened next was the problem. Kelly, still upset, jumped on her phone and tweeted, "The only reason I didn't get the lead is that @student is hooking up with @theaterdirector at my @highschool". Yes, she "at-ed" all the people, including her rival for the lead role. She took the post down within an hour, but the damage had been done; it was screen-shotted and spread like wildfire, eventually getting on the radar of the school administration. The school had to do an investigation, and even though they found nothing untoward was happening, Kelly was mortified and quickly became a pariah in her theatre group. Ultimately, the director said that he wasn't comfortable with Kelly being in the show, and the cast agreed. Kelly ended up transferring.

If you're not a theater person, you might not know how devastating it is to not get the part that you had your heart set on—it sucks! But you can probably sympathize from your own experiences. I'm sure that at some point of your life you didn't get the prom date you wanted to, or the promotion, or a place on the Varsity team, or win blue ribbon at the 4H fair (one of these days, they'll see that my apple pie is better than that Cheri-Ann). Kelly's feelings were valid, but her behavior was not. If you're a person who is prone to strong feelings of anger or upset, I beg you to put your phone in "airplane mode" when you're mad. It'll save you from yourself from sending outgoing messages that you won't be able to take back, because while the emotional context will fade, the words will live forever.

You might be wondering if starting this investigation was what Kelly meant to happen, which is a great question. She didn't, of course, she wasn't thinking clearly when she Tweeted, but that doesn't matter. It is easy for us to hide in our intentions, shouting to the heavens, "... but I didn't MEAN to!". The reality is that the impact of our actions means a great deal more. Your *intent* provides context, but the *impact* of your behavior lasts much longer. If you showed up to my book signing wearing a clown shirt, you might not have meant to upset met, but that won't change the emotions I will feel (*please* don't—Mike and Barry, I'm definitely talking to you).

Replacement Language

Many people struggle to talk about their emotions, so their communication about their feelings can be inconsistent and incomplete. Since neurodivergent people struggle to understand their emotions (Chan & Han, 2020), they are more likely to have gaps in their ability to articulate their affective states (Chapman, 2021). One example of this is the tendency for neurodivergent people to use "replacement language" when they talk about their feelings. Replacement language is when someone reacts to a feeling by saying what that feeling makes them want to do, rather than what the feeling is.

If you pay attention to your interactions with people, you've certainly heard a lot of replacement language. Your teen comes home from school and wails, "Everyone at school hates me! We need to move towns immediately". Before you call your realtor, you know—since it's unlikely that everyone at school hates your kid—that there is probably something that has upset them (the feeling), and feeling upset makes them want to move away (the behavior) because of embarrassment or shame (the feeling that they're not naming). You don't have to respond to the content of what they're saying, but you can try and co-regulate with them by acknowledging and responding to their words. If you do, they'll get to the emotional core soon enough.

Replacement language happens everywhere! Screaming "I'll kill you!" to a sibling when they take the last cookie is another example; they're mad but are jumping to thoughts of angry behavior instead of naming the feeling. An employee threatens to quit "...because I'll never be good at this job". Your romantic partner seethes, "Well, why don't you just go ask that person out on a date if they're so perfect?!" An angry football coach says, "Maybe I'll just cut all of you guys on Varsity". People are bad at naming their feelings, which makes them even worse at expressing them. Now that you know the function of replacement language, you can try to be a force for good and draw out co-regulation.

Here's another example that I often share at my talks. Neurodivergent people can provide voluminous amounts of verbal content. The more upset they are, the less regulated the content becomes. Once you know to look for replacement language, you'll see loads of it in verbal outbursts. I was once working with an 8-year-old who was very upset (I'll call him Marcus), and he looked at me dead in the eye and said, "Dr. Matt, if you ask me to talk about my feelings one more time, I'm going to chop you up with a rusty hatchet and leave your body in a culvert so it'll get eaten by raccoons!" That's a direct quote. It's the kind of thing you remember. Also, you know he's a gifted kid because "culvert" is definitely a word for precocious vocabularies.

The thing is, if I had responded to the *literal* content of what he said, I would have called the police, because he was threatening to murder me. But he was only eight years old and maybe 40 pounds soaking wet, and I was 34 years old, six feet tall, and 200 pounds. If it came down to it, I would have won that fight. Clearly, I knew that he really did not want to murder me. Marcus was very upset and expressed his feelings of anger with replacement language, i.e., threatening to murder me. I had to figure out what was making him upset so I could help him. It turned out that he had been picked last for kickball at recess. We know that being picked last for kickball is a bad reason to threaten to murder a school counselor, but we also must acknowledge that it's Marcus's right to be angry. He didn't have a right to threaten me, but I could see his fantasized behavior as an attempt to express his emotions.

When he was calmer, I was able to help Marcus solve the problem. It's amazing how offering to pitch in the kickball game can save the day. Later, when we were processing the incident, Marcus said that he was sorry for "…y'know, the murder stuff". I said that because I knew him, I knew that he was using replacement language and that I was not afraid for my life. But it was a teachable moment, because another person who didn't know him or his behavior record would have been well within their rights to escalate the situation and perhaps call the police. He had been lucky, and he knew it. He promised to work with me on developing more prosocial communication strategies and emotional awareness, and he did just that. If we want to keep our people safe, then it's in everyone's best interest to learn how to ride out an emotional storm.

The Double Empathy Problem

Like Theory of Mind, empathy is a major pillar in developing and maintaining effective social relationships (Carlson, et al., 2013). Empathy is the ability to understand and share the feelings of another person. Empathy also differs from compassion, which could be characterized as taking the feelings inherent in empathy and actualizing them into some sort of plan to remedy the situation (Moores & Oates, 2024).

For many years, one of the go-to descriptions of Autistic people was that they lacked empathy (Crompton, DeBrabander, Heasman, Milton & Sasson, 2021). I discussed earlier how Autistic people tend to track different behaviors in people and glean different information from their environments. It turns out that mirror neurons in neurodivergent brains fire differently than those in a neurotypical brain, and thus receive different information from the environment. These different rhythms of processing create disconnects in the way that neurodivergent people see, experience, and communicate with the world. Therein lies the *double empathy problem* (Mitchell, Sheppard, & Cassidy, 2021).

The double empathy problem suggests that when people with very different experiences of the world interact with one another, they will struggle to empathize with each other (Crompton, et al., 2021). This struggle is likely to be exacerbated through differences in language use and comprehension. It is important to note that these issues are not due to neurodivergent cognition, but rather to a breakdown in reciprocity, a failure at mutual understanding that happens between people with very different ways of experiencing the world (Mitchell, et al., 2021). The onus isn't on neurodivergent people to "fix" what is erroneously perceived as their failure to empathize with neurotypicals; the intervention, or repair, must be bi-directional.

You might not understand why someone feels the way that they do. Neurodivergent people tend to be flummoxed as to why neurotypical people get so upset when their sports teams lose, just like neurotypical people may not understand a neurodivergent person's sadness over the death of a beloved comic book character (they always seem come back eventually, but it's still hard when it happens!). The point is that if you can identify the feelings of another person, you can adapt your behavior to accommodate them in a prosocial way. You are not required to understand where the other person is coming from, but doing so may help you develop empathy, and achieve more positive communication.

I'll leave you with the reason that I created the talk that inspired this chapter. Several years ago, I worked at a fancy private school in the Northeast. One day, one of my favorite students (I'll call him Mikey for this story) was refusing to put his coat on to go outside for recess. It was the first really cold day of the year, and the rules required all students to wear coats outside. Mikey was refusing and was getting more and more upset as people tried to convince him that he was overreacting. It was clear that the other teachers in the room were ready to throw in the towel and just put Mikey in detention. But then someone had the bright idea to call me. I told Mikey that I could tell that he was upset, and asked if I could ask him a question about how he was feeling (there's the metacommunication). He said sure, he was feeling angry and embarrassed. Embarrassed? That's interesting; I had gotten him to name a feeling, starting the co-regulation process. I asked him if he would tell me more, which empowered him to share his story rather than just defend his feelings.

Mikey took a deep breath and said that the reason that he wouldn't go outside wasn't the rules, it was his coat. You see, Mikey's coat was from Goodwill. In a school full of wealthy kids with fancy ski jackets, Mikey was on full scholarship. And he was mortified that his peers would see his second-hand coat. Immediately there was a shift in the room; it was no longer us versus Mikey; it was us *and* Mikey versus the coat problem. Even if you didn't agree with Mikey's reasons (and remember, feelings can't be wrong), everyone suddenly understood. We all remembered what it was like to be a teen and feel lesser in comparison to your peers because you did not have *that thing* that everyone else seemed to have (for me, it was not having my own phone line different from the main house phone number–remember, I came of age in the 1990s/2000s). Mikey's mood immediately changed. He saw that we understood his feelings and he was able to utilize that knowledge to calm himself down. We still needed a solution to the immediate problem, so I let Mikey wear my coat for the day, which gained him infinite cool points on the playground. As soon as I was back inside (and warmed up—it really was cold out), I talked to a trustee about getting a donation for a proper coat, which appeared the next day.

When you're working with someone who is really upset, it is vital to remember to step out of their stream of content (what they're saying) and into their context (when are they saying these things and why?). How are your kids' actions making you feel? Whatever your feeling is—anger, upset, fear—it's a good hint as to how your kid is feeling. Your empathy is picking up on their emotional experience, but you may need to navigate the content and the replacement language to get to the core issue. So, you might say to them, "Hey, you're having a tough time. What's going on?" That might be the first time in that kid's life that an adult has taken the time to ask them how they feel. They'll feel seen because you're naming that this isn't how they normally act, which means that you've noticed them enough to care and understand their behavior. When a person feels seen by you, they're much more likely to share their story. Once you know what happened, you're able to help solve the problem and move forward.

Mikey did not make great behavior choices day. When I debriefed the incident with him, I started by saying how shocked I was that he was having such a tough time, and how proud I was that he was willing to share his feelings with us. Mikey was understandably embarrassed at how upset he got and how much he acted out. He was able to share that with me because I created an environment where he felt safe to share his emotions. I was able to meet his revelation with compassion; I understood it was hard for him to make good choices when he was so upset! The big takeaway from this story is that when you are curious, you are much more likely to get to the answer behind the emotional behavior. Most of the time, that answer won't make you mad, it'll break your heart. It will also make you wish that you had fought harder to help our people in the first place, especially if you're someone who tends to jump to problem-solving or judgment.

Emotions are messy. And complicated. And disruptive. But like a thunderstorm, they're a force of nature. When we accept that, it empowers us to understand and regulate our own feelings, and thus help others in our lives do so as well. We don't need everyone to be happy; we need them to be regulated. So, let's make room for our feelings and ride out the storms together.

CHAPTER 7
Imposter Syndrome— I Can't Really Be That Good...Can I?

Imposter syndrome is one of my favorite things to discuss when I give talks, mostly because it always lends itself to those "AHA!" moments. Most people don't know what impostor syndrome is, and when they learn that there's not only a clear definition of the condition, but it has an identifiable set of symptoms and treatments, they often burst into tears. And as my mentor once said to me, "From a therapy perspective, tears mean it's working!"

Let me ask here whether you identify with this quote:

> *"I've just been fooling everyone all these years, I'm not as _____ as everyone thinks I am. It's only a matter of time before they all find out."*

The blank word could be "smart," "talented," "athletic," "musical," "gifted," etc. If you feel that way, then welcome to imposter syndrome! You'd be amazed watching the audience when I ask them this question. People shyly chuckle, then look around, then realize that other people are slowly raising their hands, and this behavior echoes until most of the room is indicating that they, too, worry about being found out as a "fraud." Like I said before, such negative feelings make us feel alone, but we are rarely as alone as our brains try to make us think we are. Imposter syndrome is a great example of this trend.

Imposter syndrome is a psychological pattern in which an individual doubts their accomplishments and has a persistent, internalized fear of being exposed as a fraud (Hawley, 2019). To be clear, you need to have both—self-doubt, and fear of being a fraud—to have imposter syndrome. Everyone can have doubt or feel afraid. But when they're together, especially if that fear is that someone will think you're a fraud, that's imposter syndrome. Audrey Irvin, who's a leading psychologist in this area, describes it as someone who can't internalize and "own" their successes, which is an amazing description of the internal psychological processes at work (Landry, Bailey, & Ervin, 2021).

The history of imposter syndrome is really fascinating. It's based on the work of Dr. Pauline Clance and Dr. Suzanna Imes (Clance & Imes, 1978). The research starts in the 1970s in the United States on Wall Street, the financial center of the USA. At this point Wall Street was very much a "boys" club', men only, very jocular. Women had just started entering the higher reaches of financial firms, and Drs. Clance and Imes wanted to know what made these women tick. They observed and interviewed the women and their colleagues, and what they saw was overwhelmingly positive. These women were getting their own clients and making serious money. These women were largely successful: their colleagues reported that they liked them, their supervisors reported that they liked them, and their clients loved them. All good, right?

The interviews revealed something else: the women themselves were miserable. One woman interviewed by Dr. Imes said that she spent every Friday with all her stuff in a box, sure that someone was going to come in, fire her, and escort her from the building (Clance & Imes, 1978). She couldn't say exactly why she felt that way, but she was sure that she was somehow an impostor amongst all the "real" brokers. And she wasn't the only woman who felt that way! As Drs. Clance and Imes looked at this more closely, they realized that these women were made so aware of the fact that they were thought of as different *because* they were women, that they couldn't feel like everybody else. Their awareness of the difference made them question their "worthiness" to have their job at all.

Of course these women deserved their jobs; they wouldn't have been hired otherwise! But the anxiety of self-doubt is not fair, and is certainly not rational, so these women felt like impostors. That impostor feeling manifested as a negative mental health outcome and came to be known as impostor syndrome. Once psychologists knew what it was, they started seeing it in organizations all over the world, often reported by people in leadership and new to the job (Bilan, et al., 2020). But why was it happening?

When a person is made to feel at odds with their surroundings, whether overtly or with subtlety, it makes them hyper-aware of their differences. Such awareness causes anxiety and leads to what we call the "surveillance paradox": the more you look for problems, the more you find, which makes you more anxious, so you look more and find more (Feenstra, Begeny, Ryan, Rink, Stoker, & Jordan, 2020). For the women on Wall Street, it was the fact that there was no women's bathroom on their floor; they needed to walk down to flights of stairs (in heels!) to use the facilities. That difference had a major impact over time and made them aware of all the other problems in the workplace that made them feel "othered." Feeling different (and misunderstood) in an environment where there's no support is death by a thousand paper cuts.

Think about all the ways that you might feel different in your environment. Maybe you're a first-generation college student surrounded by legacy students or people for whom college was a foregone conclusion. Maybe you just got promoted to management and you're the only one without a shiny MBA on the wall. Maybe you've never done musical theatre before, but your buddy convinced you "they always need guys" (true story). Maybe everyone else in your family followed the professional track (doctor, lawyer, etc.) and you decided to work with your hands as a contractor. Either way, the narratives that you see and when you look around can make your own narrative feel sadly lacking.

People who look and feel like everyone else have the same "code". Neurodivergent people, who may or may not look different than their surroundings (but definitely *feel* different) do not have that code! Sometimes it's worse to look the same. I can easily pass as a neurotypical (as long as you don't listen to me talk or watch me try to find my keys) based on how I look, even if I've always felt very different. Some neurodivergent people "mask" their behaviors to fit in the neurotypical society, but a great source of privilege is to find that you "pass," are naturally assumed to be a part of the dominant group (Radulski, 2022). The disconnect between feeling "othered" by largely "passing" as neurotypical has caused me a lot of stress in my life, and I'm sure that it's the root cause of my own impostor syndrome because it is very easy for my brain to think: "you look like them and act like them, so why aren't you *like* them?"

People with imposter syndrome lack an internal sense of their accomplishments (Hawley, 2019). No matter how much external evidence of their competence is given, they remain convinced that they don't deserve acknowledgement for what they've achieved. Good-hearted people will say things like, "Well, I don't know what you're so anxious! You're so smart and talented and you're so successful. You've done all these amazing things—you've got this!" That's a kind intervention, and logically should provide evidence that you're not as bad as you feel. But to someone with imposter syndrome such positive feedback doesn't matter, because the counternarrative is anxiety which is strident and doesn't play fair (sure, they *said* nice things about you, but how do you know that they *really meant* it?). For a person with imposter syndrome, compliments don't stick easily.

When a person has imposter syndrome, their worldview is so warped that they attribute success to either luck or other people's failures. In therapy I often hear excuses like, "I made the team only because other kids were sick", or "I got an "A" on this test only because the teacher happened to pick easy problems", or "Anyone could do graduate level calculus if they just tried harder". While there are perhaps kernels of truth to all those sentences, the important thing is that the person accomplished their successes, regardless of what they perceive as negative context. (As I often joke to my teen clients, "...what do they call you if you run for student government president unopposed? They call you president."). On the flip side, these people see failures as proof of being an impostor. "Oh no, I've been fooling everybody all this time, and this failure is the beginning of the end!" or "Gosh, I failed at this thing; I guess I just wasn't that good to begin with. Because how could I be good at something if I failed?"

Impostor syndrome is best understood via the *impostor cycle*, which I have printed out in my office so I can refer to it to help my clients (OK, and myself). Whether we are at school or work, sooner or later we are given a project to do. That assignment leads to anxiety, self-doubt and worry. But then, because thoughts lead to feelings which lead to behaviors, the anxiety manifests as over-preparation, where you say, "I need to write a hundred pages for my 10-page paper" or procrastination, where you say, "I'm so overwhelmed, I can't possibly start this yet", or both. What ends up happening is sooner or later you're anxious enough that you get the thing done and you turn it in, and you probably did okay at it because you're a neurodivergent person.

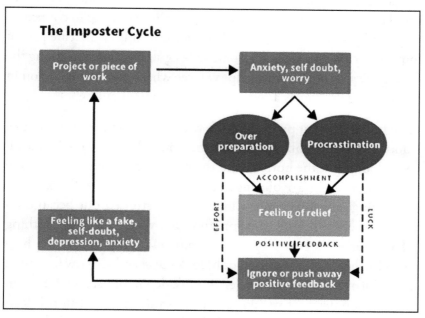

But instead of feeling good, accomplished, and proud of yourself, you know all the potholes on the road that you took to get there, including all the shortcuts you took and all the stress you had. So instead of feeling good that you did something, you feel a sense of *relief* that it's over. This feeling is the number one marker of imposter syndrome, especially in neurodivergent people, as it becomes vital to maintaining the impostor cycle. Instead of feeling good, which is the positive reinforcement that you need to keep going, you only feel relief, and you sigh, "Thank goodness nothing bad happened, so I guess I'm okay." That feeling makes you push away positive feedback, because there's some internal feeling that we *should* have done better or felt better. What rushes to fill the void where praise should be is a feeling of fraud, self-doubt, or fakeness. Before you know it, the next project comes in and the cycle starts again. You think to yourself that no one seems to struggle like this. "What's wrong with me? Do I not have some vital information or skill?"

If this cycle resonates with you, I would suggest putting this poster in a place in your office, workspace or classroom so visitors can see what's happening to them. When you can answer the question, "Where am I in the imposter cycle right now?" it puts those feelings in context so they can be better understood. Naming the feelings which are part of imposter syndrome gives you some self-regulation, and reframing the feelings as part of a process helps you see what's happening to you in context, rather than as a reflection of some awful failing.

I like to think about progress in life with the metaphor of climbing a ladder. If you're climbing a ladder and you only look straight ahead, you're looking at the horizon and the horizon never changes because it's too far away. You're putting in great effort, but you feel like you're not getting anywhere, and your body gets stressed out because it's aware that effort should equal progress, but you still feel like nothing is happening. I'd encourage you to either a) look *up* and see how much further it is to your goal or b) look *down* and see how far you've come since you started. I prefer to look down and see myself from a bottom-up perspective taking steps towards the top. But if it feels better to you to look up and say, "oh, I'm getting closer and closer to my goal," then go with that! But just remember, don't look straight ahead. Because if you fixedly look straight ahead, you're never going to feel like you're getting anywhere.

Imposter syndrome happens with many personality types, and if you're neurodivergent you'll probably recognize several of them.

○ The *perfectionists* among us are much more likely to experience imposter syndrome because of that automatic thought that says, "If I'm not perfect, I'm failing." And you'll keep trying to be perfect to avoid that feeling.

○ Also at risk for imposter syndrome are the *experts*, people who feel like they need to know everything before they start in order to have the proverbial "seat at the table." Of course, since knowing everything is impossible, the first concept or article they're unfamiliar with can send them spiraling. And they can spiral into doing so much extra work in order to somehow combat these feelings of inadequacy. For example, the first draft of my dissertation was over 250 pages when it needed to be closer to 80 because I kept finding "one more article" that would really prove my points. (sorry, Dr. Cassano!). For you gifted kids out there, there's the risk factor of being a *"natural genius."* When people are used to things coming easily—as many of us are—the idea of making an effort can be so triggering to the brain that it says, "Oh, you've always been smart, but since you have to actually try at this thing, maybe you're not so smart. Maybe you've been a fraud the whole time." You might laugh at this concept, but the first time I ever had to really study for a test (shout out to Honors Chemistry in high school), I had an existential crisis. "If I'm not the smart kid in school, who the hell am I?"

○ *Soloists* are people who are so used to working by themselves that they feel like if they ask for help, they're a failure. One of the trends I see often in the neurodivergent community is what I like to call "the curse of group projects." The stance is, "…it's too hard to work with people because they don't think and act and learn like me, so I'll just do it alone." But since life gets harder and increasingly difficult to manage alone, sooner or later you'll need help, and then come the feelings of imposter syndrome. We mustn't forget about *Super People* as a personality group at first for imposter syndrome. My superheroes are people who feel like they have to be the best at everything, and if they're not, they're a failure or a fraud. Since you know how hard it is to be good at one thing—let alone everything—you can imagine how short-lived that feeling of success might be, and how hard it is to let go of the need to be great in service of getting everything done.

Imposter syndrome doesn't come from one thing: there are many areas from which it loads (Landry, et al., 2021). There are behavioral triggers, especially in what gets reinforced for us as kids (think about what work your parents posted on the fridge growing up, and you'll get a sense of how strong the association is between "I did good" and "therefore, I have value"). There are also cognitive triggers. How much we think about things, and the value we place on their role in our lives and careers, can put us at risk for developing imposter syndrome. The more important things are to us, the more likely we are to feel imposter syndrome.

Take work, for example. I've had a great many jobs in my life; I've been a travel agent, a soccer referee, a lifeguard, a camp counselor, a babysitter, a freelance artist, a researcher—all sorts of things. But I often talk about how I liked bartending—I was a pretty good bartender! I still pour a clean draft and make a good cocktail. But the best thing about bartending was how I felt about the stakes of it; when I messed up at bartending, it didn't feel catastrophic—it was just a job. It's not that I didn't care that much about it, but I knew I wasn't going to do it forever, so it was more about passing time than it was an existential investment. But when I'm giving a talk or doing therapy, tasks that I care a great deal about, I am much more likely to feel like an impostor because I care so much more about it. Caring raises the emotional stakes, and higher emotional stakes can lead to imposter syndrome. If you explore your own life, you'll find that you don't have imposter syndrome all the time, just about the things that feel or felt important to you. The sneaky thing about imposter syndrome for neurodivergent people is that we tend to care much more about more things, and those things are what our brains tend to focus on, so we experience those feelings more often and more intensely.

Speaking of emotional intensity, intensity is also a major predictor of imposter syndrome. We know that neurodivergent people, especially gifted people, are intense. They care a great deal. This intensity comes from the brain differences that we covered back in Chapter Three: a larger amygdala, "superhighway" neuronal connections in the brain that process information very quickly, and a weaker prefrontal cortex. Because the world can be so unfriendly to neurodivergent people, they tend to over-identify with the roles or activities that bring them positivity. That over-identification contributes to intensity, because if their task at hand is challenged, they feel that you're challenging who they are.

We already spoke to the environmental factors relevant to imposter syndrome: feeling isolated, unsupported, or discriminated against. If you are neurodivergent, I expect that you or your kids have been "othered," even if you weren't aware of it. This impact is felt more intensely the more neurodivergent you are (Landry, et al., 2021). For neurodivergent people to feel successful in any environment, that space needs to be both informed about their needs and flexible to develop and evolve accommodations as needed (de Oliveria, et al., 2023). Environmental support is of heightened importance to thrice exceptional (3E) people, i.e., individuals who are gifted, have a learning difference such as ADHD, and have a socially valent identity like being black or LGBTQ (Sosland, 2022). Thrice-exceptional people can be additionally discriminated against because they have additional markers that make them susceptible to systemic bias (not to mention out-and-out racism, homophobia, etc.) at school and at work (Dahunsi, et al., 2024).

Psychological factors that amplify imposter syndrome are heightened anxiety and neuroticism. Anxiety is, well, anxiety (I have a feeling that you don't need to be introduced at this point). Neuroticism is a personality trait indicating your level of emotional stability, namely your ability to manage stress and regulate mood swings (Al-Shawaf

& Lewis, 2020). Neuroticism is usually expressed as a negative trait: someone who is highly neurotic has low emotional control. And we're just going to skip this last part because that's definitely not anybody who would be reading this book, right? (We'll just move on…)

To continue the exploration of the psychological factors, the big thing to think about when it comes to imposter syndrome is the idea of automatic thoughts. Automatic thoughts float up from the subconscious into the conscious mind (McKay, Davis, & Fanning, 2021). They're often irrational and negatively impact our self-esteem and self-concept. We have no control over them (hence the automatic part). It's vital to remember that the key to feeling better is not to try to "just stop" having automatic thoughts, it is about changing our relationship to those thoughts, especially their content (Hayes & Hofmann, 2021). We cannot stop something that's automatic, but if we learn to anticipate and manage, then we will feel differently when it arises.

There are two primary types of automatic thought that drive and maintain imposter syndrome. The first is some form of "in order to be loved or happy, I need to achieve." Many of us feel this way, right? If I don't have an "A" on the test, if I don't get the promotion, if I don't get to be first chair in the orchestra, I'm not good enough. Psychologists call this *contingent worthiness* (Zhang, Zhang, Wang, & Zhang, 2024). But there's another type of automatic thought which I have found far harder to unroot in therapy. It is some form of "What I've done before doesn't count. It doesn't matter. I need to do more. I must do more." If you are unable to give yourself credit for the good things that you have done and are doing, then you are creating fertile soil for imposter syndrome to take root. It's true that whatever job or academics you're doing will require the need for you to keep going, working, and learning, so you must learn to separate that reality from the emotional impact of "I'm never going to be satisfied with my life."

What does imposter syndrome look like? Psychologically, these people are very stressed out. They exhibit a lot of generalized anxiety disorder and depression, a lot of avoidance and procrastination leading to meltdowns, a lot of concern and rumination on failure and perfection. They are constantly moving the goalposts (which is what I call my talk on perfectionism, because the anxiety of trying to "prove" that you're not a fraud ends up with compulsively changing the finish line for the desired success. The reality is that there is no magic finish line where your imposter syndrome goes away. Tom Hanks has imposter syndrome! So, if you're an actor and you're trying not to have imposter syndrome by being the best actor possible, you have to ask yourself if there really is a level beyond Tom Hanks and, if so, is it easier to reach that 99.99999999^{th} percentile outcome or accept that you're imperfect. I know which one I'd choose.

Ultimately for neurodivergent people, imposter syndrome lives in the space between making something look easy and discounting its value *because* it was easy (Hawley, 2019). Paying attention to new things has an evolutionary benefit, so it's encoded into our sympathetic nervous systems. Neurodivergent brains crave novelty because it gives us more dopamine, but our brains also tend to ignore routine actions or events (Damiani, et al., 2017). When we ignore our routine actions (even if those actions are exceptional), our brains stop giving us credit for doing them at all, let along doing them successfully. At best, we're missing out on easy dopamine for our behavior; at worst, this can set us up for what I like to call "the hamster wheel of doom," having to do better and better and more and more to get the same level of reward for doing something.

Another thing worth noting here, one of my favorite subsections in this chapter, is the Theory of Relativity Syndrome (Treffert, 2014). It's a subset of imposter syndrome based on Albert Einstein. (Here's a fun trivia question: how many formal academic papers did Einstein write while he was a professor at Princeton University? Time's up! He published two papers. Two! So much for "publish or perish").

Einstein only submitted the two papers not because he had gotten tenure and could kick his feet up, but rather because he spent the rest of his career chasing his next big idea. When the first two papers that you write as a physicist literally change how we think about space time, the idea is that everything you do next has to be at that level. Einstein never found his "third leg of the stool," or what he called the Grand Unified Theory, or the explanation for the rest of the universe that he hadn't yet explored. While his career is by no means a failure, you could make the argument that he didn't do as much he could have because he was chasing this other extremely high-level idea. To Einstein, if it wasn't at that level, it wasn't worth publishing.

There's an old line about giftedness that says, "Talent hits a target no one else can hit; genius hits a target no one else can see." Chasing the impossible task is seductive because the potential payoff is amazing. If you have the kind of brain that allows you to even conceptualize those ideas, you've got the ceiling that allows you to get there. It's possible to get there once, twice, maybe even three times. But it's not sustainable to get there every time. When you're at Einstein's level, you can have some wiggle room to chase the impossible content, but there's also value in knowing when the task is impossible for a reason. I see this phenomenon showing up in classrooms and offices all over the country; people don't know when to quit because they're really anxious about trying to be exceptional and get something amazing done. If you've got that anxious perfectionism about not being thought of as a fraud, trying to always reach the ceiling is going to set you up for failure more often than not, because your other work is piling up while you're spinning your wheels.

We need to help our people understand that there's a lot of value in the basics. There's also a lot of value in starting slow and moving methodically. But neurodivergent brains tend to discount the basics because they come so easily. But not everything is easy for everyone. Just because it's easy for you does not mean it's easy for somebody else.

Skipping the basics can get you in trouble. Often there are kids who report these anxiously perfectionistic feelings, saying something like, "It's got to be perfect; it's got to be great; it's got to change the world!" But it might not; in fact, it really doesn't have to. Additionally, you might have the most advanced concept in the world to articulate, but if you never mastered basic writing, then your idea will fail to thrive because others cannot understand it. There is great value in contributing to the field at every level, from writing regular books to presenting at conferences, to speaking for panels, to editing papers; everything doesn't need to be exceptional to be worthwhile. Vincent Van Gogh produced over 2,000 pieces of art in his career, and while only about 110 or so are considered masterpieces, they all have value.

A colleague that I interviewed as a part of my research for imposter syndrome is an internationally famous psychologist who does meta-analysis. His career has been based on analyzing multiple studies to see if he can draw meaningful conclusions from their respective conclusions. When I was talking to him about imposter syndrome and how it impacts gifted people, he said it made sense, but it couldn't apply to him because he hasn't done anything in his career. (He felt so strongly about this that he asked me not to name him in this book—you know who you are ☺). My jaw dropped. He's a rockstar! I was lucky to get a Zoom call with him in the first place. He feels like he's not accomplished at anything because all he's done is percolate other people's research. But such meta-analysis helps us understand things, unifies the field, and illuminates blind spots in research. All this angst, and he's a person who's won international awards in psychology—not because they're pitying him or because nobody else can do it, but because he's really quite good at it. If you find your niche and you excel there, it is a good path forward. The one thing that my colleague was willing to accept as praise was that he was good at meta-analysis; at least he could be proud of his niche.

How do you find your niche? How do you know it's good enough? I'm lucky because the thing that I love to do (talking to and about people with different brains) turned into a career (being a professional nerd). Being sure of anything when you have a neurodivergent brain is tough. All you can do is try a bunch of things that are aligned with your values and see what feels best. If you're good at something, you have the potential to rise to the top. If you need a place to start, think about what you wanted to be when you were ten years old: that's the purest version of self-confidence before life gets in the way. (This means that I get to be Batman by night and a marine biologist by day. Awesome!) Just keep checking in with yourself to see what feels like the right fit and understand that it might be a long process to find your niche.

I'm reminded of the great quote from Bertrand Russell: "The whole problem with the world is that fools and fanatics are always so certain of themselves, but wiser people so full of doubts." If that doesn't sum up being a smart, sensitive, attentive person in the 21st century, then I don't know what does. The more differently your brain works, the more likely you are to be able to see things with greater nuance. My colleague knows what meta-analyses does to help us, but also is painfully aware of its limitations. Knowledge may be power, but it can also be confusion. It's important to keep that in mind that the fact of doubting oneself, losing the proverbial intellectual forest for the trees, often comes with neurodivergence.

The ability to self-reflect is a blessing and a curse. As Lin-Manuel Miranda (a true gifted kid) said, "My default state is basically painfully self-aware." As you read this book you're probably thinking about your place in your field of work or study thinking, "I'll never be great at this because what I know is but a small subset of what everybody else knows." I felt that way in graduate school when I started working on my dissertation. The legends of our field (Joe Renzulli, Del Siegel, Linda Silverman, Susan Baum, Russell Barkley, Ross Greene, Sally Reis, and so many more—but I've fanboyed enough) have done *a great deal*. It was wildly intimidating to look at the scope of their careers and realize that I was so far behind. I almost quit before I started because I couldn't stop thinking about how delayed I was, and how poorly I compared to these giants. But then I had coffee with Rena Subotnik (another legend), and she said that when they all started, there were other giants they were chasing. So, you might as well start! You'll never catch up, but you can accumulate anything if you don't ever start.

Whatever you are doing or want to do, there's likely someone better at it that you. Probably thousands of people (some self-help book, eh?). You'll never be *them*, but you can be as good as them *in your own way*.

There are things you know that other people don't know, just as there are things that other people know that you don't know. And there is an overlap. What really is true is that we are all mini-experts, and each of our niches contributes greatly to the depth of the field. The trick is not to try to *be* Bill Nye the Science Guy, but to learn from him and create your career's version of that content (like the fabulous Emily Calandrelli). Comparison is the thief of joy, but we can always learn from other people and stand on the shoulders of those giants.

You know things I don't know. That's great. I want to know *your* perspective on whatever it is you do, whether it is teaching reading, changing tires or structuring an international arms deal. Those are good things (well, maybe not the last one). I don't know as much about them because knowing those things is not my job! With luck I am showing that I know a lot about imposter syndrome and the social emotional aspects of being neurodivergent. If you need to know about those things, I hope that you call me (I mean, you already bought the book, right?). And if I need to know what you know, then I'll call you. There aren't people out there who have access to magical journals or a special Google and therefore know things you don't or can't. There are people who know things that you don't because *it's impossible to know everything*. Think about what you know and what you need to know to do your job and master those things. Everything else is gravy. This intellectual humility is the antidote to imposter syndrome.

Treatment

Cognitive Reframing

How do we help? I bet you've mentally identified someone in your life who has imposter syndrome. You think about how sad that is, and how much you want to help them, and how worthy they are of your support—all great thinking! But it also exemplifies a much larger problem: we are much kinder to other people than ourselves; we go out of our way to praise others, support others, and show up for others, *all while we're thinking <u>we</u> are the true impostors*. We are the ones that thinks this whole "imposter syndrome" thing doesn't apply to *us*, the true frauds. I tell you now, that's not true.

If I'm right, you're sitting here reading this and thinking, "Oh my gosh, my colleagues, they all suffer from imposter syndrome, but they're so wonderful, and I am the true impostor." The first part of that sentence is accurate. The second part of the sentence I want to crumble up and throw in the garbage. You *are* smart, you *are* talented, you *are* deserving of all the success you've had. You're not a phony, I promise you. If you need more proof, remember that all those wonderful people you're spending time and mental energy praising in your brain are thinking that *they* are the true impostors. We're all miserable in our own silos! You can't all be the fraud; some of you are actually good. And if you can't believe that, let's at least try to be miserable together. What? Progress is progress.

A big part of the psychology for moving forward and treating imposter syndrome is cognitive retraining, or changing your relationship to your thoughts. We talked about how we can't stop automatic thoughts, but we can change how we respond to them. The first thing is to name imposter syndrome, so we can see it when it shows up. I always tell my clients that we "name it to tame it." (Maybe I should sell bumper stickers). Naming something activates the same parasympathetic nervous system regulation that we talked about before. Every time I talk about imposter syndrome, my own imposter syndrome flares. But every time I give this talk, I know that's going to happen, so I acknowledge it when it arrives. As I manage it, the intensity level goes down and I get a little more confidence in dealing with it. I'm always working to improve. Getting better is all about seeing yourself in context.

Context

To work on understanding context, I like to suggest the 93/7 rule to my clients. Is getting 93% on a test a good score? (Yes, it is.) You're probably stuck on the fact that it's not perfect, you got seven points off. It's your right to focus on the 7% you've got wrong, even if you've got 93% right. But that 7% wrong cannot exist without the 93%, right? You must see things in context. We must make our high standards work for us, not by becoming miserable when we see the weakness and errors, but by casting those imperfections as ways to learn and grow. It's hard to like being less than perfect. It's hard to accept our mistakes when they cost us some good, especially if those mistakes were avoidable. Those feelings are normal!

It is important to understand that as we explore who we are, content is one thing, but context is much more important. Everybody feels off base at the beginning of something new, whether it's a job, meeting new people, getting a promotion, doing a TEDx talk, or going on a date. In the above 93/7 example, your content might be that you're a smart person, and smart people do well on tests. But what is the context? Is this a test that you studied for? Was something else taking up your time? Did you understand the material in class? Smart people may do well on tests, but not everyone does well when the cards are stacked against them. Context, like being neurodivergent, is never an excuse for bad behavior, but it is often a variable that we must consider to properly understand ourselves.

The Role of Perfectionism

We also should try to practice being *anti*-perfect. Nobody's perfect. Everybody struggles at times, right? Tell your kids if they play video games, if the bad guys are getting harder and the music's getting louder and things are getting more challenging, it means you're going in the right direction. Getting something wrong or failing doesn't make you a fraud. Focus on what you know rather than on what you don't, so you can build upwards towards the best version of whatever there is for you to do. I give a lot of talks and I can tell you that there is no perfect public speech (no, not even Sir Ken Robinson's TED Talk, which is basically the best thing I've seen on the internet, and yes that includes the Coldplay Pig). When I give my talk on perfectionism, I intentionally leave in two typos on my PowerPoint and challenge the audience to find them. Even if the audiences find the errors, people report that the existence of the typos don't ruin the talk. You can't wait until something's perfect to do it, and you don't have to do it perfectly. Do the thing, take notes on what happened, and then do it again. As the Patron Saint of Giftedness, Ms. Frizzle, always says: "If at first you don't succeed, find out why."

Determining reasons for failure is part of intellectual humility, which is another thing to practice when confronting imposter syndrome. If your students ask you a question that you can't answer, tell them, "I don't know, let's look it up together." Don't pretend you know things that you do not, because it implies that to be successful, we must know everything and be perfect all the time, which is both not fun and not possible. It's okay to ask for help. Maybe it violates the "code" of conduct that says we're somehow supposed to know everything and have no gaps in our knowledge, but that's not realistic. Authenticity is a much better "code".

It's okay to Google! In the past I've worked with an incredible pediatrician at a local hospital on several cases. We were working with a gifted young man who has a strange and rare autoimmune disorder. After a long meeting with his parents, we were discussing the weird presentation of the illness, and suddenly she started pounding away at her keyboard. I asked, "Oh, did you figure it out? Are you writing the medical orders?" She laughed and said no, she was Googling the symptoms. I said, "But you're this amazing doctor, what are you googling for?" She said, not unkindly, "Matt, everybody Googles." It's unrealistic to have all the knowledge we will ever need memorized. Looking things up can't be the only tool in your toolbox, but it is certainly a technique to use.

Emotional Awareness

Increasing emotional awareness and intelligence gives us words to identify and manage problems. When you know your feelings, you can activate yourself out of those feelings. Take time to know what each emotion feels like in your body: how does anger feel? Shyness? Exhaustion? Fear? Our feelings are loud and demanding but they do not always reflect reality. Learn to separate feelings from fact: just because you feel it or think it doesn't make it true (otherwise I would be the world's greatest foosball player). I often remind my clients that emotions are "data, not directions."

It's far too easy to only pay attention to our emotional trouble spots. but we have positive stimuli in the world as well. When you do this emotional work, it's vital to identify your comfort zones and safe activities. Not everything we do triggers our imposter syndrome; some tasks that we are presented with might actually (dare I say?) make us feel good. We want to have such reinforcers on speed-dial. And, yes, you need to know your triggers as well. What makes you feel more like an impostor? When you know them can plan for them and be intentional about how you approach the task, and how you reward yourself. When you get something done, you get a reward that's going help break that cycle of not getting internal reinforcement. When I'm finished writing this chapter, I'm going to go get a big chocolate chip cookie. I'm so excited to eat it that my mouth is watering. That's my reward for this writing task, and it completes the dopamine circuit and pushes back the imposter syndrome a bit more.

Managing Anxiety

Imposter syndrome is fundamentally an anxiety disorder (Landry, et al., 2021). I want you to remember this because imposter syndrome lives in abstraction. It is impossible for imposter syndrome to survive when you're taking action, because taking action proves you're not a fraud. Remember, anxiety makes us want to either fight, flee, fawn, or freeze. Especially in imposter syndrome, it's about freezing, right? No matter what direction you're moving in, as long as you're moving, you're telling your imposter syndrome, "Yes, I'm scared AND I'm going to keep moving forward." Frauds don't *do* things, they find ways to hide, reschedule, cancel, or never arrive in the first place. It's scary, but fear is the price of admission for the life you want. Sign up to do the talk, ask that person out, go for the promotion, write that paper—do the thing you need to do. Because your imposter syndrome's only ability is to scream and yell and make a big scene; it can't actually *hurt* you. Once you realize that fact, you're going to gain all the power back in that relationship.

For a great example of this reality, I'm going to be a huge nerd and refer to a podcast. I was listening to an interview with someone who runs the US Winter Olympic Ski School in Utah. They were talking about training people to ski jump. As a person who likes both feet flat on the ground, that is terrifying to me. Someone's got to do it, and I'm glad it's not me.

There is an elaborate system for training these ski jumpers, from having them jump into pools and foam pits to using bungee cords to having them go down the snowy hill. Every year, the students fall into three categories: those who successfully land the jump, those who try and crash, and those who ski past the jump and never attempt it. The US Ski Team has a lot invested in these students and they want them to succeed. What they've found is that the students who try and succeed usually end up making the team. Those who try the jump and fail also often end up making the team, because they're motivated to get it right the next time. The students who leave the program without making the team are those who, at the moment of their jumping audition, find a reason not to try the jump at all. It's too hard, too scary, too big so they do nothing. But in doing nothing, they prove themselves to be frauds, because trying risks failure and you need to be vulnerable enough to try something scary.

Sometimes in life you must literally take the leap. If you don't win the first time, you'll find that you're much more motivated to get it right in the future. Falling hurts, but as the saying goes, "What if I fall? Oh, but darling, what if you fly?"

Role-Models

From working with neurodivergent people, we know that the gifted population loves their heroes. They love other neurodivergent folks because they give us people to look up to. We want to find relevant mentors for our people. Finding these role models isn't about saying, "Look who's crazy too!", but rather it's about empathizing and showing that people can overcome such feelings. Many people that we look up to suffer from imposter syndrome, from Chuck Lorre to Michelle Obama to Neil Gaiman to Justice Sonia Sotomayor.

One of the best quotes about imposter syndrome is from the incomparable Maya Angelou, poet, activist, performer, professor, and generally amazing human being. Her quote reads,

> *"I have written 11 books, but each time I think, 'uh-oh, they're going to find out now. I've run a game on everybody, and they're going to find me out.'"*

And that's from a former Poet Laureate of the United States!

On a personal note, I had the good fortune of taking Dr. Angelou's class when I was an undergraduate at Wake Forest University in the Spring of 2006. It was a special writing class for seniors only, and you had to apply for it. It wasn't on campus because Maya Angelou doesn't teach on campus. We went to her house which was a beautiful mansion on the "nice" side of Winston-Salem. On the first day of class, we were sitting in her living room, and she came out regally and gave us snickerdoodle cookies. Everybody introduced themselves (including her, because she is polite), and it came to me and I blurted out, "I'm Matt Zakreski, I'm a Senior from New Jersey, and I don't think that I belong here in this class."

Everybody looked at me and chuckled, because I think I had expressed an anxiety that many of us were feeling. Maya grinned—and I'll never forget this—and looked at me and said, "So let's think about that for a second, shall we? Because you had to apply to get to this class. You had to submit a writing sample. One of two things are true. Either a) you fooled me, and even though your writing is awful, you presented yourself in such a way that I mistakenly let you into this class, or b) I see a talent or strength in you that you don't see in yourself. Which one of those do you think is more likely true?" There was a thunderstruck silence in the room. I was floored, and then I felt my imposter syndrome melting away, because even my anxious brain understands it's damn likely Maya Angelou knows a little bit more about writing than I do.

Another cool story about imposter syndrome is from Dr. Margaret Chan, former Chief of the World Health Organization. I knew nothing about her before I started writing this chapter. She said, "A lot of people out there think I'm an expert. How do these people think all this about me? I'm so much aware of all the things I don't know." Dr. Chan was likely the top doctor on planet Earth. If you're the Chief of the World Health Organization, you can't go any higher than that, there you are at the peak. Yet she's still beset by doubt, and the understanding that there are many things you don't know, and that's okay.

The biggest takeaway here is that the types of people who have imposter syndrome are all the smart successful people that you think have their act together, me included. So do yourself a favor, broaden the network and speak openly about this issue, because will find out that you're not alone, and that these feelings can be overcome. We overcome them by taking committed action and taking the chances that align with our values. Life is going to give us the opportunity to show up as our best self and face our fears to become the person you want to be. A fraud would find a way to say "no;" I know that you'll find a way to say "yes."

CHAPTER 8
"Improv-ing" Social Skills and Surviving Other People

I'm a theatre kid at heart—I love the stage, the lights, the costumes, the show-stopping numbers, the whole pageantry and skill of it all. I flung myself into theatre during freshman year of high school and managed to carve out a role in the theater community as someone who was willing to do anything for a laugh. I was an above average dancer and understood my limitations as a singer (plus, what local theater troupe doesn't need guys?).

I had such a good time in theatre in high school that I beelined right for Theatre Kids ® when I got to college. Even if I wasn't going to be a theatre major (said in a James Lipton-esque posh), I knew that the stage was where I felt most comfortable. I rapidly found out, despite my love of the theatre and the people in it, that I wasn't very good at acting. What a bummer. But I loved the community so much that I found ways to stay involved: building sets, making costumes, writing plays, etc. I found myself particularly drawn to improv.

Improv is a style of acting where most of what you perform is made up spontaneously based on suggestions from the audience (Amador, 2018). It's a helpful skillset for engaging with the world because most of the time we have no idea how life is going to go, and that can cause us to shut down if we don't have the skill set to navigate the twists and turns. As much as we might work to find spaces and people that are consistent and predictable (or predictably unpredictable), there are times when we will find ourselves living on the edge of our experience.

We cannot plan for every eventuality (despite what our anxiety might try and tell us), so we need to be able to lean on our ideas and creativity to make sure that we don't have to linger in awkward silence. improv requires that kind of bravery and collaboration to survive uncertainty, which is why I'm talking about it here.

It's funny to me, looking back, that I was always a better improviser than actor. When I mentioned this to my favorite theatre professor after college, she laughed and said, "Matt, you were always better with your own words than someone else's. Remember how bad it went when I tried to direct you in Shakespeare?" Well, NOW I do, Cindy! Sheesh. But speaking of Shakespeare, in *As You Like It*, he writes, "All the world's a stage; And all the men and women merely players; they have their exits and their entrances; And one man in his time plays many parts…" The poem goes on, but Shakespeare never indicates script, or lines, or stage directions. The Bard knew that we are all improvisers, because life is the greatest improv of all.

Growing up, I knew I was different. When I was in 2nd grade, I was identified as gifted, which they told me meant that I was very smart. What they didn't tell me was that being gifted meant I was also neurodivergent: the same brain that made me able to speed read also made me socially off-beat and, shall we say, quirky. My awareness of my differences made me very anxious as a kid, especially around my peers. "What are they going to say next? What will I say? What about after that?!" There were way too many variables, and that freaked me out. Everything social seemed easy to them! They had the "code" even if they didn't know it. (Which, in the 1990s, seemed to include lots of Surge Soda, Nintendo 64, liking professional wrestling, and debating who you would rather date: Jennifer Love Hewitt or Sarah Michelle Gellar).

I liked things to be a certain way, especially other people, because people are often the problem. They're so unpredictable, with foibles and quirks and needs…it's exhausting trying to keep up. I liked TV and movies more than people, because they were predictable! It doesn't matter what trap the Joker springs, Batman is always going to get out of it. The Scooby Gang unmasks the monster. G.I. Joe outsmarts Cobra. Dr. Claw, foiled again, growls, "I'll get you next time, Gadget. Next time!!!!"

Like a lot of anxious kids, I was good at saying "No" to the world and its uncertainty. I said "no" to things that were scary, unusual, strange, or new…which was pretty much everything. I kept my world small because that's how I liked it. Small meant safe. Small meant that I was in control. Anxious kids gather as much control as possible because feeling in control is a counterbalance to anxiety (Papandreou, et al., 2023). I was vaguely aware that I was missing out on things (what were those "boy-girl parties" that everyone was talking about?) but I knew that trying them invited risk. Risk meant I might fail, failing hurts, and I wanted to avoid that pain at any cost. Now you see the anxiety!

We all come up with ways of managing our anxiety, and some of them are OK in the short term; but most of them just kick our problems down the road. We must face our fears to inoculate ourselves against the feelings of anxiety and prove to ourselves that we can do so. The most important job of a parent (and to a certain extent, a teacher or a boss) is *not* to keep our people from having bad experiences and uncomfortable emotions; it is to make sure they don't experience that unpleasantness alone. How much to expose our people to stressors is a mystery: when and how do we do it without freaking everyone out? That is hard to know, and why my job as a psychologist exists!

You will learn that the harder you try to control the world, the more miserable you make yourself. The world is chaotic and resists our efforts to give everything a schedule and script (Ghamari Kivi, Jamshiddoust Miyanroudi, Mousavi, & Ghavibazou, 2023). The harder we try to fix it, the worse things seem to get. This is true for my clients, but also for their parents and bosses. The more in charge you are, the more stress you're under, and the more stress you're under, the more you feel the need to be in control. But you cannot anticipate and manage everything. Assuming you can control everything is like trying to juggle 73 tennis balls: the effort is huge, the success rate zero, and the cost in emotion and energy will leave you burned out and exhausted. We're much better off shifting our energy to surfing the uncertainty of life than we are trying to control the chaos. You can try with just a few balls, manage what you can, and the world doesn't end. How do you start on that path?

One summer, after barely surviving middle school, I was whisked away to summer camp in beautiful Carlisle, PA. And there, at my summer camp for gifted nerds, I was introduced to "Improv." At the Center for Talented Youth (CTY), they know that gifted kids need to be *voluntold* to do things outside of their comfort zones, or they would shrink right back into their small little boxes. In our clever gifted snark, we called this "mandatory fun." But I went along, bouncing between activities and trying to play as much Ultimate Frisbee as possible. One fateful Wednesday there were no good options. Or so I thought. I yelled to my roommate, "Hey, what're you doing for activity today?" and he yelled back, "improv." And since it was either that or Advanced Knitting, I tagged along.

Immediately, I realized that "improv" was some sort of acting game, which appealed to me because I always enjoy performing. I grew up going into New York City to see Broadway shows and I knew enough about that world to be intrigued. (I wouldn't get into theatre myself for a few more years—it was definitely not in the "code" of being a tween boy in the 90s. I went to the counselor in charge and asked for my lines. "Lines?" he scoffed. "This is improv. We're just going to make it all up!" I thought, "no, that's not going to work for me." I wanted to run for the door! Didn't he see that I'm anxious? I need to know what's happening, I need to have a plan. How else can I be successful? Just tell me what to do and I'll do it, I'm very smart and competent; but I can't handle the responsibility of being in charge of my own lines! Looking at my panicked face, the counselor leaned forward and told me something that I've never forgotten, profound advice that has led me to writing this book. "In improv, you don't have to know what exactly you're going to say, because you don't know what it's going to be! When we're stuck, we always say, 'yes, and…'"

"Yes, and…what?"

He smiled at me: "That's the fun part."

"No, no, no!" I wanted to shout, but we were lining up for our first activity, a classic improv game called "World's Worst." In Worlds Worst, you are given a topic, and you take turns giving a personal example of the worst version of that thing (Amador, 2018). We were given the prompt of "World's Worst person to be set up on a blind date with." Racking my brain for contemporary pop culture references, I settled on Wolverine from the X-men. This was pre-Hugh Jackman, so it made a lot more sense then.

People went one by one, and then it was my turn. The counselor said, "And the World's Worst person to go on a blind date with would be…" …and he looked up at me. I took a deep breath, ready to deliver my line, and…FROZE. There was not a thought in my head as I stared at my friends in the audience. The moment seemed to last forever (even if it was only about 15 seconds) and I was convinced that I was going to die right there in that residence hall basement (Here Lies Matt Zakreski. He Should Not Have Tried New Things. RIP).

But then something happened.

As I stood there, slaw-jacked and flop sweaty, someone from the back of the room yelled, "Dude, he's a water buffalo!" and the room cracked up with laughter. Then three important things happened.

○ I had the good sense to say, "Yep!" and run off stage (which is itself a kind of improv, since there was a part of me that wanted to stay up there and defend myself until I did my Wolverine impression). Knowing when and how to walk away is a social skill.

○ I thought that I had failed epically…but *no one had noticed or judged me.* That felt quite different than at home, where my friends seemed forever poised to knock me down for the slightest error or social faux pas. It's like people don't see errors if they're not looking for them. Weird.

○ It was so much better to laughed *with* than to be laughed *at*. I enjoyed that feeling of connection, of power. I liked being the center of attention (still do, obviously), but having people enjoy my jokes and want more from me felt really cool.

When I came clean to the counselor about my mess-up, he smiled at me. "Remember, in improv there are no mistakes, only opportunities. You may keep screwing up, but you can choose what you do with it. Sometimes the best jokes come from the mistakes, but only if you embrace them."

So, I signed back up the next day. And the day after that. And the summer after that. And then high school musicals, college theatre, a professional improv troupe, trying my hand at stand-up, going to grad school, and finally becoming a psychologist. Once I had my platform, I realized that the world needs people who live *with* their mental health challenges and get up in front of audiences to tell their story, who show people that they're not alone in their struggles, and that things can get better. That's why I do what I do, and I use improv to help because things always go wrong. I've had microphones cut out on me, lost power, had my phone play a YouTube video in the middle of talk…the gamut. In those challenging moments it's tempting to freeze, panic, or give up. But the power of improv is thinking on your feet, so when that challenging time comes, you've learned to make things up as you go.

It is a certainty that we are all going to screw up and need to recover— it's inevitable! I'm sure that is making you anxious, but we can effect positive change in our lives by thinking about how we respond to failure (I am going to spend offer a whole chapter about overcoming failure, so stick with me).

Before my intro to improv, I had to return to Fair Haven, NJ to start high school. I was leaving my happy nerd bubble and venturing into the (gulp!) real world. Would I maintain the confidence and skills I had built that summer? You're damn right I did. Because the improv trick of saying, "Yes, and…" changed me. It's not an accident that my first high school report card says things like "coming out of his shell," "really embracing change," and "rolls with the punches." Those are all lessons from improv! Developing competence in social skills increased my confidence in my social skills, which put me in more places to do more things, maintaining that virtuous cycle. (Making real friends also helped, obviously).

That's how improv helped me, but how does it help the rest of us? How does it help us embrace the uncertainty of the world? With the #1 rule in improv, we say "Yes, and...". You don't have to know exactly what to say in every situation if you have a golden rule that applies to all eventualities. It's like a social skills Swiss Army knife.

"Yes, and..." is a connection. A promise. A collaboration. It stops anxiety from shrinking our world, pushing it wide open instead. When we are anxious, we want to say "no", which grinds things to a halt. Imagine you're talking to someone at work, and they ask, "Want to grab a beer after our shift is over?" And you say, "No."

How awkward is that? The conversation just dies. That's why we want to say "yes."

Saying "yes" doesn't mean you are blindly agreeing to everything. To further the above example, what if you don't drink? The mindset is what we're shifting here, rather than the literal answer. You could go to the pub and order a coffee, or chicken wings, or just have water (with lemon, even!), and enjoy the company of others without having to worry about getting a Lyft home. Your anxious brain immediately listed all the reasons that going out for a beer was a terrible idea, but saying "yes" keeps you from missing out on the positives of the experience.

When we say "yes" to the world we open ourselves to others and the full breadth of human experience. No, it doesn't always work. Saying "yes" has embarrassed me, humbled me, lost me money, and once almost got me killed (white water rafting is HARD!).

While living in Australia, we took a spring break trip to New Zealand on an "extreme adventures tour." We climbed a glacier, rode a speed boat, ziplined, bungee jumped, skydived, bungee jumped again, and rode in a helicopter...up to the white-water rafting spot. There, the guide asked us who had been white-water rafting before, and I raised my hand because I had done it when I was 12 years old on vacation with my parents. She didn't know that context and said, "Great! You can sit up front with me; it's the second-most important seat." When we got to the most dangerous rapid on the river, I was turning to get instructions from her when I got knocked in the face by my friend's oar, fell into the water, and got sucked through the rapids on my own. I was lucky enough to pop out the other side (eventually—I was under water for a LONG time), where I was scooped up by my friends and returned to my boat. The guide looked me and said, "Well, you probably shouldn't have sat up front. But did you at least have fun on the trip?" You know what? I did. Almost dying definitely impacted by experience, but it didn't ruin it either.

That's the perfect segue to my next point. Even with those failures, I won much more than I lost by opening myself up to the world and living the lessons of improv. You can open yourself up safely by remembering that we don't just say "Yes," we say, "Yes, and...". I was saying "yes" to whitewater rafting without considering my needs in the situation, namely that I didn't know what I was doing. I should've said, "Yes I want to go rafting, AND I have no idea what I'm doing." They might have suggested I take a course, or sit in a different seat, or watch and learn. Successful relationships involve give-and-take. We use "Yes, *and...*" to show our openness, our willingness to listen, and also our personality. Improv, like life, isn't just about taking direction, it's also about adding something to the production. It might be big, it might be small, it might fail epically, but adding the "and" is your way of saying "I'm here and my needs matter too." It's a prosocial dynamic.

There are other rules of improv that are worth addressing. We should come with intention, focus on relationships, not block others, not ask too many questions, and know when to exit a scene (Amador, 2018). We should also not try to win improv, because improv is inherently a collaborative effort; it isn't a competition (Bayne & Jangha, 2016). Good improv is about lifting everyone up and having a good time without worrying about who was best. The goal is the good conversation and experience that comes from accepting and sharing each other's needs.

Imagine yourself in this situation: it's two years from now and your boss asks you if you want a promotion, but you've got to move to Singapore to do it, and you have to decide right now. You can't put it off because saying, "I'll get back to you" would be like saying, "No." You need to keep the conversation going. How do you handle the situation? Without the lessons of improv, you might blurt out, "Well this social interaction isn't going the way I had rehearsed it in my head." We are constantly faced with curveballs. Improv teaches us to be nimble, to think on our feet, to be spontaneous, which are skills that will help us time and time again in a chaotic world. You don't have to know what to say at first, you just can start by saying, "Yes, and…"

○ "Yes, and I'd like to talk about how you plan to get me out there."

○ "Yes, and I need to talk to my partner about what that means for our family."

○ "Yes, and I'd also be more interested in a promotion here in the US."

○ "Yes, it's a lovely opportunity, and I think that I'm better off where I am."

None of these are perfect answers, but life isn't perfect. Life is about doing the best you can in each situation and assessing your reactions and subsequent reflection to help grow. Trying to be perfect pulls us out of the moment and disconnects our response from the reality at hand. Improv skills give us space to practice and learn from our mistakes without the negative consequences of being mismatched with the real world.

Improv informs perspective taking, prosocial communication, executive functioning development, creativity, active listening, cognitive flexibility, and overcoming anxiety (Lerner, Mikami, & Levine, 2011).

As a psychology, I can testify to both the necessity of developing those skills and to the fact that developing them can be a long, painful process. Gamifying social skill development helps make the skills playful, and less of a tedious job to demystify the social "code". Improv games are fun, and research clearly shows that people learn more and sustain information longer when they're having fun, especially kids (Bayne & Jangha, 2016).

My favorite story about improv's ability to make important lessons fun comes from working with a neurodivergent kid at a charter school outside of Philadelphia. This young man who I will call Bryan was a charming, quirky kid who wanted nothing more in the world than to make friends. He was really well-intentioned, but he had one major thing going against him: he was a close talker. No matter how much we told him about that, it did not help to change his behavior; he just couldn't see it. It wasn't until we started improv games that Bryan finally saw the light.

We were playing a classic game called "Park Bench" in which two actors, one sitting on a bench and one who comes up to them to deliver a line creepy enough to get the other actor to move (Amador, 2018). Bryan was great at this game, not because he was creepy, but because he delivered every line about two inches from someone's nose, which was very off-putting. After several rounds, Bryan suddenly whirled around and said, "Oh my GOD! Dr. Matt! I talk WAY too close to people!" And we were like, "Oh my Goodness! That is brand new information!" And we all had a good laugh about it. He had experienced the reality of his behavior on his own, and because the experience was nested in the game, he felt supported as opposed to targeted. He was able to change his behavior because he had come to the insight *organically,* through his own efforts. Improv opened that door for him—and yes, he did end up with a date to Formal.

Another way that improv can be helpful is by offering meaningful practice in how to communicate with others, especially those who don't communicate like we do (Bayne & Jangha, 2016). One of the problems with being neurodivergent is that we struggle to understand

and parse subjective or sarcastic language (Lerner, et al., 2011). We can be *very* literal. How do we practice being less literal if we are only told what NOT to do?

People tend to think that being literal means that you don't get jokes or sarcasm, which can be true. In my experience, being literal shows up in far more complex and multidirectional ways. Here are some real-life examples from my clinical practice:

○ You feel like you have to follow precisely *all* of the stated requirements for a task, but everyone else seems to just "know" the "code" which allows you to slack in certain areas, and that's ok? What's with that? It's either a rule or it's not.

○ Perhaps you're like me and you answer rhetorical questions all the time. Answering questions is kind of my thing. If you don't want me to answer the question, perhaps you could use metacommunication and tell me it's rhetorical?

○ You know how to follow the directions but then something goes wrong or is unexpected and you don't know what to do, so you ask for help, but people say, "Well you should just know how to fix that!" Isn't it your job to teach me? And if you want me to develop independence during this project, please state that expectation ahead of time.

○ Additionally, sometimes you do exactly what people say they wanted but it turns out that what they said wasn't what they meant. Their request contained an implicit invitation to do more. It's in these moments that the response "that's great" somehow means just the opposite? I believe that this disconnect occurs because the unstated part of the "code" is that you're supposed to do what is expected of you and then add in more to differentiate yourself somehow. To me, that's working overtime, and if I'm going to be working overtime, you can pay me more. You misinterpret empty threats, sarcasm, and hyperbole as literal statements. I ask my wife at least twice per week, "Wait, was that sarcasm?" I'd rather know what I'm dealing with so I can make sense out of it. I'm happy to laugh along, but only if it's actually a joke! And if it's not, why are you being mean?

○ Being wildly frustrated with people using words incorrectly, using a less accurate word when something more specific exists.

These are all challenges that neurodivergent people face. In every social interaction, from the playground to the boardroom to the living room, there are spoken and unspoken rules that make up the "code." Neurodivergent people can become very adept at following the spoken, explicit rules (i.e., don't talk when someone else is talking, give someone your attention when they're talking, be kind with your words); but the unspoken, implicit rules get in our way (Lerner, et al., 2011). I had a client who once got yelled at by the mother of the bride at a wedding when she used her phone to take a selfie-style picture of her and the bride walking down the aisle instead of a regular picture like the rest of the audience. The MOTB hissed, "You should know better!" How do you know when a rule has extra parts? You need to be informed and practice what to do in these situations. But real life gives us few opportunities to practice.

That's why we need games, especially improv games! Improv has flexible, understandable rules. If something goes wrong, you're allowed to fix it. You can get feedback and use it in another activity almost immediately. For example, if you try a joke in improv and it doesn't work, you can talk about what didn't work and how you might fix it. When I play Park Bench with my clients and someone's one-liner didn't make the other actor move, it always opens good conversations about delivery, tone, pacing, and style, in addition to reminding the actors that some creepy content would work for some people (i.e., me and clowns) and not work for others (i.e., me and snakes—snakes are awesome). The failed one-liner doesn't mean that the content wasn't good, just that it could be delivered in a different way, perhaps to a different audience.

To deal with taking things too seriously or literally, there's a great improv game called "Irish Wake" where you tell increasingly hyperbolic short stories about a recently deceased friend (Amador, 2018). At the end of each story, you clink your imaginary drinks and yell, "To (name of the deceased)!" If you were at Bill Brasky's (that was always the name of the deceased when I played as a kid) imaginary funeral, you might start the story with, "One time, Bill gave me his last five dollars so I could get a coffee", and escalate all the way to, "If Bill had three kidneys, he would've given them all to me!" It's a great way to practice saying and responding to hyperbolic statements, because the world is increasingly filled with them. We need to be able to separate the content (no-one has three kidneys) from the intent (I'm communicating that Bill was exceptionally generous and I'll miss him).

As I mentioned before, there's another improv game called "Questions" in which you can communicate only with questions to other people (Amador, 2018). It's a great way to practice not answering rhetorical questions. It's also a great way to genuinely listen to people, rather than just biding time until it's your turn to talk. Trust me, when you don't really listen, people can tell, it's obvious, and a significant social turn-off. Since you can talk only in questions during this game, it forces you to engage the dialogue, rather than waiting for your turn to monologue.

You might feel like you can't do what I'm proposing in this chapter, living life by saying "Yes, and..." and embracing that uncertainty. It is indeed scary! Here's the sneaky truth: You're Already Doing It. From today's coffee run to your social media feed to fighting traffic on the way home, you're thinking on your feet and creating your lines in real time, based only on your wits, your experience, your courage, and your surroundings. We are all improvisers, so embrace it! Life is unpredictable and requires us to be smart, flexible, and brave, *which you already are*, because you've come this far. You can't change the world, but you *can* change how you respond to it. Leave here today encouraged with awareness, to continue to lean into that reality saying, "Yes...*and*..."

CHAPTER 9
You are Not Your Thoughts—Managing Your Inner Voice

Writing a book is hard. We might joke about all the "shoulds" of life: "We should start a band!" "We should open a bar!" "I should go talk to that girl from my math class!" Writing a book has always been on my personal list of "should". I've never told anyone this before, but I tried to write a self-help book for college students in 2004 when I was studying abroad in Australia. I called it "This Needs to be Said" and it was several pages of my well-intentioned ramblings on self-confidence, dating, empathy, and when to forgive and when to forget. If I found that manuscript today, I'm quite certain I would be utterly mortified by what I fatuously thought of as its "insights."

Self-flagellation is not why I'm bringing up this failed attempt at a book. There's no overt reason why I didn't finish the book. I had lots of time, a laptop, not a lot of friends, not a heavy class schedule (one of my four courses was in stand-up comedy, which was awesome but not academically rigorous), plenty to say, and enough skill at writing that the idea didn't feel utterly ridiculous. Yet every time I sat down at my computer, I pecked out a few words, stopped, looked around, and looked for something else to do.

Why didn't it happen? I know that my ADHD had something to do with it; writing books takes sustained focus, and my brain is not suited for that task. Living in Australia was itself a distraction; living 50 meters from one of the best beaches in New South Wales (I love you, Coogee!) is a compelling argument to not take work seriously.

Homesickness, bad wi-fi and cheap beer all factored in. But the biggest challenge was my internal monologue.

We all have a voice inside our heads. Sometimes it's nice to us, sometimes it's chaotically random (the TripleDent Gum jingle from the movie *Inside Out* lives rent free in my head). Most of you are familiar with your inner monologue because it can be downright mean. Every time I tried to sit down and write back in 2004, my brain started a compelling argument about how I wasn't good enough, focused enough, or cool enough to ever write a book—I should just give up and go surfing. And that voice won out; I did a lot more surfing than I did writing.

What is inner monologue from a psychological perspective? It is the verbalized portion of your thoughts (Alderson-Day, Weis, McCarthy-Jones, Moseley, Smailes, & Fernyhough, 2016). We are always thinking, but our inner monologue gives an internal voice to some of those thoughts. We hear the voice in our head as our own voice (though people have reported hearing that inner monologue as their parent, partner, teacher, coach, or a relative). Research shows that neurodivergent people have different types of inner monologues and a more intense relationship with them, which leads to an increased impact (Alderson-Day & Peterson, 2023). This impact stems from the emotional connections that we have formed with people, places, and events; these importance moments create memories, which turn into thoughts. They often float up unbidden, which can make their impact greater, because they seem to come from nowhere (Alderson-Day, et al., 2016).

Has it ever happened to you that you're driving along and you're in a chill "I'm just on autopilot" mode, and then suddenly your brain sends a memory of you tripping over yourself at a school dance, or dropping a catch in Ultimate Frisbee, or trying and failing to ask someone to drinks after work? The images of these painful memories are disconcerting enough, but when they come with narration it can be traumatic.

Your inner monologue acts like the automatic thoughts that have been identified as a key factor in prolonging the experience of anxiety and depression (Ghamari Kivi, et al., 2023). Throughout the day we do literally thousands of things, and our brain narrates them as a way of staying engaged in our actions and surroundings, especially if these are unique or important in some way. Thousands of actions lead to thousands of mental messages. And if your brain is sending the message that you're definitely going to fail (anxiety) because you're such a fuck-up (depression), it would get pretty debilitating over time. But because these experiences are internal, most people suffer in silence.

There are three things that make pushing back on our inner voice difficult. The external work we do matters a great deal, but it's more powerful and effective when based on strong inner work. Inner monologues are hard to ignore because 1) they sound like us (or someone we know/love/respect/fear); 2) they are constant; and 3) they are uncontrollable. Let's talk about how to manage this.

The Voice is Me.

It's easy to argue with ourselves, but very hard to win. I have a mug that reads: "Of course I talk to myself: sometimes I need expert advice." Our brains know everything that has happened to us. To engage effectively with your internal monologue, stop responding to the content and step into the *process* of the words: why are *these words* showing up in *this way* at *this time*? Our brains have a counter-argument for everything so if we keep meeting fact for fact, we'll find that we're exhausting ourselves by playing cognitive Whack-a-Mole. We keep trying to out-logic our inner voice, but it isn't ever going to play the game fair because it knows everything and it doesn't have to only recall facts; it can recall perceptions and emotional reactions, too. So, we need to change the rules of engagement.

Think of some of the iconic voices of pop culture. Darth Vader. SpongeBob. Yoda. Bane. Donald Trump. Skeletor (if you're an 80's kid like me). Siri. Caillou. (shudder). Jar-Jar Binks. Navi "hey listen!" Dick Vitale ("mental health is awesome, baby!!!") The list goes on and on. The point is that, if you've got your own voice in your head and it's making it hard to argue, then changing that voice to another character can do wonders for breaking out of that pattern. You might have trouble arguing with your*self* about whether you're worthy of that promotion at work, but an external voice would make it easier to counterargue. If you're not an impressions person, you can play with the speed of the words in your head, reading them at chipmunk-speed or in super slow-motion. Changing how our brain hears the words in our internal monologue changes our response to them and gives us more options to respond.

The Voice is Constant.

I was more a Star Wars than a Star Trek person, but Trek (and its many modern variations—shout out to Benedict Cumberbatch as Khan) has grown on me over time. I am aware of a profound quote about mental health from a Klingon therapist:

> *"The battle against mental illness cannot be won decisively. It is a long campaign against an enemy who never tires, whose forces swell to twice their size whenever you look away. Battles against a foe of such magnitude, who occupies your very mind…every moment you survive is a triumph against all odds. There is no more honorable combat."*

I've got chills. Every so often I share this quote on my social media platforms because I'm sure that someone out there needs to hear it. Sometimes, it's me.

Our voice never really shuts up, which makes it hard to deal with. A lot of my clients try to keep themselves so busy that the voice doesn't have time to catch up with them. If you run from thing to thing and never let the silence happen, you might not have to deal with the inner voice. But eventually you have to stop, rest, and sleep. If you don't, your body is going to make that choice for you. (I am a little worried about what thoughts will rush in, and in whose voice, when I'm done working all these late hours trying to finish this book by the deadline.)

I call this keeping busy strategy "Wile E. Coyote-ing." Remember those cartoons, where Coyote would be chasing Roadrunner, miss, and run pell-mell off a cliff into an abyss? He would still be fine until he inevitably noticed that he was hundreds of feet in the air, running with no ground underneath him. And then he would plummet. I don't want that to happen to you. We may feel OK in the moment but without a solid foundation underneath us, we're just waiting to fall. We need to find a way to keep our feet on the ground.

You can think about changing the relationship of yourself to the voice because, whoever is talking, it's not going to stop. We can't outrun the voice. Humans survived as a species because we are pursuit hunters; we just keep going and going until our prey gets tired and stops. Then we attack! Well, the voice is us and we are our own prey. It's going to tire us out first because it won't get tired, and then it'll strike when our defenses are down.

Have you ever gotten into a heated "war" with people in the comments section of a political post on social media? Your voice can be just like that: the words just keep coming and coming, and we end up exhausted and upset. For every good argument you make, they respond with useless nonsense like "Go Woke, Get Broke" or "Wake up, Sheeple." It's unwinnable, but we keep fighting because we believe that our logic and intelligence and sense of justice will win the day… because that's the right thing, dammit! But it just doesn't work that way. One of my mentors told me that if your plan for change involves saying, "Well, if everyone would just…XYZ", then you've already lost because there's no universe in which everyone just does XYZ. People don't always behave.

The best way to win is to not fight. You don't have to give up, but you don't have to engage. When engaging with your own thoughts—either because they're very intense or you need to get something done ASAP, you need a strategy other than fighting them or freaking out. In a behavioral situation, walking away would be an option, but you can't walk away from your own mind. In these intense cognitive moments, my favorite strategy is the "leaves on a stream" guided meditation.

Imagine that you're sitting in front of a beautiful cabin in the middle of vast woods, next to a stream. It is peaceful and safe, there is no one around for miles. You've got a pile of leaves next to you, and every time you have a thought, you reach into your head, pull the thought out, place it on a leaf, put the leaf in the stream, and watch it float away. The thought doesn't stop existing, but you don't have to deal with it anymore. You have infinite thoughts, and there are infinite leaves. You can put as many thoughts on as many leaves as you need to get this done. And you're doing it in a safe place.

This kind of guided meditation is a way to change the rules of engagement with the voice. There are dozens out there (I chose this one because it's the one that I use), so explore until you find a framework that allows you to disengage from your own voice on your terms. I think that you'll find it much more successful.

The Voice is Uncontrollable

This is the hardest part. We are used to being able to exert our will on the world in some way. Many neurodivergent folks learn early that some parts of life do not respond to our efforts to control them, which makes us less functional and happy. We adapt and find areas that we can control, even to some extent. This need to control our environment so we can be successful is why every neurodivergent person should have the option to work from home. Especially if you're gifted, you're used to most problems eventually going away, with enough effort and brain power. ("I'm giving her all she's got, Cap'n!"—told you we weren't done with *Star Trek!)*

Our inner monologue doesn't respond to effort. It doesn't respond to logic. It can't be reasoned with, bargained with, bullied, or overwhelmed. It doesn't disappear when presented with copious amounts of marijuana, shrooms, LSD, or booze; not that it stops people from trying, of course. (There's an old line from AA: "Don't try to drown your problems, eventually they learn how to swim."). The monologue keeps popping up, randomly, intruding on your day and wrecking your mood. So, what do we do?

To keep us in line, the voice says that we can co-exist if we listen to it. It knows that it cannot be controlled but it acts like a friend and fakes a compromise. The inner voice wouldn't bother us as much if we just didn't do the things that make it nervous, sad, or angry. If we stop doing those things, it'll leave us alone. Sounds great! A lot of times we would take that deal, because we just want a moment's peace. How many times in your life have you given up autonomy to have a little comfort? We all do it! (Especially my fellow parents. Thank God for the 10-15 minutes of peace that *Bluey* can buy us).

Any time you think about challenging the voice and changing behavior to move towards the thing that triggers us, then the voice gets loud: it screams, "You can't do that! We had a deal!" And you don't want to tolerate the loudness, so you acquiesce and go back to the way things were, even though the voice is telling you that you can't have the life you want. You a made a deal, and there's a lot of power in the stasis of that. You don't want that Darth Vader moment, "I'm altering the deal; pray I don't alter it any further." (In this scenario, your face definitely looks like Grand Moff Tarkin).

If this happens to you, please don't be ashamed. It's a human response to a challenging situation. I'm here to offer you another solution. There's something that you don't know about your voice; it has no body, arms, legs, teeth, or guts. Its only power is to yell at you, which can be intense and scary, but they are only words. Words cannot really hurt you. Picture your voice as an entity that wants you to think it has teeth. It talks about how sharp and pointy and vicious its teeth are, and how many people it has mauled with them. And you better not challenge it, because then those teeth are going to come out and bite you so hard! But then you realize that in all this talking about its teeth, the voice actually has no teeth. It can't actually hurt you; it just wants you to believe that it can.

Pushing back on the voice is hard, especially if doing so involves changing your behavior. For example, if you're at a party and you feel uncomfortable, and you want to scroll through your phone for a bit. You've promised your therapist that you'd try to stay more present in these moments, but the temptation is so strong! The first two minutes seconds of a behavior change are the hardest. If you can grit your teeth and survive these 120 seconds, you're going to be OK. "the two minute mountain." If you can survive the first two minutes of doing something scary, then you've already showed that you can win. And many times, even that simple fact is enough to shut your voice up for a bit. Do what you've got to do to survive those two minutes: put on an epic pump-up song, do some body-doubling, chug an extra-large iced coffee—whatever. But when those minutes are over, you'll realize that the voice could never honor the terms of the deal in the first place because its side of the deal was only based in an artificial fear, not an actual threat. You take a deep breath; your phone stays in your pocket and you find someone across the room to talk to. You're free to keep moving forward.

Between juggling intensities, our super-powered brains, and relative lack of self-control, many neurodivergent people are fighting demanding wars against their own inner monologue every day. That honestly sucks, because the world isn't getting any easier or kinder. It's easier to change our internal world than the external one, so at least we have a place to start.

Life will give us many opportunities to face anxieties. The voice in our head will give us all the reasons our plans can't or won't work, trying to convince us to withdraw and stay "safe," but at the cost of not moving forward in life. The fact remains that trying something invites a chance to fail! Going for the promotion, asking someone out, trying to find a roommate, trying to buy a house for the first time —these endeavors may not go in our favor, and there may be costs if they don't.

But who cares?! At least we tried. Make the world say no to you; don't say no to the world. If you convince yourself that it's not worth trying, you won't try, which means you have no chance of succeeding. (One of my socially anxious clients told me that she was done with dating apps and said, "If I'm meant to have a partner, they'll just manifest into my apartment somehow." This version of not trying is clearly not an effective strategy.). Your voice is going to tell you only one kind of story—one in which you fail. It's true; if you try, there's a non-zero chance that something bad might happen. But there's also a non-zero chance something positive might happen and that's worth paying attention to as well!

- ○ You might get the thing you want!
- ○ You might not get the thing that you want but get another thing!
- ○ You might get really good feedback about how to get the thing next time!
- ○ You might not get the thing that you want but you make a positive impression, and they remember you the next time they need something.
- ○ You might realize that you don't actually want this thing, now that you're up close.
- ○ And so many more!

None of these outcomes can happen if you don't put yourself in a position to try. Learning from experience is the cost *and* the benefit of doing things. Don't hesitate to try more things. I was a terrible baseball player (having bad eyesight and a fear of getting hit in the face will do that to you). I struck out a LOT. Unfortunately, I had the bad luck of coming up to bat near the end of the game when there were runners on base and a big hit would turn the tide in our favor. If life was like a movie, I would find a way to get a hit and save the day. In reality, I kept striking out.

I struck out so many times that I tried to find ways not to go up to bat. ("cough" I've got black lung, coach "cough"). My voice had convinced me that I would fail. But coaches usually saw through me and made me bat anyway. One time, near the end of my career, I went to bat convinced I would strike out, and I got hit by a pitch, which meant I got on base! And would you believe it, I ended up scoring a run because all the other players in the lineup behind me were good at hitting. I would not have had that experience if I had given in to my voice and given up. Good things can't happen to you if you're not there for them to happen.

I'll leave you with one last strategy about changing your relationship with your inner voice. In the chapter on imposter syndrome, I mentioned that we're much better at having compassion for other people than compassion for ourselves. We can apply this reality to our internal monologue by using what psychologists call "the Best Friend test." If your voice is calling you awful things and giving all the reasons that you won't succeed, stop and ask yourself, "What would I say to my friend if they wanted to do this thing?" Suddenly, your voice is going to go full Pinky Pie from *My Little Pony* (or Leslie Knope from *Parks and Recreation*, if you're an adult and don't have to watch cartoons with your kids): "OMG you got this!! You're a rockstar! A queen! An absolute legend of all things good and righteous in the realm. I'm going to go buy you some new business cards with your new title on them, because I'm that freaking confident that you're going to get this thing."

It would be great if we could talk to ourselves like that. I strongly encourage you to talk to yourself like that more often. Just saying those words in our heads has a positive impact on mood and outlook. In life, we wouldn't let a bully be mean to our friends, because our friends are wonderful, amazing humans. There's a portmanteau that I love that describes a lot of my clients: introvirtuous. Being introvirtuous means that if it were up to you, you wouldn't say or do anything outside of your comfort zone, but you will absolutely do it because your friend needs you to. A good enough cause can get us out of our own heads. Be your own good cause.

Speaking of cult classic shows, in the cult classic musical *Be More Chill*, the final number "Voices in My Head" has our main character Jeremy singing, "And there are voices in my ear / I guess these never disappear / I'll let 'em squeal and I will deal / and make up my own mind / might still have voices in my head / but now they're just the normal kind." (This is particularly relevant because he's just fought off the evil supercomputer who was controlling his behavior and attempting to take over the world). But that's what we've been talking about in action! Many of us have voices in our heads and much of what they say to us is distracting or debilitating; they pull us away from our dreams, our goals, our present, and our values. These voices say that we cannot eliminate them, so we should give in and stop trying. That doesn't mean that we should give up! We are going to work smarter, not harder. That means making space for these inner voices by changing our relationship to them.

CHAPTER 10
OK, Let's Test Drive
This Whole Concept
How to Handle Real-Life Situations

We've covered a lot of science and psychology so far. You've learned about how your brain works and where feelings come from and why you sometimes feel like a fraud. I've got to go through the foundation before we get to the intervention protocols, because the interventions mean more if they're in the appropriate context. Well, congratulations, you've officially gone through the world-building phase and now it's time to send those Hobbits to Mount Doom. Grab your Second Breakfast; things are about to get real.

One of the biggest problems with books like this is they tend to shortchange you on explaining skills themselves or how to use them. It's wonderful to spend 260 pages writing about "losing your anxiety and freeing your mind," but if you don't tell me *how* that can happen, then it's not helpful. One of the limitations of therapy is interventions discussed in session may not always generalize to the real world (i.e., it's a lot easier holding an emotional boundary with your nurturing, supportive therapist than to hold that same boundary with your CEO or soccer coach). Life is more complex than a safe lesson with a mentor; not everyone is on your side. Skills for cracking "the code" make you flexible and nimble, freeing you from a rigid script (like "the code"). If you can think on your feet and be flexible, you'll be OK in 99% of situations.

We've gone through the basics and now I'll describe situations that will come up and walk you through them, using skills that we've covered so far. I'll point out the techniques that one might use and offer a rationale for them. I'll also suggest backup plans and exit strategies. You don't have to memorize a script; find the version of these concepts that works best for you. Make sure that you practice before you use them; go through the words in your head to "hear" how they sound. Your competence will lead to social confidence.

Since this book is written for all neurodivergent types (if the LOTR reference above didn't make that abundantly clear), we're going to cover a variety of social situations and give tips for being as prosocial as possible. I have scenarios that are applicable to everyone, some that are applicable to kids and their parents, some that best work for teens and college-age folks, and some that are uniquely adult (though I work with some elementary school students who are concerned about their 401K). They're all about identifying the spoken or unspoken "code" and developing the skills to navigate social challenges. Feel free to read them all or skip to the ones that are most relevant to you.

Small Talk

Small talk—everyone's favorite topic! I am good at small talk, which is unusual for a neurodivergent person. (I thank my paternal grandfather Chester, who was the king of small talk and a huge ham; he remains my spiritual North Star.) Small talk is defined as the polite conversation about unimportant matters that is necessary in social situations, from weddings to networking events to being stuck in line at the airport (Bristoll & Dickinson, 2015). Small talk gets a bad reputation because it can feel awkward; no one wants to start a conversation and risk discomfort, but everyone wants to connect, so we all stand there uncomfortably, pretending to be interested in our phones.

There are two ways to have a better relationship with small talk. The first is to see it for what it is: a way of navigating social situations, not just to pass the time, but to see who you can go deeper with. You can't get close with everyone. Small talk is a way to be polite and prosocial while seeking that "spark" of connection (Yu & Sterponi, 2023). When you feel it, you sense some similarities: things in common, sense of humor, awareness of the awkwardness of the situation, etc. You can create a "code" in that moment together.

The second way to improve small talk is to think about the difference between potential and kinetic energy. Like potential energy, the hardest part is getting started. Every *thing* has potential energy in it, just like every person is a potential connection, even if they never move past small talk. Once you ask an initial question or otherwise start the conversation, you've moved into kinetic energy. Maybe, like rolling rocks down a hill, it flops over once and stalls; that's OK, you tried. At that moment it's better to acknowledge that you don't have the power or tools to move that rock, your energy is better spent elsewhere. You bow out gracefully and try again. Maybe the next rock keeps rolling, picking up speed as this connection with a new friend gains momentum.

When it comes to making small talk correctly, you can start by revisiting the Core Four skills of relationship building (see Chapter 2):

- ○ Active Listening
- ○ Asking Good Follow-up Questions
- ○ Seek Connection
- ○ Metacommunication

They're all relevant here. To get things started, you can try using a small similarity (Bristoll & Dickinson, 2015). A small similarity points out something that you share, even if just for this moment. Think about the classic cheesy pick-up line: "Come here often?" Though it is "cringe," it does speak to a small similarity; you're both here, aren't you? Still, we can do better. How about, "How many weddings/conferences has it been for you this year?" That's a better observation and invites several lines of further chatting.

More prosocial versions would be commenting on something shared that's more accessible. If you're at a wedding, you might comment on someone's shoes and note how pretty they are and ask where they got them. If you're at work, you might comment on the quality of the office coffee, or how much you like coffee. If you're in line behind someone at a baseball game or a concert, it's fine to keep to yourself and share a companionable silence (hi, introverts—we haven't forgotten you!). But alternatively, you could ask if they're having fun, if they've seen this band before, or what it's like to be charged $17.99 for a knish and a light beer.

These examples might seem shallow and saccharine, but that's OK. The point is to navigate the potentially awkward social moment by filling the silence in a prosocial way; it's far too soon to be thinking about making a lifelong friend (Yu & Sterponi, 2023). Commenting on a shared experience binds you to that person, even for just a moment, and might invite reciprocity. Once they respond, you'll be able to use your Core Four skills to keep the conversation moving. Most people dislike small talk because it feels shallow; people want the kinds of connection that allow them to go past the basics into deeper conversation (Bristoll & Dickinson, 2015). Keep passing the conversational ball back and forth and you might just get there.

The biggest advice I could give you with small talk is not to get too far ahead of yourself. Anxiety tends to pull us to the future; desperation to connect with others can lead us to over-share or put too much weight on the simple moment. (An anxious overshare might be, "Oh my goodness, you're also outside? I love being outside! I was outside last summer when I lost my pants at a birthday party…"). Remember, most people are hoping for connection as well. Focus on light-hearted observations that invite response: "I hope this ice cream is good after such a long line"; "Well, we've reached the conversational lull of the first date right on time"; "I spent four years at high school and all we're getting in return is to stand outside in vinyl robes to get a piece of paper?"

There are entire books written on the art of small talk if this interests you, and I won't belabor the point further. You can take these strategies and reframes to change your relationship to small talk and let it be a tool to improve your life, if even in a small way. Small talk should have small goals in terms of execution and expectations (Yu & Sterponi, 2023). Little comments. Sharp observations. Shared, surface connections that are easy to see. Before you know it, small talk can lead to big relationships, especially if you have the confidence to let things grow apace.

Someone's Mad at Me...Right?

Human beings are notoriously bad at decoding ambiguous situations (Lee, 2011). Socializing is full of ambiguity, even for neurotypical people (Moscovitch & Hofmann, 2007); neurodivergence makes more situations seem more ambiguous (Lee, 2011). We tend to get anxious when things are ambiguous, and when we are anxious, we assume the worst in ourselves and others. This kind of catastrophic thinking can lead to intense feelings and behaviors that manifest in socially destructive behavior (Alderson-Day, 2016). We want so badly to connect and have healthy relationships that we unwittingly set ourselves up for emotional upheaval that could likely be easily avoided.

If your brain creates a catastrophic explanation of someone else's neutral behavior (let's say that Kelsey is walking down the hallway and I wave to her, but she doesn't wave back), the temptation is to run with the anxiety. "She's mad at me! Otherwise, she would have said hi!" This is highly unlikely, so we start casting about in our brains to find other explanations.

The first few might also be catastrophic! "She heard a rumor about me and hates me!" "She saw me talking to her ex at the party last week!" "She thinks I took her parking place!" But eventually other options come up. "Maybe she's just having a bad day." "Maybe she didn't see me." "Maybe she's got her earphones in." Our brains have a tough time sustaining challenging emotions, so if you can stick with seeking alternate (more positive) explanations for a person's behavior, you're bound to find some that aren't quite so alarming. This kind of cognitive flexibility is a healthy social skill, because first impressions are rarely accurate (Lerner, et al., 2011). If you have a tough time with this, try leading your thoughts with ridiculous or sci-fi answers: "She's clearly a Cylon." "I guess the lobotomy worked." "Is this a *Freaky Friday* situation so the person in the body-swap doesn't actually know me?" The more possible explanations we can give our brain, the more we blunt that initial emotional alarm. With fewer unchecked emotions, we can usually make better decisions (Al-Shawaf & Lewis, 2020).

Most of the time, a person's behavior has very little to do with us. If their behavior does relate to something that we did or didn't do, then at some point they have an obligation to let us in on the facts so we can address them and attempt to move forward. If we let our anxiety get the better of us, we fall victim to a self-fulfilling prophecy and create an environment where our behavior is obnoxious enough to make that person mad at us.

You're BORED

OK, so you're bored. There are many things that you could do, but you don't want to do any of them. It might be homework, it might be your new job assignment, it might even be practicing the theremin. None of them are alluring, and you can't figure out why. One way to think about being bored is that "bored" is often replacement language (which we talked about in Chapter 6). What concept is conveyed by talking about being bored? For many people, it's being overwhelmed or underwhelmed (Westgate, 2020). When we are at a suboptimal level of stimulation, our brains are not engaging properly with the dopamine circuit, so we are essentially spinning our wheels hoping that something will happen.

One way to move forward when you're bored is to use the Yerkes-Dodson Law (Corbett, 2015) to find what we call the "leading edge of learning." The Yerkes-Dodson Law shows that everybody has an optimum level of stress. Too little stress makes us underwhelmed, and we disengage. If it is too easy, we don't care. If you were a high-level soccer player and I asked you to dribble the ball in a straight line, that's boring, you wouldn't want to do it. On the other hand, if I say, "You're good at soccer, go play Leo Messi one-on-one." That's probably too hard and you disengage because it's too difficult. When we're seeking the optimum level of performance, we must be curious about what is the right level of stress for that person to learn.

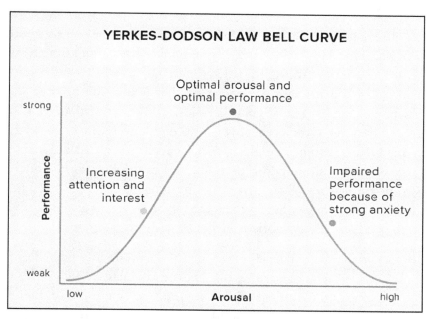

Why say "bored" when you mean something else? It can be hard to articulate your needs socially. Such communication requires emotional awareness and self-confidence, which is hard to come by. Saying that you're bored is a statement that protects the ego (psychologists call that ego-syntonic) because it doesn't acknowledge your personal stake in the problem. Saying that you're bored invites people to give you solutions or suggestions, which can maintain your sense of control because you can reject their ideas as not what you need (every parent reading this just nodded).

Skill levels in neurodivergent people vary widely across different domains, but individual skills are often badly mis-matched with the standards of those domains. You might be a coding genius in elementary school, but your teacher still asks you to make that CodeMonkey pick up all the bananas before you can write an epic Mortal Kombat emulator. Or people assume that you know how to tie a tie because you're an adult and mock you when you show up at a formal event looking like you were hit by a rogue wave. To help people, we need to meet them where they are; otherwise, they run the risk of hiding in their "boredom."

Let's use math as an example. Many neurodivergent people are good at math, but that's not one-size-fits-all because we're not going treat math like a monolith, right? Three divided by one is a lot different than 6,124 divided by 197. I can't do that one in my head at all. Maybe you can, which is cool! Let's just acknowledge that there is differentiation in skill levels. If you're going to meet someone's needs in any subject, you need to do a pre-assessment phase. If a kid is able to do addition, subtraction, division, and multiplication, it might be time for algebra. Who cares what the curriculum says! If we find the right level, that's where we need to be, because when we find the level, you have an appropriate challenge to motivate growth.

This is a good time to talk about the idea of the productive struggle, or the effortful process of learning that goes beyond passive engagement with the material (Murdoch, English, Hintz, & Tyson, 2020). Being able to struggle productively builds resilience and grit in a way that simple "hard work for the sake of hard work" does not. The challenge here is to find the content and presentation modality motivates you to engage and keep engaging. When our brains are engaged, we hold more information in our short-term memory, which allows for more storage and deeper connections to be made across content. Set up a challenge to get unbored. (For more on this, check out Andi McNair's "Genius Hour" content, listed in the Appendix).

Hanging Out

(Sings: "Down the street / The same old things / we did last week." Hello, Wisconsin!). Ah, social life. It seems so easy from the inside, but it can be ridiculously challenging to conceive when you're on the outside looking in. There are too many rules about "hanging out" to possibly fit in a book, let alone in a chapter, let alone in a subsection of said chapter. But I want to highlight a few core ideas.

○ If you're making a friend and you want to hang out, it is better to have something concrete to pitch them with. Initial meetings should be planned and on neutral or productive ground (i.e., studying at the library, grabbing lunch on Thursday). It is easy to give in to our nerves and say something to the effect of, "Let's hang out sometime!" which *sounds* great, but doesn't give the other person something to hang on to. To lower the barrier, you can tie the hang-out to something that you're already doing, like getting a drink after work or hitting the gym together while your kids are at dance class.

○ When other people are making plans around you, it can be hard to know whether those plans involve you or not. At my 20th high school reunion, I had a very pleasant conversation with my friend about the after-party he was planning on having. After a while, I said, "Well, dude, have fun!" and he looked at me like I had two heads before saying, "Dude, you're invited. Why do you think I was telling you?" I legitimately didn't know. Since everyone won't be as straightforward as my friend, it is totally appropriate to ask whether you're invited. If you're not comfortable asking the whole group, you can find the person that you're most comfortable with (even if they're a comfort level "three" amongst a bunch of "one") and ask where you stand. It's a good idea to use metacommunication here, perhaps saying, "Hey, I never get these social cues; am I actually invited?" or "If I was invited, you'd let me know, right?"

○ Body-doubling can be a helpful way to hang out. I've noticed that people can find it easy to make what I call "big moment" friends, i.e., people you invite to parties, see at work events, tailgate with, etc. But I think that where friendships are most valuable (and, often, where they are forged) is in the little moments, the day-to-day tasks that we all must do and are often better done with a friend. If you're looking to hang out more with someone, especially if you'd like to deepen the relationship past the "I see you at parties and we always say, we should SO hang out but never do" phase, then you can leverage common daily activities into an excuse to hang out. You need to go grocery shopping: can you do it with a friend? Who doesn't need an excuse to go to Target? I'm running to the Post Office after school; can I drop you off after? You'll be amazed at how much people appreciate those little moments as ways to connect.

○ When you're choosing who to hang out with, remember that you have value, and that you have values. It's better in many ways to have friends, but not at the cost of selling yourself out. Know what matters to you and what kind of people espouse or respect those values. If you don't know, take the time to figure that out. Moving forward without knowing what matters to you in a relationship can set up a downward spiral in which you're hanging out with someone just to have someone to hang out with; you don't feel comfortable with them, so you're not having fun at the event, which makes you not want to go to future events. But since you need a friend, you say yes anyway. Sometimes, to have the social life we want, we need to take a step backward to be able to move forward in a better way. You're worth taking that time to determine your standards and you're worth having people who honor and celebrate those.

Seeing Someone Breaking the Rules

Why do they have the rules if some (but not all!) are bendable, if not downright breakable?

One of the toughest parts of being outside the "code" is understanding what rules you can break and what rules must be followed. The more neurodivergent you are, the more you're going to struggle with that ambiguity (Lee, 2011). Many of us deal with this challenge by taking every rule very seriously—by the "letter of the law" (Bradley & Noell, 2022). If you memorize the rules, our brains tell us, then you won't have to worry about anything because you'll always know what you're allowed and not allowed to do. And that's true...until it isn't.

The challenge is twofold. The first challenge is ambiguity. Some rules are OK to be broken regularly (like littering), some are OK to be broken in different contexts (you normally wouldn't drink a cocktail at 8am, but people do so in airports all the time!),illustrate:

A few years ago, one of my old clients called from college. I hadn't seen him in a while and was thrilled to hear from him, until he started talking. "Dr. Matt," he whispered. "I have to call the police!"

"What?!" I yelped. "Are you OK? What's wrong? Aren't you at college now? Are you safe?"

"Yes," he replied, "but there's a big, huge, major problem. My room-mate has a bottle of alcohol in the room."

I paused, waiting for the rest of it. "Um, and?"

"It's ILLEGAL!" he scream-mumbled. "And when people do things that are illegal, you call the police." A pause. "Right?"

We had a great conversation about the nature of rules and how some are more able to be broken in different contexts. It is much more socially acceptable to drink alcohol underage at college than it is in middle school, for example. I pointed out to my client that he didn't have to like his roommate's behavior, and he didn't have to tolerate it either because it was his room too, but there were better ways to handle it than calling the police (even if it was just Campus Security). I reminded him that they could have a conversation about what to do next as a cohort, and while I don't think that he had considered doing so until that moment, he handled it quite well! His roommate apologized for making him uncomfortable and resolved to store the alcohol in 2-liter soda bottles, which gave them a comfortable level of plausible deniability.

The second challenge is that some rules are spoken, and some are unspoken. When I work with businesses, I always ask their HR representatives to name all the unspoken company rules. We know what the written ones are, they're in the employee manual (which my Autistic clients read cover to cover, my gifted clients skim, my ADHD clients immediately misplace, and my dyslexic clients advocate for an audio-book version). But what are the unspoken rules, what is the ethos of the company? In a lot of companies, that unspoken standard of comportment is more important than the written rules, which is unfortunate, because that's where a lot of my clients get into trouble: they break rules that they didn't know existed.

For example, when I was in my early 20's, I worked at EF Educational Tours in Cambridge, MA. If you've ever been to Boston, it's across from the Museum of Science and near the end of the Duck Boat tour. During the orientation, they told us the company rules (one of which was "work hard, play hard" and is very relevant to this story) and then explicitly named the unspoken ways that we honored those rules. Of all the jobs I've ever had, this was the best onboarding I ever experienced; I really understood what they wanted from me.

Right after I started there, we had our legendary holiday party. The drinks would be flowing, and the venue would be open late (a rarity in Boston). And it was on a Thursday night. Wait…really? As they told us about the party, our managers mentioned the most important thing: no matter how much you drink at the party or how awful you feel in the morning, you come to work. It's an expected behavior. It's a badge of honor. Many people at other companies would sleep in, groan off the hangover, and give themselves a nice three-day weekend. But at EF, you came in and worked that Friday (how *much* work was actually done is an entirely separate thing). So I went, and I drank, and I stumbled home. And in the morning, I staggered into the shower and got dressed for work (and drank a 64 oz. Gatorade I had put on ice). When I arrived at work, there were Egg McMuffins waiting for us in the lobby (God bless you, EF) and an ovation from the leadership team. They had said what they meant and backed it up. I think that every organization would be more successful and harmonious if they communicated so openly.

Another thing to remember when it comes to people making mistakes is the concept of Hanlon's Razor (Walmsley & O'Madagain, 2020), which states that most erroneous human behavior is better explained by ignorance than malice. So, if someone is doing something that they're not supposed to, they are much more likely to be unaware of the rules or, crucially, not aware of the impact their rule breaking is having on someone else. I distinctly remember as a kid getting yelled at for taking pictures during a Broadway production of *Rent*. I wasn't being a bad kid; I genuinely didn't know that it was a rule. The usher took one look at my face and decided not to confiscate my disposable camera, thank goodness. If you can keep the concept of Hanlon's Razor in mind, I think you'll be pleasantly surprised at how many good opportunities you will find to give people the benefit of the doubt when they make mistakes.

Leaving an Event Before You're Supposed To

How is that some people just seem to *know* when they can duck out of an event? It doesn't matter if it's a pep rally, a staff "all-call," their second cousin's wedding, or a professional conference—some people just know when and how to make an exit. Neurodivergent people love following rules (as we just discussed), but there are social nuances to leaving events that need to be explained because they apply in school, at work, and in social life (Bradley & Noell, 2022). There are four things that are relevant to being successful when leaving:

○ You could do what's called an "Irish goodbye" and just leave the event without saying anything to anyone. It's not a bad strategy *per se*, but it doesn't build social skills. It can also increase future anxiety because you're not addressing the thing (talking) that is making you anxious in the first place, so the anxiety can just grow.

○ You can ask permission to leave. That's a more social adept move, but there's a problem with this strategy. If you ask someone, there's a chance that they could say no, or ask for a *quid pro quo* in return, like "you can duck out early today, but I'll need you to work a double shift this weekend for me." (My old boss was a master at this.) There are some things that you must do in life without permission because you need or deserve them.

○ You don't owe anyone an explanation, though you are welcome to give one. If you're leaving because you don't feel well, then that's appropriate context to give. You probably don't want to say that you're leaving because their event sucks; some opinions are better left unsaid. Saying that you're tired, or done with the night, or have a big day tomorrow are all fine pieces of context to share. Just be careful giving that context, because it can invite either push-back like "Aw, c'mon, the night is young!" or follow-up like "You said you had a big day on Sunday; what do you have to do?".

○ Remember that "No" is a complete sentence. If you're somewhere and you don't want to be there anymore, you don't have to stay. If people try to make you stay and you feel uncomfortable, then you say, "No." That's it. Repeat as necessary. And call a cab or a friend or your adults so you can get out of there. It's better to take the small social hit of leaving than being in a place that might not be safe and doesn't fit your values.

Someone has Made a mistake!

Quick, it's time for my favorite joke about gifted kids. Where does a gifted kid get their water? From a "Well, actually…" ☺

I truly believe that no neurodivergent person starts out wanting to be egregious when it comes to people making mistakes. We really want to be helpful! Perhaps they don't know that it isn't encycloPEEdia, but encycloPEDia (cue Hermione Granger, a gifted kid if there ever was one, saying, "It's LeviOsa, not LeviosA."). And if they did know, they might change their behavior for the better. But the problem is that many people are comfortable in their lack of knowledge and content to stay there; it is not our task (nor our responsibility) to change that for them. Neurodivergent people tend to miss the "code" rule that says that we shouldn't correct people because we have strong senses of justice and a desire to be right. But being right doesn't always mean that we're doing the right thing.

Several years ago in a therapy session, I was working with a client who was trying to create the perfect best man's speech for his friend's wedding. His initial plan was to "just wing it" which I quickly shot down. His response was that he didn't want to write down every single word he was going to say and read it off "like a high school book report." That's true as well; we want to find the middle ground (the "third door solution," you might say) between flying blind and feeling bound by our plan.

As we crafted the speech, we started by doing a brief survey of his strengths and weaknesses. He was comfortable in front of a crowd, but he was worried about not sounding "fancy enough." He was a blue-collar guy, and he and his friend had grown up in a tough part of Philadelphia. But his buddy was marrying a girl from the "Main Line" of southeastern Pennsylvania (where the streets aren't paved with gold, they're done in platinum), so there was a poshness to the event that we needed to consider. I offered some suggestions to his speech, emphasizing some points over others, and then sat back to listen to the rough draft.

It was great! He was funny, sincere, honest, and humble. His speech was going to bring the house down. And at the end of his rehearsal with me, he said, "Now, would everyone raise their "champ-pagney" glasses."

Their what?

I realized quickly that he had meant to say "champagne'" (pronounced sham-pain, not champ-pagney). But he had clearly never said that word before! So, I offered what we call "the compliment sandwich." I told him something I liked about his speech, that he had great comedic timing, that he's really funny. Then I told him something that I thought that he needed to change: the pronunciation of the word "champagne." I ended by saying what I think that he should do the next time he practiced giving the speech.

He took my feedback well. Then he realized what I had said about his word pronunciation and got a little embarrassed. But after a moment, he was able to tell me that he felt OK about my critique, and that he appreciated that I hadn't thoroughly disparaged his speech because of a minute problem. Then he started laughing and told me that he had "absolutely" been the kind of person in school that would've interrupted a classmate for making a small error. He said that it would have been "karma" if he had gone forward with the mispronunciation in his speech and had people burst out laughing at him. I laughed along with him and pointed out that there are better ways to help someone than to make a big deal about it; the best lessons are more subtle.

Accuracy matters and we want to help people do better. When we call out someone's mistake publicly and loudly, we are making their error about *us* and our need to be right. If I point out his error as silly, then I am just claiming superiority while not helping him to improve in any meaningful way. When we act like that, regardless of intention, we make other people feel awful. Remember that unsolicited feedback is often received as criticism by the target of the feedback. Think about a time when you made a mistake; how were you treated? Did it feel good or bad? What would you change about that experience? You can use that memory to make your own behavior more prosocial.

I want to highlight responses to mistakes here, because dealing with them can be a major challenge for neurodivergent people in social situations. You may not like the mistake that's been made; your feelings are your feelings. I won't tell you that the mistake "isn't a big deal" because it may in fact change the way that you feel about that person in the moment. But that's the necessary context: *in the moment.* Let things breathe until the next break in the event or lull in the conversation. There are ways to navigate those moments that protect the dignity of everyone involved (not the least of which is you). We can always say what we need to say later, in private, and with care. When in doubt, use the compliment sandwich to guide you. People respond much better to critique if it's nested in compliments, and there are almost always good things to say.

Conflict in a Relationship

People are imperfect. When you let someone into your life, you're letting them in for the best parts of who they are: their charm, their intelligence, their compassion, their parents' beach house—whatever. But when you let someone in, you also must let in their flaws. We can't cherry pick the parts of people we like and exclude the rest of them. The less good parts of people are going to disappoint you and let you down, and hurt you on occasion (maybe by accident, hopefully not maliciously).

When people hurt you, there's going to be conflict. People want to talk about their happy relationships and offer glowing reports of their partners, and we know those things are true. But there are also bad parts, uncomfortable parts, and fights. People fight! They argue! They become petty and insecure and say things they don't mean. I remember being in high school and hearing people crow about their relationships how "we never argue". I'm not looking for an argument, but I have always understood that conflict is a part of a healthy relationship. If you're not standing up for yourself or holding a boundary or advocating for something, then you're a doormat in the relationship.

It is important to note that arguing in a relationship is normal and healthy. Abuse in a relationship is not. If the arguing escalates to threats or becomes physical in any way, then that's not a healthy relationship. There are lots of resources out there, like calling the National Domestic Violence hotline at 800-799-7233 or texting BEGIN to 88788.

Conflict can stem from many places, but usually it's about miscommunication (see any number of "rom-coms" or Shakespeare plays for examples). We are all idiosyncratic and monolithic in our thinking, especially if you're neurodivergent. We all experience most of the world from our own brain, so we tend to think that *our* way is the way that things *should* be—why would they be any different? When people are talking about the same concept (say, a night out on the town) in the different ways (Peter wants a candlelit dinner for two, but Jack wants to watch the game together at a sports bar), or are used to their needs being met in a certain way (think about how you like to be treated when you're sick—do you want to be coddled or do you want to be left alone? Now how does your partner feel?), there's room for things getting complicated, quickly.

Here's another example. When my wife and I were dating (this was the winter of 2012), we spent a lazy Sunday together. It was a day after a rather ambitious night out on the town, and we were laying low and binge-watching the Food Network at our . I had made our typical hangover brunch of scrambled eggs and toast, and the day staggered inexorably forward. Around mid-afternoon, I had reached that semi-Zen state of coach potato bliss when my wife suddenly bolted upright and shouted at me, *"So I guess you're just not going to feed me!?!?"*

She was immediately mortified, clasping her hands to her mouth in shock, because I don't think that she thought that she would ever speak to me like that in a million years. And once I got over the initial shock, I was quick to thank her for being so direct with me. I didn't know that she was hungry, and if I had known, I would have been off like a shot to the kitchen for some homemade pasta! (OK, Mac and Cheese). Coming from a family of indirect communicators, this kind of clear declaration of need was new to me, but it was immediately refreshing. Why dance around the issue when we can just talk about it? (Though preferably not in a shout, if that's cool).

Having to guess what someone needs is exhausting, but unfortunately it isn't quite as simple as just saying what we need all the time, because sometimes it isn't welcome to do so. We are all responsible to communicate so that people's needs can be shared safely, just as we need to be able to advocate for ourselves when the time is right. Standing up for yourself takes courage, because it involves facing your fear (especially fear of the unknown, fear of how your relatively new boyfriend will respond to a screamed demand for food RIGHT NOW). Managing your anxiety takes awareness of your sympathetic nervous system (fight or flight) and a strong parasympathetic nervous system (rest and digest). Standing up for yourself makes relationships stronger, because you've taken the conflict and turned it into something productive.

Consent

Late in the writing process, I started to freak out because the book wasn't perfect, because I needed to cover *everything,* and there was no way that I could do that. My wife and I sat down, and I asked her (because she has a master's degree in sex education and is far more level-headed than me) whether I should add an entire chapter in this book about sex and dating. She used her level-headedness, thought about it for a while, and finally said that sex and dating are too big of a concept to cram into a chapter, but too important to leave out entirely. So here is a subsection on consent, because consent overlaps physical, emotional, sexual, platonic, and romantic relationships. I'll talk about sex and dating in my next book.

If you've never met me, I'm a pretty big guy—six feet tall and about 215 pounds. I have a beard, a big personality, and a booming voice. I tend to work with people who are much smaller than me, usually kids, but some short teachers, too). I am aware of my size and the impact that it can have on other people. For example, if I come up to a kid and say, "Give me a hug!" it might come across as a demand, not an invitation. If a person cannot say no safely, then they cannot genuinely give consent.

We strive for affirmative consent to all our actions (Bell, 2020). Affirmative consent means that a person understands what they are agreeing to, wants to do it (the "Yes!" test) and feels safe to say "no." Consent cannot be assumed, is not forever, and is not transferable. Consent is a dialogue, a co-creation, should be respectful, and should be sought every time (i.e., not presumed). I still ask my wife if I can kiss her, just like she asks me if she can have a back rub. The person might say yes most of the time, but you still should honor their choice to say "no". There are times that you might be able to get consent from body language and other non-verbal behavior, but you must establish those guidelines as part of the consent creation process.

Affirmative consent a high standard, but it's the only standard that works, especially for neurodivergent people who struggle with reading social cues and prosocial communication. Affirmative consent is often tied to sex and dating, where it is requisite, but it is also important in other interpersonal things. If you want to greet someone, you can ask for a hug or offer a high-five. If your grandmother wants to pinch your cheek (my dad's mom was legendary at this), you can say "no thank you." My parents know that they need to ask my kids for a hug or kiss hello or goodbye. You can ask someone before you interject a story or add something to what they're saying, or even "go old-school" and raise your hand to be called on.

Affirmative consent works very well for neurodivergent people because it gives them a way to navigate uncomfortable social situations when beset by the neurotypical "code" and need options (Bell, 2020). Why do we cheek kiss at weddings? What if I don't want to do that? You can model consent language and say, "I'd love to say hi, but I don't feel comfortable kissing you. Can we hug? Or fist bump?" It might feel a little awkward at first, but you can think of affirmative consent as another way to use metacommunication; instead of just saying "NO!" or running away, you're using your words to place your behavior in context. The other people might not understand it, but they'll respect it because you've given them scaffolding.

Lastly, in the dating space, some people might think asking, "Can I kiss you?" is uncool. It certainly isn't modeled in most of popular media, where Lover A grabs Lover B as she's walking away and passionately kisses her. Dramatic, sure, but not necessarily good practice. My thought is that affirmative consent can be sexy. Also, it is an important prosocial skill in the dating, romantic, and sexual parts of our lives. Why would you want to have to guess if someone wants to kiss you, just trying without words or certainty? I'd rather know for sure. I feel like asking such questions and maintaining a respectful dialogue honors the values and person of each person involved. When anxious we shut down or make suboptimal choices. Knowing more clearly allows us to do better, and there are a lot of great experiences to be had with other people when we know what's up (yes, like sex).

Group Work

Rare indeed is the neurodivergent person who enjoys group work. When you are as asynchronous as we are, with our very idiosyncratic brains and fast-thinking styles, it can be easier to just go it alone. But life requires—even demands—that we find a way to get along with others. It's a hard thing to practice before you're in it. If you cannot prepare mentally before the challenging situation, then you're likely to be heading into it with bad feelings and a hair trigger and eventually snap, "You know what? I'll just do it myself!" As soon as you say this, your other erstwhile group members silently cheer and go on playing with their phones as you do all the work, and they share in your "A+." You end up left out and isolated.

Let's get our mindset organized to work with others. I often discuss planning group work through the idea of planning a group theme party. If you're working with other people and you're planning a theme party, you're naturally going to be drawn to the activities and tasks you want to do best. To use myself as an example, I love a good party, and there are many skills within the party structure that I am particularly good at. I'm a good host, I am an above-average cook, I've bartended professionally, and I even know my way around a DJ station. Those are all the jobs you should want me to do. You don't want me negotiating with a venue or taking money at the door or organizing the spreadsheets, because I'm not good at those things. I'm not drawn to those things, which doesn't make me good or bad, it just makes me *me*.

The reality in the party situation is that you're rarely ever alone for the planning (in terms of scale I'm thinking more prom committee than "drinks at my place this weekend"). Thankfully, the presence of other people means that you don't have to be good at everything. And that is a great realization because no one is good at everything! If I am allowed to play to my strengths, I'm going to feel better and do better, and be far more likely to make meaningful social connections because I'm feeling and doing so well. If there are multiple people who want to do the things that I want to do, then I'm going to either connect with those people (you need many bartenders, after all) or their choices will organically prompt me to be more prosocial and opt into another task that I can do that serves the needs of many. Conversely, if you pigeonhole me into a task or role that I'm ill-equipped to do, I'm going to be less successful and thus less happy; the vicious cycle could also swallow any relationships that could form.

If we're not careful, work and school can create these vicious cycle environments. Think about the parts of your job or education that you hate. Chances are that you didn't *choose* to do them, but instead were *assigned* to do them. When we arbitrarily decide what people need to do and push them into those tasks without consideration or consultation, we're risking burning them out (or losing them altogether). The idea behind the theme party exercise is that it's a structured way to explore your values and skills, rather than just figuring it out as you go along. Knowing yourself allows you to be more successful personally, which leads to increased success interpersonally, which is what we want in this modern age of work and school. But if we don't give people time and space to figure their needs out, they will have underdeveloped senses of self or may not know at all what to do. Let people try a variety of roles until they find one or more that suit them, and *then* let them get to work.

Missing Out in a Conversation

In Chapter 3 I talked about how the neurodivergent brain can run fast, operating on a different wavelength than to neurotypical people. Our relative weaknesses in the prefrontal cortex, especially the inability to sustain attention, have been discussed *ad nauseum*. I would be remiss if I did not mention that neurodivergent people can suffer with auditory processing disorder, which contributes to missed or garbled audio cues. These factors put us at enhanced risk for missing out in conversations, which is an unnecessary deprivation, and at worst can feel like others were rude.

When you zone out or miss information during a conversation, the temptation is to roll the dice to fill in the missing words. You don't want to make someone repeat themselves, so you assume the information based on your preconceived notions and context clues. "Dr. Smith asked me to go do *something-something*…well, Dr. Smith always needs their copies picked up from the main office, so that must be it." You might get away with it sometimes. You are smart, after all, and many times the answer will reveal itself if you ask enough questions later. But guessing and flying by the seat of your pants is *not* a sustainable strategy! (ADHD readers may be scoffing loudly right now, but it's true!). The times that you guess wrong can create big problems.

For example, I worked at summer camp for twice-exceptional kids, and each camper had a house chore. One kid, Allison, had the responsibility to wash the dishes every night, which she took great pride in. As she was putting the dishes away after dessert one night, another camper, Leah, came up and asked for a "clean glass, because that's what I like to drink from." Allison got really upset! Obviously, *all* the glasses were clean—she had washed them! Allison stormed off in a huff, leaving me to explain to Leah how her words had hurt Allison. But Leah had said "green glass", not "clean glass". Big difference. We were able to resolve the situation quickly, but Allison might've avoided a meltdown if she had owned the fact that she had guessed wrong about what she thought she heard, and asked Leah to repeat herself.

Since you don't always want to guess, and asking people to repeat themselves may not feel like a viable option, here are some strategies that I offer my clients for when this happens. You don't have to use the suggested words exactly, but the frameworks are solid. Note that all these strategies use metacommunication. This situation doesn't happen to neurotypicals as often, so you won't find as much of a "code" here to violate (they may still be put off because it doesn't happen to them as often).

- ○ "Sorry, I was stuck on what you said earlier, and I missed what you went on to say. Can you repeat the last sentence?" This strategy shows that you *were* listening, but you got stuck on something they had said earlier. You're offering the speaker an easy do-over to move the conversation along.

○ "Boy, there's so much noise in here I'm in total sensory over-load and having trouble hearing you. Can we go somewhere else to talk about this or could you text it to me?" This strategy shows that you *want* to listen, but the environment is getting in the way. If you go to a place with less stimulation, you'll be able to hear them and respond. Offering the option to text (or write it down, if you're old-school) accommodates the social norm that this person might not want to change locations or otherwise feel controlled.

○ "Oh, my goodness, this is a topic that I love! I could totally infodump on this. How much do you need or want to know? Give me some limits or I could talk all day!" This strategy names the fact that you're very interested in what they have to say, and notes that you might have trouble regulating yourself. If the person sets the standards, however, you'll know how to follow (and blog about the rest later).

My experience is that in all situations, metacommunication brings situational context and self-awareness into play, allowing me to navigate the conversation more easily. Understanding the thoughts and feelings that come up in these social scenarios is vital for giving yourself the context to navigate your behavior in a positive way. I hope that I've given you a playbook to begin to navigate these common social situations in all their intrapersonal and interpersonal complexities. The most important point is that you *can* do this, and do it in a way that feels authentic to yourself. Try these strategies and let me know how they work for you.

CHAPTER 11
Failure:
You're Eventually Going to Fail, So What Are You Going to Do About It?

"I hate failing," my clients say to me.

"That is shocking information!" I reply. "That definitely puts you in the minority!" Once again, I need my sarcasm font.

We're here to talk about *failure*, which is great because I am almost certainly going to *make some mistakes* during this chapter. Despite my best efforts, this chapter isn't going to be perfect; it will contain some mistakes. But I will soldier on, knowing that submitting something imperfect still provides value and illustrates many of the points I'm trying to make. Plus, I'm really tired of editing at this point of the process.

Here's an example of a famous failure: Jennifer Lawrence. You might be thinking to yourself, Jennifer Lawrence is a beloved and award-winning actress, she's not a failure! You're right. But I'm still going to talk about a time that she failed.

The year is 2013, and our girl Jennifer Lawrence has made history! She's just won the Academy Award for Best Actress. They call her name, and looking genuinely stunned she goes to walk up on stage in front of thousands of her peers and an international audience of millions of people. And what does she do? She takes two steps up the stairs and then falls on her face. It's painful to watch; it's one of those nightmares that you can imagine, where you've reached the pinnacle of your career and you fall, failing at a thing you have done thousands of times, walking up a flight of stairs. It's like my nightmare of showing up at high school realizing that I haven't' studied for my Spanish final, except infinitely worse because it's in front of the entire world.

When I came of age on the internet, the term "epic fail" was very much in vogue. You've probably seen the clips: dudes trying to ski jump but crashing into pine trees, dogs tackling kids while crashing a ball, people thinking that they've parked their cars when they haven't put on the handbrake, and so many more. A quick Google search shows us that an *hourlong* YouTube video by FailArmy has over 77 million views. (Heck, I'm probably one or twelve of those views.) There's something very compelling about failure. It's fundamentally human and visceral. We've all failed, and surely don't want to do it again, but we unquestionably want to watch *others* do it. Failure is a great unifier.

What is failure? Failure is a lack of success (Ronnie & Philip, 2021). You tried to do something, and it did not work, you were not successful at it. Failure is also an inability to meet an expectation (Ronnie & Philip, 2021). This second definition is relevant for our work here, because sometimes the expectations we are held to are unfair, ill-informed, and even aggressively incorrect. Such standards represent "the code" of successful behavior for neurotypicals, but we're neurodivergent! I'm not saying that we shouldn't be held to any standards, but I don't think that we should be held to theirs. With that "code" in mind, we're going to talk about how to adjust expectations internally and externally to reformulate what they call failure into viable concepts of growth.

First, let's define the stages of failure. The first is a failure of **vision**. In this stage, the person says, "I don't even know where I want to go or what I want to be. I know my life needs to change, but I don't even know what that could look like, so I can't get started. Help!" A lot of people come to therapy with this self-concept, which is why just going to therapy is an achievement worth celebrating—they know they need help and took the first step. Treating change like a monolithic roadblock makes it feel impossible to attempt, let alone complete. How can you make progress if you can't even picture a goal? Left untreated, this level of failure can lead to existential depression, especially in neurodivergent folks.

The second stage is a failure of **tactics**. This person says, "I know what I want, but I don't know how to get there." A lot of people come to me and they say, "You know, I want to lose weight, but I don't know what to do. Should I run, should I do pushups, should I eat better? Help!" We need to have tactics that actually work to meet our goals. This is especially challenging in the era of information overload, with millions of ads and hucksters on the internet telling you that their plan (and *only* their plan) can solve your problem.

Next, we have failure of **strategy**. This is the client that says, "I have a plan. I have followed the plan, but I haven't yet achieved my goal. Help!" I see this a lot with gifted kids who must finally learn how to study, whether in high school or college. And they say, "Okay, I'm trying to learn this whole studying thing, but it's not really working out. My grades haven't started to improve yet."

And finally, we have failure of **adherence**. This client says, "I had a plan and I followed it and it worked! Hooray! But I couldn't sustain the success, and now I feel even worse than before I started. Help!" For you parents out there, I have a six-year-old and a four-year-old. Every so often the house gets messy, and my wife and I talk to our kids about cleaning up. We agree that *this* is how we're going to organize the toys from now on; we have a plan, and we implement the plan, and the toys get put away, and we feel good about ourselves. And three weeks later and the playroom is a mess again. *Adhering* to a strategy is very challenging.

Why do neurodivergent people feel failure more? Let's count the ways! There are F.I.V.E. (OK, there are actually four reasons indicated by the literature; I just love an acronym. I feel like you're looking at me like the mom from *Turning Red* when she sees 4*Town has five members.)

1. *Fusion.* Many gifted people experience a fusion between their giftedness and their sense of self. Many of us say, "If I'm not the smart person, if I'm not a *genius*, then who even am I?" We wrap up a lot of our identity into the idea that we are gifted, and if too much of our identity fuses to that concept, failure doesn't feel like just a poorly executed thing, it feels like a judgement against your entire self.

2. *Isolation.* Gifted and other neurodivergent people tend to be isolated. They tend to struggle to find community (to learn more about the power of community, read the chapter on Hope). If you fail, that feeling is felt more because you've been isolated; being alone removes us from emotional support, removes us from people who could challenge our internal narrative that we are terrible, and nothing will get better. We need to find community to help support us through failure.

3. *Valence.* Giftedness is a lot of things, but especially, it is intensity. The physical and neuropsychological differences of the gifted brain create intense emotional interplay (see Chapter 6), which means you care about things *a great deal*. But more than just the intensity of the emotion is the valence of it—the extent to which an emotion is positive (comfortable) or negative (uncomfortable). If you're gifted, you're likely to feel the valence at an extreme, without moderation. More valence leads to bigger feelings leads to bigger behaviors (which is why you see people throw their golf clubs into the lake when they shank a drive, screaming, "*I quit this stupid game!*")

4. *Experience.* If you've never failed or rarely failed, then you don't necessarily have resiliency skills. For example, if you've always gotten "A" grades on tests, and suddenly you get a 72 on your first high school chemistry test, the grade itself feels bad, but overall you feel much worse because you don't have the prior experience on how to navigate those moments. That's exactly what happened to me in high school, and I freaked out because I realized, for the first time in my life, that just working harder

would *not* be enough to solve the problem! I was going to need help, and I had no idea how to get it. People don't get to experience failure because they're afraid they'll become numb to the feeling; trust me, I've failed plenty and it still hurts. Experiencing that first big failure is important! First failure is like first heartbreak; you remember it forever.

Since we neurodivergent people can't change what got us here neuro-logically or experientially, I think it's important to start a conversation about failure with the idea that failure is inevitable. That sounds like a huge bummer, but it's helpful. You have probably worked hard in your life to keep failure from happening; it's human nature to avoid pain! (If you know neurodivergent people or if you're neurodivergent yourself, you know that we will go to the ends of the earth to make sure failure doesn't happen). We have all had times where no matter how hard we worked, we still screwed it up and were left to deal with the consequences.

For example, I used to work at a bar in New Jersey where I grew up. One night right after I got promoted to bartender, I got one of my best life lessons about managing failure. It was a Thursday night, and I'd worked a double shift. It's the end of the day, closing in on 2am, and I'm exhausted. My coworker and I are loading cases of beer into the beer fridge, so the bar is ready for the weekend rush. I had loaded seven cases of beer without incident. But when I went to put the eighth one in there, I dropped it, and it shattered all over the place. As a gifted person and an intense human, also already exhausted and feeling insecure about not wanting to look bad after my recent promotion, I looked down at my mistake and started having a small meltdown.

Before I could spiral too hard, though, my colleague looked at me and said, "You know what? Here's something that might help you out. I think one of the things you've got to think about is that today your success rate was one out of eight. You put eight cases of beer in there, but you dropped only one. Your failure rate was only one out of eight today; not great, honestly. So, tomorrow, try and make it one out of 20, and then one out of 24, and then one out of 30, one out of 33, 1 out of 37, on and for forever, OK? You're never going to get that top number to zero, but you can make the bottom number as big as you possibly can." And then he got a mop and started helping me to clean up my mess.

That speech really helped me because it's the sort of reframe that can change the entire way that you view something. You're never going to reach a point where that failure rate, that top number (of course, my gifted brain was shouting "the numerator!") to zero. It doesn't work that way, but you have control over how big the bottom number ("the denominator!") is. As you know, there's a big difference between one out of eight and one out of 80 and one out of 8,000. We might not be able to control the specific number, but we can control how much we are exposed. Control is important for mental health, and by accepting failure as an inevitability, it might feel like you're giving up control, but I disagree. I think that you're moving smartly to something that you can control versus something that you cannot. You can control your improvement, which means that you have a fighting chance of controlling your rates of, and reactions to, failing.

As a psychologist, I tend to look at life through the therapy lens. Therapy is great because you cannot fail at therapy, nor can you win therapy. It is a judgment-free and valuation-free zone! Therapy is a place to process your feelings and be validated. And it's also a place to practice failing and recovering. I can't tell you how many times I've sat in session and gone through dress rehearsals with clients for so many of the important moments in their lives: "Here's how I'm going to ask this person to the dance," or "Here's how I'm going to apply for this job," or "Here's how I'm going to break up with this person," or "Here's how I'm going to give this speech at a wedding." Therapy gives us space to refine those approaches so that you get a little better at it. It's an opportunity to fail gracefully and get meaningful feedback to improve, *before* the big moment (and its high stakes) arises. When you fail in a safe environment, it helps you grow and inoculates you against catastrophic feelings from future failures.

There are many approaches to therapy, but they're all based on two fundamental concepts. The first is we change our relationship to our thoughts, especially our *automatic thoughts*. The second is we want to decrease the frequency, intensity, and duration of challenging thoughts (in psychology it is The Big Three, F.I.D). We want to impact how *frequently* the feelings arise, how *intense* the feelings are, and their *duration*. We will likely *not* get any of those numbers to zero! But we can make them smaller and smaller, and that's what growth in mental health looks like. If you try to never have a panic attack ever again (a very understandable goal, of course, panic attacks are the worst), you are guaranteed to fail. Try instead to reduce the frequency of panic attacks from once per week to once per month, the intensity of the attack from ten (on a scale of 1-10) to six, and the duration from forty-five to 15 minutes.

One therapeutic approach that I have found works well for neurodivergent people is acceptance and commitment therapy, or ACT (often attributed to Steve Hayes and Russ Harris). We want to experience *all* human emotions, not just the fun and pleasurable ones. To do so we aim to develop cognitive and psychological flexibility, which creates emotional openness. When you do ACT, you're being more accepting of the things that happen in your life, whether we like them to or not. You learn that the power of interventions is best when it is appropriate to the challenging emotion, rather than when intervention is used to merely quash any challenge (Hayes, Strosahl, Wilson, 2011). I find the thoughtful nature and suite of tools that make up ACT (not to mention its tendency to rely on elaborate metaphors, which fits my thinking and speaking style), play into the cognitive strengths of being neurodivergent. Like the Neurodiversity Movement, ACT posits that differences are not deficits, and we must meet people where they are without judgment to best help them.

ACT is organized around an idea we call the Hexaflex (see below). The Hexaflex is comprised of six concepts that, when used properly, will flow into psychological flexibility. Psychological flexibility is the ability to respond nimbly to the impact of events in our lives, and especially the thoughts and feelings that flow from them (Hayes, et al., 2011). One of the ideas behind ACT is that we are constantly trying to increase psychological flexibility and benefit from it as much as possible, because it isn't a finish line to cross. The strained effort of trying constantly to be anything (including flexible) prevents us from achieving it (just as trying to be calm makes us more stressed out). Rather, flexibility is a state of mind to appreciate and cultivate.

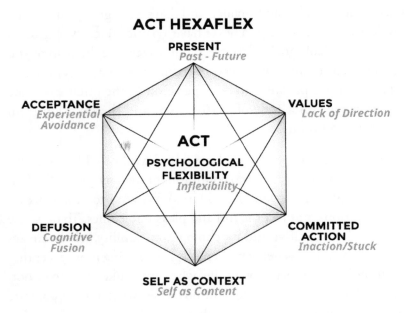

ACT HEXAFLEX

The bold text up top are the things we want:
- ○ Present moment focus
- ○ Living our values
- ○ Taking committed action
- ○ Seeing our self as context
- ○ Diffusing ourselves from our thoughts
- ○ Accepting what happens to us

Adapting these stances can increase psychological flexibility. The italicized texts underneath are the less-helpful things that we do, which are probably bringing us to therapy. For example: getting stuck in the past or stuck in the future, not living our values, being inactive, seeing ourselves as merely content without context, fusing to our thoughts, and avoiding the things that happen to us. We're going to talk about how to use each of the six steps of ACT, as defined by Hexaflex, to increase our flexibility and deal with failure.

Acceptance

Let's start by talking about acceptance. As you see here, we have a picture of a beach ball. Imagine that I ask you to take this beach ball, go in the pool and hold it under water.

No matter how big you are or strong you are, sooner or later that beach ball's coming back out of the water, right? That's what it wants to do. You're going to fail at that task of holding it under water, not because you're not smart or clever or strong or talented or any of those things, but because the task is not possible in the first place. Eventually, the ball comes splashing out of the water, and not only did we fail our task, we also got soaking wet. This experience triggers a thing we like to call the "struggle switch." (Harris, 2006)

The ball is out of the water and you're wet, and you're not at all happy about it! You're understandably upset that you've failed, but you don't want to be upset. Now you're upset that you failed and angry at yourself for being upset. But who wants to be angry? Now you're sad that you're angry that you're upset. And you've been working on not being sad in therapy, so now you're worried about being sad that you're angry that you're now upset. And that's where meltdowns come from, because these feelings just cascade on top of each other so that you're not just dealing with one feeling, you're dealing with several at the same time.

Instead of fighting to keep the beach ball under the water, let the beach ball come to the surface. The beach ball represents our failure, our unwanted emotions, the things we're trying to hold back, hold under, push away—but they're still there. They're floating on the surface of the water. And you think, "Well, I don't want them there." Of course you don't. We'd rather the beach ball not be in the pool at all. Acceptance doesn't mean giving up; it means changing our focus (Hayes & Hoffman, 2021). Since we can't take the beach ball out of the pool, we change our relationship to the problem by letting it move slowly across the top of the water, ultimately floating away. When the ball is on the surface, it gives us the ability to deal with it in a different way. If the beach ball floats towards us while we're swimming, then we swim to the other end of the pool, or we push it away, or even get out. It's not about getting rid of the feelings; it's about learning to live with them by accepting their presence.

The idea is that you become more flexible and capable by accepting the existence of the problem. Don't spend all your energy trying to do the impossible, i.e., hold the beach ball under water indefinitely—you will not succeed. If you give yourself permission to move the beach ball or move yourself in relation to the beach ball, you get your capability back. The undesirable feelings are still there, but they are not as scary because you're not focused on hating them and trying desperately to make them go away. You are learning to deal with them.

Failure is unavoidable, so stop taking on the impossible task of trying to avoid it. When we embrace failure, it doesn't stop existing, but it bothers us less because we're working less hard to keep it from happening. Failure triggers more uncomfortable feelings that can combine into the struggle switch that we discussed earlier. When you're able to just let things be—when you turn the struggle switch to "off" —you gain your flexibility and creativity back and become more resilient in the offing.

Present Moment Focus

The next piece we're going to talk about is *present moment focus*. Psychological stress pulls us away from the present (Weissman &

Mendes, 2021). If something bothers us, for example, anxiety, such feelings whisk us right away to the future. When we worry, our brains say something to the effect of, "I have to pass this test. Okay, well if I don't pass this test, then I'm not going to get a good grade in this class, which means I'm not going to have a good transcript for high school, which means I'm not going to go to a good college, which means I'm not going to get a good job, which means I'm not going to meet a good partner, which means I'm going to end up sleeping under the third street bridge!" It's like you just pulled yourself 24 years ahead into a dark future. All we're talking about is a biology exam, right? When we get pulled away from the present, we must try to pull ourselves back to where we are *now* so we can deal with the problems in front of us, because those are the only ones we can change.

Depression does the same thing, except it yanks us to the past. You start thinking about the file folder of every single failure you've ever had (mine is more of a library wing at this point). When you look in the folder, it usually reveals something relevant in theme: "We lost the basketball game. I remember that time I missed the game-winning shot in tennis." Then the pages in the folder start flipping like a time-lapse in an old movie: "That reminds me of other shots I missed in hockey. And the time I missed the goal in soccer, and the time I struck out in baseball, and when I got turned down for prom..." and every other bad thing that's ever happened to you until you're questioning your self-worth and whether anyone has never really loved you (depression, it must be said, is a jackass). Successfully managing these thoughts isn't about fighting them off or the feelings that come with them. The thoughts come on their own, that's why we call them automatic. Remind yourself that the only thing you can do is affect the present. You can't change what's going to happen in the future and you definitely can't change what's already happened.

If we focus energies on the present moment, we are more likely to succeed and be better prepared to manage when negativity tries to yank us away (like the Time Variance Authority from *Loki*). When we are less present, we are less able to receive the good things that are happening to us right now. We become less willing to accept that good things can or will happen because we're busy fighting imaginary wars in the future or reliving our low moments from the past. We become less able to recover, respond, and reach out. One of the things you can do if you're worried about failure is to you remind yourself that no matter what happens—good or bad—all you can do is try to positively impact the world you're in right now.

To emphasize this concept (I say this in therapy all the time), say to yourself, "Don't stumble over something behind you." A lot of us have baggage, stuff in our past we don't like. We all have embarrassing memories that we're not proud of and we wish didn't happen. I would raise my hand on that one because in my experience it's absolutely true (you should see the pictures of me from middle school…yikes). But such things are behind us, for better or worse. Try and move forward by learning from that experience because it can still instruct us. One of my clients was bemoaning about how close-minded she used to be: "I hate that I was so awful back then, Dr. Matt. I cringe when I think about the stuff I used to say to my mom and my friends." I thought about it and replied, "Well, maybe it's good to have cringe memories. Because if you do, that's a sign that you've grown. If they didn't feel cringey, then you'd still be that person." I am happy to be able to give such good advice.

One of the great theater aphorisms is that *the show must go on*. Failure happens in every show—sometimes big things, sometimes little things (I've seen curtains fail to open, props misplaced, and a kid get knocked unconscious by a set piece)—but the show goes on. How do we make sure the show goes on? Accepting that it must go on naturally puts us in a creative problem-solving mode: we can't just crank to a halt and say, "well, that's the end of the play, we're just not going to do the second act of *Wicked*." No way! We going to figure out how to make it work.

One great example in theater of overcoming failure is in *The Tragedy of Julius Caesar* by William Shakespeare. You may have heard of him. In the play, Brutus says, "Peace. Count the clock." And Cassius says, "The clock hath stricken three." Now, if I was doing this live, I would ask the room, what's wrong with this statement? And some people would talk about the grammar. The grammar is not wrong, "stricken" is still correct English, and more importantly, it fits with the rhythm of Shakespeare's language, which in this instance is iambic pentameter. Finally, somebody says, "Wait a second. Clocks didn't exist in ancient Rome, right?" They didn't! This play has a clock in a scene 1700 years before they were invented. Shakespeare didn't miss this event by a couple of months; he missed this by the better part of two millennia. And if William Shakespeare can make a mistake in a play, a play that is performed all over the world and is probably being performed right now, I'm sure we can give ourselves the flexibility to make a mistake.

Committed Action

The next thing to talk about is committed action. If we were together in person, I would have you guys play a game called "Zoot." In Zoot is you count in order, trying to get as high as you can go. I'd bring five people up on stage, have them count 1, 2, 3, 4, 5, 6, and so on. Sounds easy, right? The trick is that there's a hidden pattern not revealed to the players; based on the pattern, you don't say some numbers and instead you say, "Zoot!" I don't tell the players what that pattern is; they have to figure it out through trial and error—*through failing*.

The players count anxiously, knowing that at some point I'm going to tell them that they are wrong. They get to the number seven I yell "Zoot!" Now they've learned their first piece of information about the pattern. Since they made a mistake, they have start over in their counting. They start again at one, and after six they say "Zoot!" instead of saying seven; they then climb to 14 and I say "Zoot!" again. Now they're starting to figure it out. When they get to 17, I say "Zoot!" again, but they get confused because the pattern is different than they thought. It begins to come clear that the pattern involves replacing multiples of seven with "Zoot!", but it also includes any number with the number seven in it. So, the zoot numbers are 7, 14, 17, 21, 27, 28, etc. You don't have to use just seven; it could be five or eleven or whatever you choose. The key idea here is that you did a committed action, you faced your fear and moved ahead anyway.

This is a game you cannot play without failing. Failing is baked into the game, and thus playing the game normalizes it. When you get up there to participate, you're taking a committed action to face your anxiety, face your fear of failure. Additionally, because this is a game where inevitably everybody makes a mistake, it moves failure from "oh it's your fault" to "this can happen to anyone." By democratizing the experience of failure, you create empathy and a sense of unity, as the team works together, solves the pattern, and overcomes its mistakes. As a team, it's a challenging thing to do, but it's a pleasant and simple game to play with your people.

One of the things that keeps us stuck and inflexible in life is our fear—fear of pain, or failure, or loneliness, or embarrassment. In a world where the "code" of conduct seems capricious and unfair, it's far too easy to *not* try because you want to stay safe, especially if you're neurodivergent and have learned that the odds are stacked against you. The only way to grow is to do things, risking initial failure for the potential of joy and evolution on the other side. You may fail, which means that you can try again. You may fail at some aspects of things but succeed in others. Heck, you might find out that you suck at it but want to do it anyway (like me and acting, or my client who cannot code for her life but still participates on her school's Robotics team). There are many possibilities for success.

One of those possibilities is that you could be awesome at it. You might not be awesome at the task in the way that everyone else is, but that's fine. Either way, you could find that you enjoy this task and quickly want to do more of it. You might find that just practicing this thing feels as good as playing it, or winning at it, or being celebrated for it. We want to embrace such feelings because they're rare. You're never going to have those good feelings if you don't embrace the flexibility required to try new things.

Self as Context

Next, we will consider self as context, not self as content. Failure is an event; it's not who we are. When we personalize failure (identify our self with it), we increase its impact on us. Our brains really like to center on what happens to us; we have what the kids like to call "main character energy." Psychologically speaking, our brains *hate* not knowing what's happening, so they create an understandable but false narrative instead of not having a narrative.

For example, if you come home from work and your partner's upset, your brain's going to say, "Oh no! Did I do something? I feel like I did something. What did I do? Or NOT do? I'm really sorry!" Maybe your partner just had a bad day at work, or maybe they just stubbed their toe on the kitchen counter. Or any of a billion other options. In the process of making our selves the center of the problem, we rob the person who was hurt and upset of their emotional needs. They end up having to manage us instead of managing their own feelings. What happens is that we make them mad at us for asking, "What did I do? What did I do?!" This is a classic example of a self-fulfilling prophecy. They end up mad at us and our brains say, at some level, "Oh good, now I understand what's happening; they're mad at me. I feel better now." But at what cost? Your partner is still upset, and now they're *also* mad at you.

Context always matters. There are always external factors that contribute to our failure. Many times, the context has nothing to do with us. Here are some key failure contexts.

○ *Novice*—Are you a novice? Have you never done this before? Neurodivergent people, especially gifted and ADHDers, are notorious for thinking, "I'm pretty good at ice hockey and field hockey and golf, so I should be good at paddle ball." Why would you be, it's not the same thing. If you've never done it before, we need to grade you on a different scale. When you're new at something, you're more anxious and tend to be less knowledgeable of what to do and how to do it. I once was asked by my dear friend Dianne Allen to write the forward for her book, to which I of course said yes. I've done a lot of writing (and that's before I took on writing this book!) and I figured that writing a forward would be easy. And I was dead wrong! It took me weeks to figure out how to marry the right tone of the forward with the appropriate content with the right length. I finished it right at the deadline and it was fine, but talk about a steep learning curve!

○ *Ambiguity*—Were the directions or tasks presented to you in a way that was clear or fair? One of my favorite exercises to do in session (and during talks) is to pick someone from the audience and ask them to stand up, and then to sit down. They inevitably sit back in their chair, which gives me the opportunity to ask them why they did that. The person always replies, "Well, you told me to." No! I just said, "sit down". I knew what I meant in my head, but I didn't articulate that to you. Often the people giving us directions (bosses, partners, family, teachers, even therapists) are giving instructions that are *unwittingly* vague because they know what they mean inside their own heads (Alderson-Day, et al., 2016). When you follow your own interpretation of that "code" and guess wrong, you're immediately chastised. But was it really your fault if it was not made clear what you were supposed to do?

○ *Environment*—Are you trying to succeed in the wrong environment for you? Could the environment be better? How can you adapt the environments or scale them? I run my own psychology practice, and I do a great job at it. Part of the reason I work for myself is that I don't work well in group practices—I need to have autonomy. You need to make sure that the context you're trying to succeed in is the right one. Determining that is important because very often, choices about school, religion, where we live, etc., are choices that were made *for* us, not *by* us. These are things you are allowed to change. I wouldn't take a STEM genius and enroll them at Julliard unless that's where they wanted to be. You can't take a weekend golfer and put them on the Olympic team. When I was single, I realized that what little flirting skills I had were absolutely useless at clubs and concerts, so I stopped trying to meet people there and instead talked to people at baseball games, coffee shops, etc. If you know how you operate best, personally or professionally, then you can seek out places that amplify your real self.

○ *Systemic Bias*—We live in a society where certain organizations have practices and beliefs embedded in them that hurt different groups. Not all of that is intentional, though obviously some of it may be. If you are in a minority—racial, sexual, a neuro-minority, etc.—you may be in an environment that is working against your success based on aspects of yourself that you cannot control. This is why DEI work is so important and must include neurodivergence as part of its mission statements (Dahusi, et al., 2014). It's one thing to say that you want diversity as a part of your organization (and not all organizations even say that), but if you don't create systems and structures to recruit a diversity of people and keep them there, then your words aren't worth much. When it comes to overcoming systemic bias, you have to walk the walk, not just talk the talk.

De-fusion from Our Thoughts

The next thing to discuss is de-fusion from our thoughts. Neurodivergent people tend to become overidentified with their thoughts, and when you fuse with something in your thoughts, it can easily overtake you. We are not our thoughts! Working against this is the fact that some thinking styles actively *maintain* cognitive fusion, and unfortunately neurodivergent people are susceptible to many of them.

○ The first is *black and white thinking,* where you convince yourself that something is either perfect, or it was bad. If you get a 98 on a test, I'm here to tell you, as a mental health professional, that 98 is a very good grade on a test. You don't need to get a hundred for it to be excellent, exceptional, as good as perfect.

○ The next maladaptive thinking process is *all or nothing thinking,* where you convince yourself that because a part of a thing or event didn't go well, you failed. I was talking to a client last year who is a very talented musician, and he said he was depressed because "I was playing a piece of music and in the seventh movement I was a little bit flat on one of the notes. Clearly, I suck at the French horn." And I said, "dude, I don't think anybody could tell". And even if they could, you played hundreds of other notes and those all went well, right? That context matters a lot.

○ The next maladaptive thought process is the *self-fulfilling prophecy*. We talked about this earlier, but if you act like you knew you were going to fail, sooner or later you're going to behave in a way that proves you right, because our brains love to be right. You can unwittingly sabotage yourself by convincing your brain that an outcome is predestined, which causes the brain to act in a way that ensures that response. Try to shift into an accepting stance, acknowledging that you've done what you could and the results are what they are.

○ The last thing is *catastrophizing*, which is assuming that all failures are terrible, whereas most failures are quite small and inconsequential, especially in the long term. One of the hardest parts of being a therapist is honoring a client's emotional response to something that feels very big in the moment ("I can't believe I lost my glasses") knowing that in the long term, it's going to be less than a footnote in their story. Both things—the giant emotion and its ultimate inconsequentialness—can be true. If you spell your name wrong on a test, it doesn't mean you're going fail middle school, it just means you spelled your name wrong on a test. Things happen.

The way that we diffuse from these thoughts is to shift to *bottom-up thinking* as opposed to *top-down thinking*. Top-down thinking is results-driven and punitive: if you get a 98 on a test, and you're doing top-down thinking, you're going to be sad because you want things to be perfect, and if it's less than perfect, it's bad. Your brain reframes getting a 98/100 as, "I got one problem wrong, so it's not perfect, I want to be at the top and I'm not". Bottom-up thinking, on the other hand, is aspirational and cumulative. It allows for the process of learning and growth, and it shows you how far you've come. If you think, "I got 98 on the test! Wow, that means I knew 98% of the material. Hot damn, that's much better than knowing 0% of the material." I always tell my clients that doing nothing is the default. If you don't do anything, nothing changes. But on the flip side of that, anything you do is value added, which is very powerful.

There's a great quote from Amanda Gorman from Joe Biden's inauguration.

> *"Somehow we've weathered and witnessed (something) that isn't broken but simply unfinished."*

If you fuse to the thought "I failed, therefore I am broken," it's going to be difficult not to see yourself as broken because you see yourself *as the failure.* But if you allow yourself to see yourself as unfinished, as in "I got that note wrong in rehearsal because I haven't ever played that song before so I should practice more," you're going to diffuse from thoughts of failure. Defusing may help you find that failure is a thing that happened *to* me; it is *not* who I am. That's a powerful reframe.

Psychological Flexibility

All these areas of development are in service of psychological flexibility. We know that failure is inevitable. It's going to happen to us, regardless of how much we try to keep it from happening and how much we don't want it to. Surely you have thoughts about failure already, based on years of experience. Here's the truth: you don't have to change how you feel about failing. If you hate it, you'll keep hating it. Failing sucks; who wants to feel that way? You don't have to be psychologically flexible to merely *survive* in the world, but psychological flexibility is key to *thriving* in the world.

Whether you hate or love the snow, you'll have the same amount of snow in your life; the question is how much fun are you going to have with it? Failure happens *to* us, but it also happens *for* us. Failure can teach us important lessons, increase our resiliency, amplify our motivation, and improve our resolve. The fact is that you're already learning from failure. Trial and error are pieces of human learning.

This is baked into our genetic code, and error (failure) is part of that process. We learn by trying and failure. You might as well try to find some joy in it.

You want a good teacher about failure? Watch a toddler (I have two kids, so this is a relevant example for me), toddlers fail all the time. They try to walk, and they fall down. They try to put blocks together and they stumble. They try to eat pureed peas and it's like trying to thread a needle in a hurricane: the spoon is all over the place. Toddlers know they're learning through doing. A toddler accepts failure as part of engaging in the world. They might get upset by it and cry, but they don't give up. Can you imagine if a toddler said, "Well I clearly can't figure out this spoon, so I'm going to give up on eating." They keep trying: if they smear 78% of the pureed peas on their face to eat the rest, that's a win for them.

Experiencing failure strengthens us. Pressure turns coal into diamonds; we learn from the pressure of our mistakes. My dad often said to me, "you either win or you learn." I never got that as a kid, but as an adult and a professional psychologist, I get it now. I have learned a lot more than I have won in my life. Every time I have failed, there's been a lesson to figure out, to make me a little bit better next time.

For example, let's say you're driving a car, and a tree suddenly falls in front of you. You've got no time to react, and you slam into the fallen tree. You're fine but your car looks totaled. You might be sitting there thinking that you're an idiot and a terrible driver, because honestly, who hits a tree? (Austin Powers voice). But zoom out for a second—that's a freak accident! Nobody would prepare for a tree to suddenly falling in their path, that's not a realistic thing to prepare for. Getting into that accident doesn't make you a bad driver. If, on the other hand, you were changing the radio and playing Pokémon Go and yelling at your kids in the backseat when you slam into the car in front of you, then there are different lessons to be learned.

Role Models (Again? Again.)

Gifted people love to learn from their heroes. There are lots of gifted people who are famous failures. Steven Spielberg was rejected from film school. Someone once told Elvis Presley he had no charisma. (I mean, I'm not a big Elvis fan, but that makes no sense to me.) Michael Jordan was cut from his high school basketball team. Winston Churchill lost five elections, and he's also the source of my favorite quote on failure:

> *"Success is not final. Failure is not fatal. It is the courage to continue that counts."*

We've just got to find a way to keep going. There are a million examples of famous people who failed and overcame. Whatever you or your kids or your clients are interested in, I'm sure you can find a relevant example so they can learn from their heroes.

My favorite one concerns Ruth Wakefield and chocolate chip cookies. Everybody loves chocolate chip cookies, and they were in accident! Ruth was trying to mix the chocolate into the batter, and she didn't know that they would cook where they were. And yet, chocolate chip cookies are an international phenomenon. Her mistake literally changed the course of human history. Not in a big way, but in a delicious way.

What happened to Jennifer Lawrence? She climbs up the stairs, she falls down, and the entire world gasps. But she gets up there, and what she says in her acceptance speech is: "You guys are all clapping for me just because I fell." The place exploded with applause and cheers. From a psychology perspective, especially from an ACT lens, it's the best possible answer. She didn't pretend it didn't happen, she didn't act like everything is fine (looking at you, Will Smith). She also didn't sprint away off the stage, which nobody would've blamed her for. She stepped into the spotlight and owned what happened to her. She accepted it and thus gained the power to take committed action: she acknowledged what happened and went on to give her speech. When you fail, you fail. We're not going to let failure define us, we're going to let it *refine* us.

Final Lessons from Failure

There are only three ways to truly fail.

- One: Never trying in the first place.
- Two: Giving up.
- Three: Stopping improving.

The last one is probably the trickiest thing for gifted kids, because they can get so far with their natural abilities. They're smart, they're talented, they're clever, they're creative—all the wonderful things that come with being gifted. But at some point, the smartness isn't a match for how hard life is. Neurotypical people have developed coping strategies to navigate those moments, but gifted kids haven't because they never had to. That's when you've got to change your approach and find another pathway to start learning and growing more intentionally. Because if you never improve, everybody else who's working hard is going to catch up with you and probably pass you at some point.

Let me tell you guys about my most epic failure. It's not my favorite story to tell, but it has a happy ending. In college at Wake Forest University, I was an editorial cartoonist for the school newspaper. In 2007, I was nominated along with many fellow colleagues from all over the country to go to the American Association of Editorial Cartoonists Annual Gala in Washington DC. There were 10 regions in the country and each region nominated *four* students. But that year there was a mistake and *five* invitations went out to the Midwest. So, five kids showed up—there were supposed to be 40 people but instead there were 41 people. That's going to be important, I promise.

Part of this conference experience is your network: you sit on panels; you buy art supplies (SO many Sharpies!); and you meet famous cartoonists. But the major reason to go is to get your work adjudicated by a famous cartoonist. In my case, the adjudicator was Annette Balesteri. She won the Pulitzer Prize, she's a big deal. I'm sitting there in my suit and she's looking through my portfolio; as a gifted kid and professional artist, I was used to being good at stuff and people telling me how awesome I am. Annette finally finishes flipping through my portfolio, she looks up and she says, "You're not that good at this." I stammer out, "I'm sorry, what?" She goes on, "How did you get nominated for this conference?" At that moment the penny dropped for me; oh gosh, this isn't an elaborate joke. She actually means these awful things. She proceeded to rip my cartoons apart as unoriginal and uninspired. She didn't agree with my politics, and she definitely didn't like my drawing style. I was mortified, but what was I to do? I sat there and took my lumps. When she finally dismissed me, I grabbed my portfolio, and I hid in the bathroom for a while and cried.

It was not pleasant.

I was supposed to sit on a panel that afternoon, but I bailed. I went to the train station and got an early train back to New Jersey. I was really upset and, when I got home, I told my parents that I was never drawing again, and they should throw my portfolio into the ocean. To my mom's everlasting credit (love you, mom!) she didn't listen to my melodrama. Instead, she validated my feelings and then said, "Matt, there's a lesson in this. We don't know what it is yet, but at some point, a meaningful lesson will come from this." So, I spent a couple of days licking my wounds, and then finally on day three, I sat down and asked grumpily if the lesson had emerged yet. My mom smiled and said, "Okay, I've found something in her critique that I think is going to help you out." And despite myself I wanted to listen. Mom had found the very last thing that Annette wrote in her feedback: "He's not a very good political cartoonist, but he would make a good comic book artist."

I went on to launch my web comic, "My Roommate's a Superhero," and ran that for two years in the late aughts. Then I created some art for schools, had a side gig as a caricaturist, and I'm working on a graphic novel (coming soon!). I get to work professionally with the fabulous artists at the Joe Kubert School here in New Jersey. I'm not saying that without that challenge I wouldn't have created these other successes; I don't know if that's true. But I do know that this catastrophic moment—getting absolutely shredded by somebody I looked up to—showed me that you can recover from failures like that.

Now remember how I said there were 41 kids there when there were supposed to be only 40. I finished 41st in the adjudication. I was literally worst of the worst. I finished behind the kid that wasn't supposed to be there! But when this book comes out, I'm going to mail a copy to Annette with a thank you because I learned from that failure. I learned how to be more intentional with my errors. I know I learned how to take myself more seriously and prepare rather than just showing up and hoping my talent would take me the rest of the way. When a failure happens, people say, "Do you wish it didn't happen?" Most of the time, the answer is clearly yes. But with this one I can tell you now, I'm glad it did.

CHAPTER 12
Hope—When Life Feels Impossible, How do we Keep Going?

Two years ago, my friends at the Davidson Institute in Reno, NV asked me to give the keynote address at their 2022 annual symposium. Little did they know, this was my *first ever* keynote address. They told me that the theme for the conference was the work of Mr. Rogers, and I was thrilled. I had always Mr. Rogers to be one of the sincerest and authentically hopeful people I had ever seen. This was a perfect opportunity to talk about hope. (Interestingly, I'm finishing this chapter as I'm packing up to go back to Reno for the 2024 Davidson Institute Symposium).

The day before my flight (three years ago), I got an email that my flight had been changed to 6am from Newark out to Los Angeles, and then on to Reno. I grumbled to my wife but changed my alarm and woke up early (so early) to get to the plane on time. Yet when I got there, I couldn't check in. It turns out that United Airlines, in all their wisdom, had changed my flight from 930am on Friday to 6am—not on Friday, but on Sunday!—the day *after* the conference. I was livid and flabbergasted. Thankfully I used to work as a travel agent, so I knew what to do.

After trying to get into Reno that day (not possible, I was told), and then every surrounding airport within a two-hour radius (none possible), I got them to change my flight to San Francisco, which put me four hours away from Reno by car, which I would of course have to rent. And once all that mess was sorted, I would be driving up I-85 northeast from the Bay Area on roads I had never driven, exhausted, and stressed. I called the team at Davidson and explained the situation. They were obviously concerned, both for my safety but also for the conference that they were putting on for 1100 people who were expecting me to speak.

"Can you do it?" they asked.

"I hope so!" I replied.

When I landed at SFO and got my rental car, I called three people. My wife, to update her. My parents, to vent. And my therapist, for hope. Because, despite my bravado, I was terrified. It's a long drive in the dark and I was already very tired. It was not like I could sleep in the next day; I was expected to be *on* in less than twelve hours. We chatted for a while and then my therapist told me something that still sticks with me: "If all you've got is hope, that's a start but it isn't enough. You've got to have a plan as well to back that hope up." That's why I see him!

Why do most people come to therapy? If you haven't looked around recently or read the news or watched outside or checked on social media, it feels like everything is on fire and everything is terrible all the time. That is one of the reasons people come to therapy, especially over the last few years, as we navigate Covid-19, political turmoil, and climate change. Talking to somebody who's neutral and supportive can be a helpful thing. I don't have answers to all the world problems (if I had the answers, I would've called Dr. Fauci years ago). But I can sit with you and hold space for those feelings. Ideally, you leave the hour with me with a little more hope than you showed up with.

So...what is hope? To have hope is to want an outcome that makes your life better in some tangible way (Corn, Feldman, & Wexler, 2020). Hope is the expectation that one will have positive experiences, or that potentially negative or threatening situations will not materialize, and your life will develop into a favorable state of affairs. That latter definition is from the American Psychological Association (2017), and I like it because not only is it a positive experience, but it also honors the fact that sometimes hope is about bad not happening, and that's okay too. For example, I hope that you like this book; I *also* hope that you don't hate it.

Where does hope come from? Hope is a very personal thing. It comes from confidence in your own life, your personal values, and your dreams. It's also a very human thing. We as a species, are not content to be content. If you look through the developmental and fossil records of human behavior, you will see that humans have consistently reached for the stars and aim to make things better. We don't settle. We constantly tinker and improve and seek to make things better. Sometimes we fall on our collective faces, but every so often, something beautiful happens.

From a therapy perspective, our brains are simple. Our brains like to make a story and stick to it. Simple stories mean that our brains are spending less energy on that and more energy on other things, like keeping us alive. Our brains will pick a story that makes things easy to tell. They will find pieces of information that fit the story, and they'll pay less attention to ones that don't. Hope gives us a guiding principle to be the main characters of our own lives.

It's tough to have a conversation about hope without quoting one of my favorite movies. "Hope is a good thing, maybe the best of things. And no good thing ever dies." I love this quote for many reasons, but I particularly like it in the context of the movie. Very few characters in modern cinema have had it quite as bad as Andy Dufresne, played memorably by Tim Robbins in this classic film *The Shawshank Redemption*. When he speaks about hope to Red, played by Morgan Freeman, we know he has had a terrible time in prison: he has been sexually assaulted, he's been starved, and he's been physically beaten. He knows that he took the rap for a crime that he didn't commit (the murder of his wife) and, heartbreakingly, that the real murderer is out there. And because he participated in large scale fraud while at Shawshank at the behest of the warden, there are liabilities involved with allowing him to leave, so the warden makes sure that he stays put. In the midst of all that turmoil, he grabs onto hope and doesn't let go.

Oftentimes I say to my clients, "I can't make the bad things in your life not happen to you. And I can't keep more bad things from happening to you. But as long as you were nurturing yourself with that little glimmer of hope, that tiny ember, then we've got a chance to make things better. Or at least suck less." The people who come to my office, sometimes they don't even want to have hope anymore. They've said, "You know what, Dr. Matt? I'm just done with hope. I don't even know why I'm still doing my life, just putting one foot in front of the other." That admission allows me to say, "I don't know why or how you do it either, but it's amazing that you do." Let's work together to find out how you're doing it.

We should talk about the difference between hope and optimism. Hope is linked to optimism (Corn, et al., 2020). They're like cousins, but not the same thing. Optimism is the attitude or outlook that good things will happen and that your wishes will ultimately be fulfilled; optimism is looking on the bright side. Hope is the gas that runs the engine of optimism. Hope sets the goals that make the possibility of change tangible and leads us to be optimistic about meeting those goals.

Hope provides us with goals and the motivation to meet them (Pleeging, van Exel, & Burger, 2022). Hope looks to the future and makes the present easier to bear. We live constantly with one foot in the present and one in the future. For those of us who have more hope, the future seems bright, or we hope that it will be brighter. It allows us to tolerate things as they are now, by hoping that they will get better. Hope connects us to the broader cosmic or spiritual universe, because hope represents something bigger than us. For some people, that's religion. For some people, that's faith in the universe. For some people, that's faith in nature. However, you get your spiritual connection is wonderful: it is a thing to be celebrated. Part of what's connecting you to that feeling of something bigger than us is hope.

If we're going to use hope to make goals, we should talk about what makes a "good goal." Goals should be SMART. SMART is an acronym for Specific, Measurable, Achievable, Relevant, and Time-Bound

(Latham, 2020). I like SMART goals, something I've worked very hard on helping my clients to achieve. Let's walk through it together.

○ Goals should be *Specific*. The goal should not be, "I hope that I am good at soccer." That's not really a very specific thing. What does good mean? Good like Leo Messi, good like not the worst player on the team, good like I remember to tie my cleats on my feet, not my hands? Because the word "good" is so vague we cannot know precisely what it means, so the goal falls apart. A better goal would be, "I want to score two goals this season in soccer." That's a specific goal.

○ That specificity leads directly into *Measurable*. The thing that you want should be measurable so you know when you hit it and then can celebrate. "Two goals" is measurable. "Lead the league in scoring" is measurable. "I want to score!" starts to fall apart. Consider a different goal: clients will come to me and say, "I want to lose some weight." I respond with, "Cool, how much does 'some' mean?" because some doesn't mean the same thing to every person. When clients respond, "I don't know. I'll know it when I see it." I say "That's a great idea, but it's a bad goal. Let's say you'll lose 10 pounds. Let's lose 10 pounds by Christmas." We're making it measurable—both a measurable achievement and a measurable outcome.

○ Then we make our goal *Achievable*. The goals we make must be things you can reasonably do. I work with an 8-year-old right now who really wants to be a professional basketball player. He told me, "My goal is to be able to dunk. I want to be able to dunk a basketball like LeBron [James, arguably the greatest NBA player ever]." I think that's awesome for a goal. I love his confidence and passion. Also…there's virtually no way an 8-year-old can dunk a basketball in a 10-foot hoop. He can't even pick up the ball with one hand yet! An achievable goal for him is to hone the skills that he's physically capable of doing right now—dribbling, shooting and playing defense are things he can work on now. When puberty inevitably happens and he can jump out of the gym, we'll talk about dunking.

○ The goal also must be *Relevant*. Specifically, the goal has to mean something to the person who is setting it, not the other people in their life. This is where adults and teachers often mess up when they're trying to give kids hope. A kid comes to you and says, "I don't have any friends." We tend to respond with, "Well, someday you'll have so many friends and you'll be the 'big man on campus'." Not only is that patronizing, maybe that's not what your kid wants to be. Maybe the relevant goals are having two or three good friends to go to the comic book shop with, or a half dozen friends to have over for a movie. Those goals are fine, and also accurate for the neurodivergent experience, because we tend to seek quality over quantity people when it comes to friendships.

○ Lastly, we have the *Time-bound* piece of goal setting, which is a challenge for the neurodivergent brain and its propensity for rushing (especially given all the executive functioning challenges that we talked about in Chapter 5). I work hard to ensure that the goals my clients set are relevant to them and what they're trying to achieve, and also that they fit into a realistic timeline. If you're trying to build a pitch perfect replica of Helms Deep out of Legos and your goal is to build it as fast as you can, that's not a very good goal for that project. You need to be thoughtful and methodical to complete difficult things. I often must remind my clients that you don't gain extra points for speed in hobbies. Rushing can make us far less likely to be successful. But time-limits cut both ways! If you want to lose 10 pounds, doing so by Christmas is a realistic time limit. When we're anxious or ambivalent about the goal, we tend to use nebulous terms like, "I'll do it later," or "before I'm 40" or "definitely before the inevitable heat death of the universe." I can guarantee you that at some point between now and the inevitable heat death of the universe, you will lose 10 pounds. But the "magical land of later" doesn't exist; you need to start sooner and with a timeline so that the goal is actually achievable.

To that end, hope is a wonderful thing, but it's not enough. It's not going to completely solve the problem. You can pray for rain all we want, but you should dig a well as you do it. I often tell my students, it's great that you hope to get an A on the test. Maybe when you're done *hoping* for that, you can *actually study* a little bit. You need to have your feet on the ground, too. Structuring plans with SMART goals will make success much more likely.

Hope is like psychological capital (Pleeging, et al., 2022). It's the ability to look within yourself and identify a thing that you can connect to because it's something that you want in your life. The more psychological capital you have, the longer you're able to keep going because you can make more withdrawals as needed. Hope enables us to keep putting one foot in front of the other, believing in our heart of hearts that a better outcome is coming. Hope is a force for many positive outcomes across different domains of functioning:

○ **Health**—Increased hope is positively related to better health outcomes. People with more hope are more likely to go to the doctor, more likely to take medication, and report feeling less sick for shorter periods.

○ **Athletics**—Belief in the ability to succeed makes us run faster and jump higher. The more anxious (less hopeful) you are about something, the more relaxed and focused your body becomes. Looser (less anxious) bodies are more confident and allow for better performance.

○ **Academics**—This is where the "hope vs. optimism" question comes up again. We want our students to do more than just hope for an "A" on the physics test, we want them to actualize that hope by studying. Students who are more hopeful tend to get into better schools, get better grades, and feel less overwhelmed by their workloads (even if the stress stays the same).

○ **Work**—Choosing a career is tough and we'd like to be optimistic that we made the right choice. But what if we didn't? Hope allows us to seek that positively be also prepare ourselves to be wrong. If you hope you're going to get a promotion or break into your ideal field of work, you will work harder and be more successful. If you're reading this and thinking, "but that doesn't describe my job, I don't have any path forward where I work", then you have my permission to change jobs. Because you need hope to drive you forward to actualize your potential.

Hope acts with a cumulative effect (Pleeging, et al., 2022). Hope instigates what we call a virtuous cycle: when we feel better, we do better, and when we do better, we feel better. When more engaged with the world, we feel better and achieve more, which encourages more engagement. It fuels positive relationships with ourselves, with our loved ones, with the community, and in our workplaces. *Hope feeds itself* in a positive way. Since so many mental health challenges involve a vicious cycle (I feel bad, so I did badly, which made me feel worse, and then I did worse), I strive to get somebody into a hope cycle, and then I get an "A+" in the therapy business.

The effectiveness of using hope in life (especially in therapy) comes down to what I call the *paradox of hope*. Neurodivergent people crave authenticity. They crave someone to be real with them, to tell the truth and say, "Hey, I'm with you and I'm going be real with you." To have hope implies that things are not as we want them to be: they might be terrible, and we want them to be less terrible; they might be good, and we want them to be great; they might merit a "99", but we want a "100". Having hope implies that things are not as we want them to be. If there are things in your life that you have hope about, you must acknowledge that things are not the way you want them to be now.

That can be scary. There's a lot of vulnerability in that process, and that's okay. If one of your values is to be a good friend and you hope that you can fix your relationship with that person, that implies that your relationship is not the way you want it to be now. It doesn't matter whose fault it is: there is power in acknowledging the reality and saying, "I would like this part of my life to be different." Maybe it's the relationships you're in (or not in). Maybe it's the job you have, or the career you want. Maybe it's the way your body looks in the mirror. The options for identifying the need to change are as varied as our likes, dislikes, and values.

Whatever it is that you'd like, saying "I hope I can do better" releases you from being bound to where you are right now by saying, "Things are what they are right now, and there's value in that. But there's more value in what could possibly come next." The therapeutic side of the paradox of hope is: **you already don't have the thing you want.** You already don't have the date or the job or the salary or the partner (or partners) or the body or whatever it is you want. So, you might as well go out and try to get it. The worst thing that can happen is that nothing changes. If you ask your boss, "Hey, I want a promotion," and your boss says "no", that sucks, but you still have your job. There's a certain freedom in realizing that you don't have what you want. If you can internalize that as a worldview, you're a lot closer to getting the things you want.

Hope also benefits meaningfully from community (Corn, et al., 2020). That's why you attend conferences, that's why you listen to speakers (and read authors) like me; that's why you go on Facebook and find groups of like-minded people, because ultimately hope benefits from community (just don't read the comments section, there are some places hope cannot go). It is certainly possible to be hopeful alone, but it's much easier to be hopeful in a community.

We are social animals. We learn from and for others. If other people have hope, it blips on our radar and we think, "what are they hopeful about? I want to know what they know, so I can feel that way too." The reason Andy Dufresne was such a threat to the warden in *Shawshank Redemption* is that he kept having hope despite all the terrible things that were happening to him; with hope as his guide, all the other prisoners were learning from him to have hope and try to better themselves. That was a dangerous thing for the Warden's plans for Shawshank Prison, but it certainly improved the mood within the walls.

When we have our bad days, the power of community for hope activates. Community helps us limit our negative and self-defeating beliefs (Corn, et al., 2020). If you are down on yourself and everybody in your community sees it, they're not going walk by and say, "Oh, there goes Mike, crying himself to sleep again." Instead, they'll say, "Whoa! Hey Mike, I know things didn't go the way you want. You didn't get the promotion, your prom date bailed on you, the Devils didn't win the Stanley Cup, etc. Whatever the thing might be, we're here for you." And because this community knows you, or at least knows about the thing that you're here for in the first place, they can speak your language (or "code") so there's a shared perspective.

Community feedback doesn't make us immediately feel better, but it gives us a path to feel better and the support of allies to go along on the journey (Corn, et al., 2020). Community also gives multiple perspectives to allow for multiple avenues to follow on the journey towards success (Pleeging, et al., 2022). We know that neurodivergent people can be myopic, but the idea here is that were used to solving problems one way, and you've always solved problems that way, until BAM! one day your go-to strategy doesn't work. You might feel lost and hopeless if that happens. But if your normal strategies for coping don't work or are not available, your community provides hope by saying, "Well, I know a lot about this thing, too. What if you tried this [fill in amazing idea]?" Or "what happened when you tried this [other amazing idea]?" It gets the ball rolling and plants seeds for success which will manifest in different ways.

Community benefits all of us, creating a critical mass of positivity that raises everyone up. If you've experienced it, you know what I'm talking about. If you haven't, that brings me to a story that I think is a particularly powerful demonstration of the power of community for hope. Let me paint you a quick picture to set the scene. The year is 2011. One Direction and Carly Rae Jepsen are on the charts, and planking is a thing. Everyone is playing Angry Birds, and the US men's national soccer team is playing a home game in Philadelphia, where I lived at the time. This game is against Mexico, our archrivals, and unlike us they are very highly rated. Nevertheless, I show up at the stadium, Lincoln Financial Field, and I'm decked out in all my America gear. I've got my American flag cape and an Uncle Sam hat; I'm wearing red, white, and blue socks. I'm in it to win it. You'd think that I'm in a sea of Old Glory, right?

Wrong. All I'm seeing is the El Tri colors (that's Mexico's nickname and kit, for the uninitiated). I think to myself, "how are we outnumbered in our own country, in our own stadium, in the birthplace of liberty of all places?" I start to feel a little overwhelmed, and I realize that I'm a man on an island right now: I don't have community. As I'm slinking my way through the stadium to my seat, I see in a far corner a bunch of people jumping up and down and yelling and screaming. Of course this interests me, so I walk closer, and then I hear through the din of stadium noise:

> "I!" *(The crowd responds, "I!")*
> "I believe!" *(The crowd responds, "I believe!")*
> "I believe that!" *(The crowd responds, "I believe that!")*

I think, "What?! I believe what? Tell me!" I also think that this is the slowest sentence in human history.

Then the crescendo: "I believe that we…WILL WIN." Then several thousand people start chanting as one, "I believe that we will win! I believe that we will win! I believe that we will win!"

It's hard to communicate just how powerful this felt in writing, so search YouTube for the "I believe that we will win" chant. Seriously, I'll wait. It's worth it!

How good was that!? It still gives me chills.

"I believe that we will win," I said to myself. And in that moment, I knew exactly where I wanted to be. I ditched my assigned seat, and I ran to the seats with the excited people, and I crammed in with them. So, what if that wasn't where my ticket was for? I spent the next 90 minutes of soccer action jumping and screaming and playing a drum and chanting with everyone there. I felt so much better as a fan with those people during the game.

My newfound community didn't change the outcome of the game. Weirdly, I couldn't remember the score, so when I was writing this chapter I had to look up. (We tied 1-1). But I do remember feeling hopeful and feeling connected to other people. I had found community. The fact that their "code" was easy to understand made it all the easier to join. The feeling of being surrounded and supported is my takeaway from that game—the change from feeling alone to feeling happily connected to a community. It inspired me not only to want more but to hope for more.

If you want to build hope in your life, you can't always go to a 60,000-person soccer game to find an immediate community of like-minded people (though I would highly recommend it). Let's figure out other ways to build hope in yourself.

The first thing is to look back on past wins. The best predictor of future behavior is past behavior, and you have almost certainly won a lot more than you're giving yourself credit for. Our brains are good at ignoring or minimizing past successes, especially if you have trauma or depression. Be intentional and draw those minimized successes to mind on purpose. Think about them—small or large, recent or distant, globally important or entirely singular. The important thing is that they're there, and they matter. One of the biggest mistakes that we make when we try to improve our lives is that we ignore our prior successes in lieu of a belief that we must go out and find "new" things to be good at. You've already got some of what you need!

Once you have this list of past successes to draw from, you don't have to go out and achieve new things. You're giving yourself credit for stuff that's already happened. It's free money. It's the psychological equivalent of finding a $20 bill in a pair of old jeans: "Ooh, that's $20!" You had it the whole time, but now you've found it, and you're very excited about it. The intentional action of celebrating yourself and the wins you already have comprises the "Yes!" test. You pick something good that you did, you bring that action to mind, and you shout "Yes!" to yourself. If you're reading this and you ate breakfast—the most important meal of the day—give yourself a "yes!"! Go ahead, do it.

Cue the awkward silence. ::twiddles thumbs:: You're done? Good. Thanks for playing along at home.

Whatever good thing you did—shower, brush your teeth, put on clean clothes, leave the house, go for a walk, feed your cat—it matters! Whatever that thing is, give yourself a "yes!". Our brains take shortcuts and don't pay attention to everything we do, especially daily rote things (McKay et al., 2021). But all those things matter, they all have value. The best thing about that value is that you are the one assigning it, so the valuation is personalized and bespoke; it doesn't have to meet anyone else's "code" but your own. I'm not saying that because you had a cup of coffee this morning you get to kick your feet up and take the rest of the day off, though that would be lovely. The point is that you get to give yourself credit for the good things you do.

Life is hard and it isn't getting easier. There are lots of reasons to be discouraged and to want to give up. But there's something audacious about having hope (Obama was spot-on in his book title), in modeling it for ourselves, our families, our friends, and our colleagues, in the face of all this despair. Hope connects us to something bigger than us all and gives us not only a glimpse of a better life, but a potential pathway towards it. I want you have a better life, and I hope that this chapter gives you the playbook to go get it.

CHAPTER 13
Conclusion
So How Do I Use All this Stuff?

When I announced that I was writing this book on social media, most of the comments were quite positive and supportive. Seriously, thank you for that. Writing is so much harder than I could have ever imagined, and the support of people in this community really makes the grind worthwhile. One negative comment stuck out to me, so much that I decided to re-write the introduction to my conclusion to address their point.

Person: "I can't believe that you'd write a book like this, Matt. I'm so disappointed in you. Neurodivergent people don't need more help masking! They need support to be their authentic styles. ND people shouldn't always have to accommodate NT (Neurotypicals) any more than they already do. Where's the book making them learn how to help US?"

Well, damn.

The person raised a good point. Am I perpetuating an ableist stance? Am I furthering tired clichés about dorks and nerds desperately trying to look and sound cool? Am I selling out my neurodivergent community to make a quick buck?

I thought about it. I slept on it. I journaled about it. I talked to my wife about it. I talked to my parents about it. I talked to my friends, colleagues, mentors, and family about it. I talked to my therapist about it (hi, Mike!). And I came to an inexorable conclusion.

Probably not, but maybe.

Many people describe me as "'ggressively pragmatic," and I think that's a good descriptor for me. Whether it's my giftedness or my ADHD or the fact that I am a product of the internet generation, I have never had much patience for waiting and agonizing over whether I am making the Best Possible Decision ®. I'd rather do it, learn from it, and try it again. This book is my attempt at codifying that process.

Would it be great if I could write a book for neurotypicals about how to communicate with neurodivergent folks? Absolutely! I could even try to do it someday, but I don't think that they'd read it. About 80% of the population is neurotypical. We are, to paraphrase Judy Singer, "neurological minorities." Our neurodivergent community and culture (yes, it is a legitimate culture) matter a great deal. I wouldn't trade my happy ND spaces online and in the real world for anything. I don't want to sell those out, and I hope to never do so.

The reality is that there are more of them than there are of us. They built and continue to build the world, as well as the systems that maintain it. They wrote the "code" and live by it, using it to protect social spaces and rituals. And when we neurodivergent people finally get a toehold, that's the moment they update it without telling us. It sucks, and it's unfair. I don't think that it's malicious in nature, but it is unquestionably impactful (and like we discussed, there is a difference between intention and impact)

This book is my strategy to combat those harsh truths. If we can adapt skills and knowledge to allow us to play their game within acceptable parameters, then we can readily crack their "code" while staying true to ourselves. These strategies are more about "code switching" than they are about "masking" or "selling out." Code switching is when a person alternates between two or more languages or language varieties during a conversation based on the changing situational needs and audience membership (Myers-Scotton, 2017). In the broader context of this book, being able to code switch into the neurotypical "code" is not only effective, it is also a prosocial communication skill.

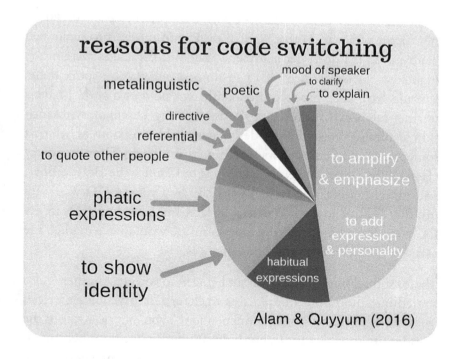

reasons for code switching

metalinguistic

poetic

mood of speaker
to clarify
to explain

directive

referential

to quote other people

to amplify & emphasize

phatic expressions

to add expression & personality

to show identity

habitual expressions

Alam & Quyyum (2016)

In high school, I lived in two worlds (no, this is not a *Hannah Montana* reference). I played on the soccer team and moved in the spaces and rituals consistent with high-level athletics. I wore a dress shirt and blazer on game days and carried an oversized soccer bag. For lack of a better phrase, I spoke their language, though it never felt like I fully cracked their "code". I also was a theatre kid (and the mascot, but that's a story for another book). In those spaces, I was brand new at the beginning, but I quickly grew fluent with their language, their rituals, and their expectations. I felt like I was able to share that "code"; and it's not an accident that the theatre space was filled with neurodivergent people (kids *and* teachers). So, if anything, I was Finn Hudson from *Glee*, though if you switched out Finn's "Can't Dance" with Mike Chang's "Can't Sing."

What does this have to do with code switching? I learned early on that the only way that I was going to survive living in both worlds was to keep them separate. The theatre kids didn't really care about my soccer exploits; they were more upset that I was never able to audition for the Fall play. They supported me, but in a passive, "you're my friend and you do that 'sports' thing and it seems to make you happy, even if I don't get it myself" way. But the stakes were much higher on the soccer field: if I had slipped into theatre-speak there, I would have been mocked incessantly as a nerd or a geek. I have a distinct memory of listening to music (on my Discman, with anti-skip technology) on the bus rides to away guides, anxious as hell that someone would find out I was listening to a mixed-CD of Broadway classics while everyone else rocked out to Coolio, the Beastie Boys, and more. (Parents, please tell your children what a CD was.). It's not that I didn't like those artists! In fact, I had all their CDs in my CD case. I just knew that my taste in music would have marked me as a true outsider, with real consequences.

There's something honorable about being who you are, but there's also something stubborn about refusing to change. In psychology, we call this kind of thinking "context independent": you may be aware of the broader situational context, but it doesn't factor into your behavioral choices (Liang, et al., 2011). One of the biggest advantages of being neurotypical is the ability to be more complex dependent; they are more naturally able to read and adapt to the specific situation that that they find themselves in: playing nice with the in-laws, sitting quietly in church, getting rowdy while watching UFC. It's a social skill to be that adaptable, though certainly you run the risk of losing your true self in that process. Neurodivergent people tend to be context independent; we are who we are, accept no substitutes (Cain, 2020). And that sometimes hurts us!

When one is aware of the power of context and allows it to influence (if not wholly alter) their decision-making, that's context-dependent thinking (Liang, et al., 2011). As an adult, you don't want to talk to your boss the same way you talk to your buddies from marketing at happy hour. As a kid, you don't want to act around the principal as you would at a sleep-over with friends. Changing communicative strategies and techniques is a social skill; frankly, it's a survival skill. I cannot tell you how many calls I've gotten about my clients over the years that begin with some authority figure saying, "Well, they're a good kid, but honestly, my biggest problem is that they really just can't talk to me that way."

Sometimes that stance has been clearly articulated, especially by teachers who have "had it up to HERE" with the neurodivergent kid's behavior in class, and have had to draw that boundary several times; I empathize with that feeling. But often, the person who is upset and reflecting on my client's behavior is articulating a standard of behavior that has never been said out-loud, simply implied. It's the "code" striking again; the person in power thinks that the neuro-divergent person should "just know" how to operate around them, because neurotypical people are able to do so. But that's an inherently unfair standard.

I often do an exercise with my clients concerning this phenomenon which I call the "blue shirt rules." Let's say that I have a rule concerning the fact that I find it offensive if a client wears a blue shirt in therapy. My reasons are my reasons, but I get really upset when people wear blue. I'm allowed to feel that way, but if a client doesn't know about that rule, then I must adapt my response to their blue shirt because they didn't know the rule. I can express frustration and remind them to change their behavior in the future, but to hold that against them the first time is unfair. If they continue to wear the blue shirt in the future, then that behavior is wholly their responsibility, and they are opening themselves up to critique and consequences.

Changing how we act is hard; otherwise, my job wouldn't exist. You're not going to use every technique in this book, but if you agree with my broader concept, I hope that you see how we can crack "the code" of neurotypical communication by being willing to learn about our differences and use that knowledge to strategically adapt our behavior. As I've said, the differences in neurodivergent brains may make these skills harder to master, but they're still worth it, despite the difficulty. As I say to my clients, "being neurodivergent is a context for our behavior, but never an excuse."

Sometimes life will make you the kid on the beach, staring up at your "friends" as they weaponize an unspoken or unknown "code" against you. That sucks! Since I cannot keep that from happening to you, I want to give you the tools to manage such moments. The best way of living life isn't about keeping all bad things from happening, it's about making those bad things feel less bad when you can. That may not be the most aspirational goal out there, but it's real, achievable, and very human (you might even say it's SMART).

I will leave you with this idea. Many people in the neurodivergent support world joke that every gifted person has the potential to be a supervillain (look at the number of supervillains with doctoral degrees in the Batman and Spider-man universes if you don't believe me). With that in mind, I tell my clients that they should use their powers for good. If you want to change the world, it requires disruption. You can be kind about it, which might mean that you pull your punches and end up not being as effective you'd like, or you can be hardcore about it, which means that you might stop people listening to you. Or, you can be prosocial and advocate firmly, with intention and grace. If you want to see recycling buckets in your school or office, for example, you don't start by handcuffing yourself to the CEO's office door, but you can do more than just write a polite email. That "third-door solution" is your best path forward.

If recycling is your passion, then follow it. Recycling may not be a glamorous pursuit, especially from those in the old school that neurodivergence should be used as a pathway towards "eminence." I'll make my stance on this very plain: if you enjoy doing it and it doesn't hurt anyone, then it has all the value it will ever need. There is an unfortunate amount of gatekeeping and stonewalling within the neurodivergent community, and it breaks my heart to see it. We must be on our own side here; we must advocate for each other, even if we don't like each other all the time (or ever). Once again, I don't have to "get" you to be able to or want to help you. Nothing that we do is a "waste" of our talent, because talent blooms most when it is combined with passion. There is no "wrong way" to use your neurodivergence. If you want to win a Fields Medal, go for it! If you want to be the best damn community librarian in Boise, that's got just as much value. You don't owe anyone anything (but yourself!). Putting yourself in a position to follow your dreams increases the chances that you positively impact the world.

It might sound crazy to believe it now, but life will eventually put you in the position where you have "the code" and other people are on the outside. It might be an audition or a job interview; it might be helping someone with your computer knowledge; it might be acting as a mentor for the neurodivergent folks who will follow in your footsteps. What you do in those moments will define the kind of person you want to be. I hope that you remember what it felt like to be the outsider. I hope that you take that knowledge and welcome people in. It's always better to build a bigger table than a higher fence.

At the end of my first keynote speech, I told the audience that if they wanted to do what I was doing right now, they could reach out to me and I'd share the skills and steps that got me to where I was. Some people gave me criticism for my offer to help others! "There are only so many keynote speaking gigs," they said, "aren't you increasing your competition?" Listen, I've been that gifted kid who felt that the only role in a group was to be In Charge. I don't miss feeling that way. I want to lift others up; thankfully, it's an ethos shared by many people in the speaking community (go see my friend Ben Whiting's Keynote on "Connecting like a Mind-Reader" and thank me later). I was proud to offer that guidance and proud of the people who reached out to me, because I remembered how hard I worked to break that ceiling and get on stage. I remembered what it felt like to be separated from the thing I truly wanted and feeling that there was some magic secret (a "code") that everyone on the inside "just knew" and was keeping from me. I don't want to be exclusive; I want to be inclusive. When we help each other, everyone wins! There's nothing wrong with making the pathway challenging, as long as you're making a pathway. We can all have space at the top. I'll be waiting for you there, whatever your path up the mountain might be.

I hope that you've learned something and had a few laughs. I hope that you can use this book to make your life better. Mostly, I hope that you understand that you're wonderful and awesome just how you are, neurodivergent or neurotypical. We all can stand to learn more about our brains and communication styles, as well as practice the interpersonal skills that smooth the way forward. I truly believe that if we all communicate authentically, intentionally, and empathetically, the only "code" we'll need is this quote from Harold Kushner:

> *"When you are kind to others, it not only changes you, it changes the world."*

May it ever be so.

References

Andrade, J. (2010). What does doodling do?. *Applied Cognitive Psychology: The Official Journal of the Society for Applied Research in Memory and Cognition, 24*(1), 100-106.

Agnew-Blais, J. C., Polanczyk, G. V., Danese, A., Wertz, J., Moffitt, T. E., & Arseneault, L. (2020). Are changes in ADHD course reflected in differences in IQ and executive functioning from childhood to adulthood?. *Psychological Medicine, 50*(16), 2799-2808.

Alamu, F. O., Adesina, A. M., & Awokola, J. A. (2021). Emotional Regulation of Stress Disordered Patients using Trivia Games. *Lautech Journal of Computing and Informatics, 2*(2), 11-28.

Alderson-Day, B., Weis, S., McCarthy-Jones, S., Moseley, P., Smailes, D., & Fernyhough, C. (2016). The brain's conversation with itself: neural substrates of dialogic inner speech. *Social cognitive and affective neuroscience, 11*(1), 110-120.

Alderson-Day, B., & Pearson, A. (2023). What can neurodiversity tell us about inner speech, and vice versa? A theoretical perspective. *Cortex. 168*(Nov), 193-202.

Al-Shawaf, L., & Lewis, D. M. (2020). Evolutionary psychology and the emotions. *Encyclopedia of personality and individual differences*, 1452-1461.

Amador, S. (2018). *Teaching Social Skills Through Sketch Comedy and Improv Games: A Social Theatre ™ Approach for Kids and Teens including those with ASD, ADHD, and Anxiety.* Jessica Kingsley Publishers: London, UK.

Apperly, I. A., Lee, R., van der Kleij, S. W., & Devine, R. T. (2023). A transdiagnostic approach to neurodiversity in a representative population sample: The N+ 4 model. *JCPP Advances*, e12219.

Armstrong, T. (2015). The myth of the normal brain: Embracing neurodiversity. *AMA journal of ethics*, *17*(4), 348-352.

Baldassarri, D., & Abascal, M. (2020). Diversity and prosocial behavior. *Science*, *369*(6508), 1183-1187.

Barenberg, J., Berse, T., & Dutke, S. (2011). Executive functions in learning processes: do they benefit from physical activity?. *Educational Research Review*, *6*(3), 208-222.

Bayne, H. B., & Jangha, A. (2016). Utilizing Improvisation to Teach Empathy Skills in Counselor Education. *Counselor Education and Supervision*, *55*(4), 250-262.

Bell, M. C. (2020). *Changing the Culture of Consent: Teaching Young Children Personal Boundaries*. University of South Florida.

Berger, A., Kofman, O., Livneh, U., & Henik, A. (2007). Multidisciplinary perspectives on attention & the development of self-regulation. *Progress in neurobiology*, *82*(5), 256-86.

Bierman, K. L., & Sanders, M. T. (2021). Teaching explicit social-emotional skills with contextual supports for students with intensive intervention needs. *Journal of Emotional and Behavioral Disorders*, *29*(1), 14-23.

Bilan, Y., Mishchuk, H., Roshchyk, I., & Joshi, O. (2020). Hiring and retaining skilled employees in SMEs: problems in human resource practices and links with organizational success. *Business: Theory and Practice*, *21*(2), 780-791.

Böckler, A., Knoblich, G., & Sebanz, N. (2010). Socializing cognition. *Towards a theory of thinking: Building blocks for a conceptual framework*, 233-250.

Bradley, R. L., & Noell, G. H. (2022). Rule-governed behavior: teaching social skills via rule-following to children with autism. *Developmental neurorehabilitation*, *25*(7), 433-443.

Breedlove, L. (2022). Characteristics of gifted learners. In *Introduction to gifted education* (pp. 59-79). Routledge.

Bristoll, S., & Dickinson, J. (2015). Small talk, big results. *Newsli*, *92*, 6-13.

Brown, C. G. (2010). Improving fine motor skills in young children: an intervention study. *Educational Psychology in Practice*, *26*(3), 269-278.

Brown, R. L., Chen, M. A., Paoletti, J., Dicker, E. E., Wu-Chung, E. L., LeRoy, A. S., …& Fagundes, C. P. (2022). Emotion regulation, parasympathetic function, and psychological well-being. *Frontiers in psychology, 13*, 879166.

Bucaille, A., Jarry, C., Allard, J., Brochard, S., Peudenier, S., & Roy, A. (2022). Neuropsychological profile of intellectually gifted children: A systematic review. *Journal of the International Neuropsychological Society, 28*(4), 424-440.

Butler, E. A., & Randall, A. K. (2013). Emotional co-regulation in close relationships. *Emotion Review, 5*(2), 202-210.

Cain, P. (2020). "How do I know how I think, until I see what I say?": the shape of embodied thinking, neurodiversity, first-person methodology. *Idea Journal, 17*(2). 41-55.

Carlson, S. M., Koenig, M. A., & Harms, M. B. (2013). Theory of mind. *Wiley Interdisciplinary Reviews: Cognitive Science, 4*(4), 391-402.

Carpenter, K. L., Baranek, G. T., Copeland, W. E., Compton, S., Zucker, N., Dawson, G., & Egger, H. L. (2019). Sensory over-responsivity: an early risk factor for anxiety and behavioral challenges. *Journal of abnormal child psychology, 47*(6), 1075-1088.

Cavilla, D. (2019). Maximizing the potential of gifted learners through a developmental framework of affective curriculum. *Gifted Education International, 35*(2), 136-151.

Chapman, R. (2021). Neurodiversity and the social ecology of mental functions. *Perspectives on Psychological Science, 16*(6), 1360-1372.

Chapman, R., & Botha, M. (2023). Neurodivergence-informed therapy. *Developmental Medicine & Child Neurology, 65*(3), 310-317.

Chan, M. M., & Han, Y. M. (2020). Differential mirror neuron system (MNS) activation during action observation with and without social-emotional components in autism: a meta-analysis of neuroimaging studies. *Molecular autism, 11*, 1-18.

Clance, P. R., & Imes, S. A. (1978). The impostor phenomenon in high achieving women: Dynamics and therapeutic intervention. *Psychotherapy: Theory, research & ractice, 15*(3), 241.

Corbett, M. (2015). From law to folklore: work stress and the Yerkes-Dodson Law. *Journal of Managerial Psychology, 30*(6), 741-752.

Corn, B., Feldman, D., and Wexler, I. (2020). The science of hope. *The Lancet.* 21(9). 452-59.

Costa, H. J. T., Abelairas-Gomez, C., Arufe-Giráldez, V., Pazos-Couto, J. M., & Barcala-Furelos, R. (2015). Influence of a physical education plan on psychomotor development profiles of preschool children. *Journal of Human Sport and Exercise, 10*(1), 126-140.

Council on School Health, Murray, R., Ramstetter, C., Devore, C., Allison, M., Ancona, R., …& Young, T. (2013). The crucial role of recess in school. *Pediatrics, 131*(1), 183-188.

Courchesne, V., Bedford, R., Pickles, A., Duku, E., Kerns, C., Mirenda, P., …& Pathways Team. (2021). Non-verbal IQ and change in restricted and repetitive behavior throughout childhood in autism: a longitudinal study using the Autism Diagnostic Interview-Revised. *Molecular autism, 12*, 1-10.

Crompton, C. J., DeBrabander, K., Heasman, B., Milton, D., & Sasson, N. J. (2021). Double empathy: why autistic people are often misunderstood. *Neuroscience, 9*(554875), 4-11.

Dahunsi, O., Robinson, N., Parks, C., & Nittrouer, C. (2024). How a DEI Climate Can Enable Allies and Support People Who Are Neurodivergent. In *Neurodiversity and Work: Employment, Identity, and Support Networks for Neurominorities* (pp. 207-230).

Damiani, D., Pereira, L. K., & Nascimento, A. M. (2017). Intelligence neurocircuitry: cortical and subcortical structures. *Journal of Morphological Sciences, 34*(03), 123-129.

de Oliveira, C., Saka, M., Bone, L., & Jacobs, R. (2023). The role of mental health on workplace productivity: a critical review of the literature. *Applied health economics and health policy, 21*(2), 167-193.

Dirzyte, A., Patapas, A., & Perminas, A. (2022). Associations between leisure preferences, mindfulness, psychological capital, and life satisfaction. *International Journal of Environmental Research and Public Health, 19*(7), 4121.

Dovidio, J. F., Piliavin, J. A., Schroeder, D. A., & Penner, L. A. (2017). *The social psychology of prosocial behavior.* Psychology Press. Washington, D.C.

Doyle, N. (2020). Neurodiversity at work: a biopsychosocial model and the impact on working adults. *British Medical Bulletin, 135*(1), 108.

Eagle, T., Baltaxe-Admony, L. B., & Ringland, K. E. (2023). Proposing body doubling as a continuum of space/time and mutuality: An investigation with neurodivergent participants. In *Proceedings of the*

25th International ACM SIGACCESS Conference on Computers and Accessibility (pp. 1-4).

Ellis, L., Hoskin, A. W., & Ratnasingam, M. (2018). *Handbook of social status correlates*. Academic Press. Washington, D.C.

Feenstra, S., Begeny, C. T., Ryan, M. K., Rink, F. A., Stoker, J. I., & Jordan, J. (2020). Contextualizing the impostor "syndrome". *Frontiers in psychology, 11*, 575024.

Flouri, E., & Panourgia, C. (2014). Negative automatic thoughts and emotional and behavioural problems in adolescence. *Child and Adolescent Mental Health, 19*(1), 46-51.

Frye, K. E., Boss, D. L., Anthony, C. J., Du, H., & Xing, W. (2022). Content analysis of the CASEL framework using K–12 state SEL standards. *School Psychology Review*, 1-15.

Gardner, H. (2021). *Disciplined mind: What all students should understand*. Simon & Schuster. New York, NY.

Gary, A., Kiper, V., & Geist, R. (2022). An introduction to motivational interviewing. *Nursing made Incredibly Easy, 20*(2), 32-39.

Ghamari Kivi, H., Jamshiddoust Miyanroudi, F., Mousavi, S., & Ghavibazou, E. (2023). Role of Types of Inner Speech in the Prediction of Symptoms of Anxiety, Depression, Somatization, and Distress in the Normal Population. *Practice in Clinical Psychology, 11*(4), 341-348.

Gilbert, S. J., & Burgess, P. W. (2008). Executive function. *Current biology, 18*(3), R110-R114.

Goswami, U., Huss, M., Mead, N., & Fosker, T. (2021). Auditory sensory processing and phonological development in high IQ and exceptional readers, typically developing readers, and children with dyslexia. *Child development, 92*(3), 1083-1098.

Greene, R. W., & Ablon, J. S. (2005). *Treating explosive kids: The collaborative problem-solving approach*. Guilford Press.

Gross, M. U. (2009). Highly gifted young people: Development from childhood to adulthood. *International handbook on giftedness*, 337-351.

Gueldner, B. A., Feuerborn, L. L., & Merrell, K. W. (2020). *Social and emotional learning in the classroom: Promoting mental health and academic success*. Guilford Publications.

Hai, T., & Climie, E. A. (2022). Positive child personality factors in children with ADHD. *Journal of Attention Disorders, 26*(3), 476-486.

Haier, R. J., & Jung, R. E. (2018). The Parieto-Frontal Integration Theory. *Contemporary intellectual assessment: Theories, tests, and issues, 219.*

Hart, S. C., DiPerna, J. C., Lei, P. W., & Cheng, W. (2020). Nothing lost, something gained? Impact of a universal social-emotional learning program on future state test performance. *Educational researcher, 49*(1), 5-19.

Hasan, M. M., Fatima, Y., Pandey, S., Tariqujjaman, M., Cleary, A., Baxter, J., & Mamun, A. A. (2021). Pathways linking bullying victimisation and suicidal behaviours among adolescents. *Psychiatry research, 302,* 113992.

Hayes, S. C., Strosahl, K. D., & Wilson, K. G. (2011). *Acceptance and commitment therapy: The process and practice of mindful change.* Guilford press. London, UK.

Harris, R. (2006). Embracing your demons: An overview of acceptance and commitment therapy. *Psychotherapy in Australia, 12*(4), 70-6.

Hawley, K. (2019, June). I—What is imposter syndrome?. In *Aristotelian Society Supplementary Volume* (Vol. 93, No. 1, pp. 203-226). Oxford University Press.

Hayes, S. C., & Hofmann, S. G. (2021). "Third-wave" cognitive and behavioral therapies and the emergence of a process-based approach to intervention in psychiatry. *World psychiatry, 20*(3), 363-375.

Hayward, L., Whitworth, M., Pepin, N., & Dorling, S. (2020). A comprehensive review of datasets and methodologies employed to produce thunderstorm climatologies. *Natural Hazards and Earth System Sciences, 20*(9), 2463-2482.

Ho, T. C., Pham, H. T., Miller, J. G., Kircanski, K., & Gotlib, I. H. (2020). Sympathetic nervous system dominance during stress recovery mediates associations between stress sensitivity and social anxiety symptoms in female adolescents. *Development and Psychopathology, 32*(5), 1914-1925.

Hodges, V. C., Centeio, E. E., & Morgan, C. F. (2022). The benefits of school recess: A systematic review. *Journal of School Health, 92*(10), 959-967.

Kapp, S. K., Gillespie-Lynch, K., Sherman, L. E., & Hutman, T. (2013). Deficit, difference, or both? Autism and neurodiversity. *Developmental psychology*, *49*(1), 59.

Kapasi, A., & Pei, J. (2022). Mindset theory and school psychology. *Canadian Journal of School Psychology*, *37*(1), 57-74.

Karpinski, R. I., Kolb, A. M. K., Tetreault, N. A., & Borowski, T. B. (2018). High intelligence: A risk factor for psychological and physiological overexcitabilities. *Intelligence*, *66*, 8-23.

Kaufman, S. B., & Sternberg, R. J. (2008). Conceptions of giftedness. In *Handbook of giftedness in children: Psychoeducational theory, research, and best practices* (pp. 71-91). Boston, MA: Springer US.

Keeley, T. J., & Fox, K. R. (2009). The impact of physical activity and fitness on academic achievement and cognitive performance in children. *International review of sport and exercise psychology*, *2*(2), 198-214.

Kelly, C., Martin, R., Taylor, R., & Doherty, M. (2024). Recognising and responding to physical and mental health issues in neurodivergent girls and women. *British Journal of Hospital Medicine*, *85*(4), 1-12.

Khalil, R., Tindle, R., Boraud, T., Moustafa, A. A., & Karim, A. A. (2018). Social decision making in autism: On the impact of mirror neurons, motor control, and imitative behaviors. *CNS neuroscience & therapeutics*, *24*(8), 669-676.

Kiamos, K., & Lumme, D. (2020). Find and Be True to Your Personal & Professional Core Values: Leader, Mentor, STEM Advocate. *Naval Engineers Journal*, *132*(3), 66-70.

Kipping, J. A., Tuan, T. A., Fortier, M. V., & Qiu, A. (2017). Asynchronous development of cerebellar, cerebello-cortical, and cortico-cortical functional networks in infancy, childhood, and adulthood. *Cerebral cortex*, *27*(11), 5170-5184.

Kircher-Morris, E. (2022). *Raising Twice-exceptional Children: A Handbook for Parents of Neurodivergent Gifted Kids*. Routledge. New York.

Kolk, S. and Rakic, P. (2022). Development of prefrontal cortex. *Neuropsychopharmacology*. *47*(1), 41-57.

Kopnina, H. (2020). Education for the future? Critical evaluation of education for sustainable development goals. *The Journal of Environmental Education*, *51*(4), 280-291.

Kuhn, T., Blades, R., Gottlieb, L., Knudsen, K., Ashdown, C., Martin-Harris, L., ...& Bookheimer, S. Y. (2021). Neuroanatomical differences in the memory systems of intellectual giftedness and typical development. *Brain and Behavior, 11*(11), e2348.

Lambek, R., Tannock, R., Dalsgaard, S., Trillingsgaard, A., Damm, D., & Thomsen, P. H. (2011). Executive dysfunction in school-age children with ADHD. *Journal of attention disorders, 15*(8), 646-655.

Landry, M. J., Bailey, D. A., & Ervin, A. (2021). You are not an impostor: the registered dietitian nutritionist and impostor phenomenon. *Journal of Nutrition Education and Behavior, 53*(7), 625-630.

Landry, P. (2021). A behavioral economic theory of cue-induced attention-and task-switching with implications for neurodiversity. *Journal of Economic Psychology, 86*, 102423.

Latham, G. (2020). Goal-setting: A five-step approach to behavior change. *Organizational Collaboration.* 10-20.

Lee, S. Y., Olszewski-Kubilius, P., & Thomson, D. T. (2012). Academically gifted students' perceived interpersonal competence and peer relationships. *Gifted Child Quarterly, 56*(2), 90-104.

Lee, H. (2011). *Interpretation of Ambiguous Emotional Cues of Children with Developmental Cognitive Disabilities and Its Relation to Their Social Skills.* University of Minnesota.

Lerner, M. D., Mikami, A. Y., & Levine, K. (2011). Socio-dramatic affective-relational intervention for adolescents with Asperger syndrome & high functioning autism: Pilot study. *Autism, 15*(1), 21-42.

Levitin, D. (2015). *The Organized Mind.* Dutton Publishing. New York, NY.

Liang, B., Runyan, R. C., & Fu, W. (2011). The effect of culture on the context of ad pictures and ad persuasion: The role of context-dependent and context-independent thinking. *International Marketing Review, 28*(4), 412-434.

Logan, D. E., & Marlatt, G. A. (2010). Harm reduction therapy: A practice-friendly review of research. *Journal of clinical psychology, 66*(2), 201-214.

Lovecky, D. V. (2011). Friendship and the Highly Gifted. *Greatest Potential, Greatest Need: Soaring Beyond Expectations,* 142.

Marlatt, G. A., Larimer, M. E., & Witkiewitz, K. (Eds.). (2011). *Harm reduction: Pragmatic strategies for managing high-risk behaviors.* Guilford Press. New York, NY.

Martin, R. A., Brown, D. A., Diamond, M. E., Cattaneo, A., & Fernández De-Miguel, F. (2020). *From neuron to brain.* Oxford University Press. Oxford, UK.

Matthews, D. J., & Dai, D. Y. (2014). Gifted education: changing conceptions, emphases and practice. *International Studies in Sociology of Education, 24*(4), 335-353.

McKay, M., Davis, M., & Fanning, P. (2021). *Thoughts and feelings: Taking control of your moods and your life.* New Harbinger Publications. New York, NY.

Mitchell, P., Sheppard, E., & Cassidy, S. (2021). Autism and the double empathy problem: Implications for development and mental health. *British Journal of Developmental Psychology, 39*(1), 1-18.

Molenberghs P, Cunnington R, Mattingley JB., (2009). "Is the mirror neuron system involved in imitation? A short review and meta-analysis". *Neuroscience and Biobehavioral Reviews.* 33(7): 975–980

Moreno, A. (2022). *Purpose-Driven Learning: Unlocking and Empowering Our Students' Innate Passion for Learning.* Taylor & Francis. United Kingdom.

Moscovitch, D. A., & Hofmann, S. G. (2007). When ambiguity hurts: Social standards moderate self-appraisals in generalized social phobia. *Behaviour Research and Therapy, 45*(5), 1039-1052.

Mrazik, M., & Dombrowski, S. C. (2010). The neurobiological foundations of giftedness. *Roeper Review, 32*(4), 224-234.

Murdoch, D., English, A. R., Hintz, A., & Tyson, K. (2020). Feeling heard: Inclusive education, transformative learning, and productive struggle. *Educational Theory, 70*(5), 653-679.

Myers-Scotton, C. (2017). Code-switching. *The handbook of sociolinguistics,* 217-237.

Ne'eman, A., & Pellicano, E. (2022). Neurodiversity as politics. *Human Development, 66*(2), 149-157.

Neipp, M. C., Beyebach, M., Sanchez-Prada, A., & Delgado Álvarez, M. D. C. (2021). Solution-focused versus problem-focused questions: Differential effects of miracles, exceptions and scales. *Journal of family therapy, 43*(4), 728-747.

Nesayan, A., Hosseini, B., & Asadi Gandomani, R. (2017). The effectiveness of emotion regulation skills training on anxiety and emotional regulation strategies in adolescent students. *Practice in Clinical Psychology*, 5(4), 263-270.

Nicpon, M. F., & Pfeiffer, S. I. (2011). High-ability students: New ways to conceptualize giftedness and provide psychological services in the schools. *Journal of Applied School Psychology*, 27(4), 293-305.

Olive, C., McCullick, B. A., Tomporowski, P., Gaudreault, K. L., & Simonton, K. (2020). Effects of an after-school program focused on physical activity and social–emotional learning. *Journal of Youth Development*, 15(6), 292-305.

Ott, T., & Nieder, A. (2019). Dopamine and cognitive control in prefrontal cortex. *Trends in cognitive sciences*, 23(3), 213-234.

Pagliaccio, D., Luby, J. L., Bogdan, R., Agrawal, A., Gaffrey, M. S., Belden, A. C., …& Barch, D. M. (2015). Amygdala functional connectivity, HPA axis genetic variation, and life stress in children and relations to anxiety and emotion regulation. *Journal of abnormal psychology*, 124(4), 817.

Papandreou, A., Athinaiou, E., & Mavrogalou, A. (2023). Conforming and Condescending Attitudes of Gifted Children in Response to Their Social Anxiety and Asynchronous Cognitive and Emotional Development. *Biomedical Journal of Scientific & Technical Research*, 50(2), 41539-41545.

Papacek, A. M., Chai, Z., & Green, K. B. (2016). Play and social interaction strategies for young children with autism spectrum disorder in inclusive preschool settings. *Young exceptional children*, 19(3), 3-17.

Pedrini, L., Meloni, S., Lanfredi, M., & Rossi, R. (2022). School-based interventions to improve emotional regulation skills in adolescent students: A systematic review. *Journal of Adolescence*, 94(8), 1051-1067.

Peterson, H. (2014). An Academic 'Glass Cliff'? Exploring the Increase of Women in Swedish Higher Education Management. *Athens Journal of Education*, 1(1), 33-44.

Perlman, S. B., & Pelphrey, K. A. (2011). Developing connections for affective regulation: age-related changes in emotional brain connectivity. *Journal of experimental child psychology*, 108(3), 607-620.

Pleeging, E., Van Exel, J., and Burger, M. (2022). Characterizing Hope: An Interdisciplinary Overview of the Characteristics of Hope. *Applied Research in Quality of Life*. 17(3). 1681-1723.

Praszkier, R. (2016). Empathy, mirror neurons and SYNC. *Mind & Society, 15*, 1-25.

Prescott, J., Gavrilescu, M., Cunnington, R., O'Boyle, M. W., & Egan, G. F. (2010). Enhanced brain connectivity in math-gifted adolescents: An fMRI study using mental rotation. *Cognitive Neuroscience, 1*(4), 277-288.

Probine, S., & Perry, J. (2021). Does the more knowledgeable other and the established discourses that accompany it have a place in EC today?: Rethinking and re-casting Vygotsky for the twenty-first century. *Early Education, 67*, 5-13.

Rabinovici, G. D., Stephens, M. L., & Possin, K. L. (2015). Executive dysfunction. *CONTINUUM: Lifelong Learning in Neurology, 21*(3), 646-659.

Radulski, E. M. (2022). Conceptualising autistic masking, camouflaging, and neurotypical privilege: Towards a minority group model of neurodiversity. *Human Development, 66*(2), 113-127.

Rao, B., & Polepeddi, J. (2019). Neurodiverse workforce: Inclusive employment as an HR strategy. *Strategic HR Review, 18*(5), 204-209.

Raymaker, D. M., Teo, A. R., Steckler, N. A., Lentz, B., Scharer, M., Delos Santos, A., ...& Nicolaidis, C. (2020). "Having all of your internal resources exhausted beyond measure and being left with no clean-up crew": Defining autistic burnout. *Autism in adulthood, 2*(2), 132-143.

Reese, W. J. (2011). *America's public schools: From the common school to" no child left behind"*. Johns Hopkins University Press. Balitmore, MD.

Reuben, C. E. (2024). Attention-Deficit/Hyperactivity Disorder in Children Ages 5-17 Years: United States, 2020-2022. *Centers for Disease Control Brief.*

Rodriguez, R. (2021). *Employee resource group excellence: Grow high performing ERGs to enhance diversity, equality, belonging, and business impact.* Wiley & Sons. New York.

Rolls, E. T. (2015). Limbic systems for emotion and for memory, but no single limbic system. *Cortex, 62*, 119-157.

Roberts, J. (2024). Ableism, Code-Switching, and Camouflaging: A Letter to the Editor on Gerlach-Houck and DeThorne (2023). *Language, Speech, and Hearing Services in Schools, 55*(1), 217-223.

Robinson, A., Shore, B. M., & Enersen, D. (2021). *Best practices in gifted education: An evidence-based guide*. Routledge. London, UK.

Rocha, A., Almedia, L., & Perales, R. (2020). Comparison of gifted and non-gifted students' executive functions and high capabilities. *Journal for the Education of Gifted Young Scientists, 8*(4), 1397-1409.

Rong, Y., Yang, C. J., Jin, Y., & Wang, Y. (2021). Prevalence of attention-deficit/hyperactivity disorder in individuals with autism spectrum disorder: A meta-analysis. *Research in Autism Spectrum Disorders, 83*, 101759.

Ronnie, J. B., & Philip, B. (2021). Expectations and what people learn from failure. In *Expectations and actions* (pp. 207-237). Routledge. New York, NY.

Salimova, K. R. (2022). Neurophysiological correlates of impaired development in autism spectrum disorder (ASD). *Biology Bulletin Reviews, 12*(2), 140-148.

Sapey-Triomphe, L. A., Timmermans, L., & Wagemans, J. (2021). Priors bias perceptual decisions in autism, but are less flexibly adjusted to the context. *Autism Research, 14*(6), 1134-1146.

Schlegler, M. (2022). Systematic literature review: Professional situation of gifted adults. *Frontiers in psychology, 13*, 736487.

Schulz, S. E., & Stevenson, R. A. (2019). Sensory hypersensitivity predicts repetitive behaviours in autistic and typically-developing children. *Autism, 23*(4), 1028-1041.

Sergerie, K., Chochol, C., & Armony, J. L. (2008). The role of the amygdala in emotional processing: a quantitative meta-analysis of functional neuroimaging studies. *Neuroscience & Biobehavioral Reviews, 32* (4), 811-830.

Shell, G. R. (2021). *The Conscience Code: Lead with Your Values. Advance Your Career*. HarperCollins Leadership. New York, NY.

Shermer, M. (2014). *How the Survivor Bias Distorts Reality*. Scientific American. 311(3). 94.

Shore, B. M., Chichekian, T., Gyles, P. D., & Walker, C. L. (2018). Friendships of gifted children and youth: Updated insights and understanding. *The Sage Handbook of gifted and talented education*, 184-195.

Siedler, A., Gałkowski, T., & Pąchalska, M. (2019). Self-reported individual differences in inner speech (internal monologue and dialogue) in adolescents with Social (Pragmatic) Communication Disorder (SCD). *Acta Neuropsychologica, 17*, 39-53.

Silverman, L. K. (2017). The construct of asynchronous development. In *Charting a new course in gifted education* (pp. 36-58). Routledge.

Silverman, L. K. (2021). Counseling asynchronous gifted students: A 30-year perspective. In *Handbook for Counselors Serving Students With Gifts and Talents* (pp. 327-349).

Sinha, T., & Kapur, M. (2021). When problem solving followed by instruction works: Evidence for productive failure. *Review of Educational Research, 91*(5), 761-798.

Solé-Casals, J., Serra-Grabulosa, J. M., Romero-Garcia, R., Vilaseca, G., Adan, A., Vilaró, N., ...& Bullmore, E. T. (2019). Structural brain network of gifted children has a more integrated and versatile topology. *Brain Structure and Function, 224*(7), 2373-2383.

Soma, C. S., Baucom, B. R., Xiao, B., Butner, J. E., Hilpert, P., Narayanan, S., ...& Imel, Z. E. (2020). Co-regulation of therapist and client emotion during psychotherapy. *Psychotherapy research, 30*(5), 591-603.

Sosland, B. E. (2022). *A call to action: Identification and intervention for twice and thrice exceptional students.* Rowman & Littlefield. Lanham, Maryland.

Steinbrecher, E., Jordan, S. S., & Turns, B. (2020). Providing immediate hope to survivors of natural disasters: A miracle question intervention. *The American Journal of Family Therapy, 49*(2), 204-219.

Sullivan, D. M., & Bendell, B. L. (2023). Help! Lonely at work: Managerial interventions to combat employee loneliness. *Business Horizons, 66*(5), 655-666.

Swain, J. E., Bogardus, J. A., & Lin, E. (2021). "Come on Down": Using a Trivia Game to Teach the Concept of Organizational Justice. *Management Teaching Review, 6*(3), 210-222.

Thomas, M. S. (2016). Do more intelligent brains retain heightened plasticity for longer in development? *Developmental cognitive neuroscience, 19*(1), 258-269.

Tistarelli, N., Fagnani, C., Troianiello, M., Stazi, M. A., & Adriani, W. (2020). The nature and nurture of ADHD and its comorbidities: A narrative review on twin studies. *Neuroscience & Biobehavioral Reviews, 109*, 63-77.

Toth, G., & Siegel, L. S. (2020). A critical evaluation of the IQ-achievement discrepancy based definition of dyslexia. In *Current directions in dyslexia research* (pp. 45-70). Garland Science. New York, NY.

Treffert, D. A. (2014). Savant syndrome: Realities, myths and misconceptions. *Journal of Autism and Developmental Disorders, 44*(3), 564-571.

van Geel, M., Goemans, A., Zwaanswijk, W., & Vedder, P. (2022). Does peer victimization predict future suicidal ideation? A meta-analysis on longitudinal studies. *Aggression and violent behavior, 64*, 101577.

Walmsley, J., & O'Madagain, C. (2020). The worst-motive fallacy: A negativity bias in motive attribution. *Psychological Science, 31*(11), 1430-1438.

Waters, T. (2014). Of looking glasses, mirror neurons, culture, and meaning. *Perspectives on Science, 22*(4), 616-649.

Weissman, D. G., & Mendes, W. B. (2021). Correlation of sympathetic and parasympathetic nervous system activity during rest and acute stress tasks. *International Journal of Psychophysiology, 162*, 60-68.

Westgate, E. C. (2020). Why boredom is interesting. *Current Directions in Psychological Science, 29*(1), 33-40.

Wittek, R., & Bekkers, R. (2015). Altruism and prosocial behavior, sociology of. *International encyclopedia of the social & behavioral sciences, 1*, 579-583.

Wood, V. R., & Laycraft, K. C. (2020). How can we better understand, identify, and support highly gifted and profoundly gifted students? A literature review of the psychological development of highly-profoundly gifted individuals and overexcitabilities. *Annals of Cognitive Science, 4*(1), 143-165.

Yu, B., & Sterponi, L. (2023). Toward neurodiversity: How conversation analysis can contribute to a new approach to social communication assessment. *Language, Speech, and Hearing Services in Schools, 54*(1), 27-41.

Zelazo, P. D. (2015). Executive function: Reflection, iterative reprocessing, complexity, and the developing brain. *Developmental Review, 38*, 55-68.

Further reading

https://www.arthurmorganschool.org/home/importance-of-free-time-for-students/

https://www.apa.org/monitor/2021/06/cover-impostor-phenomenon

https://www.davidsongifted.org/gifted-blog/play-partner-or-sure-shelter-what-gifted-children-look-for-in-friendship/

https://onemindatwork.org/the-business-case-for-investing-in-workforce-health/

https://mhanational.org/sites/default/files/Work%20Health%20Survey%202019.pdf

https://www.psychologytoday.com/us/blog/cutting-edge-leadership/202004/lying-is-social-skill-should-you-use-it

https://www.health.harvard.edu/blog/co-regulation-helping-children-and-teens-navigate-big-emotions-202404033030

https://add.org/the-body-double/

https://www.autism.org.uk/advice-and-guidance/professional-practice/double-empathy

https://www.forbes.com/sites/christinapark/2015/03/30/an-introverts-guide-to-small-talk-eight-painless-tips/

https://www.wendaful.com/2018/06/how-to-plan-schedule-your-days-to-get-things-done/

https://www.betterup.com/blog/code-switching

https://www.psychologytoday.com/us/blog/play-your-way-sane/202301/no-joke-improv-comedy-reduces-social-anxiety

https://www.forbes.com/sites/sallypercy/2024/03/05/how-leaders-can-instill-hope-in-their-teams/

https://greatergood.berkeley.edu/article/item/how_to_learn_from_your_failures

https://disabilityin.org/resource/neurodiversity-at-work-playbook-employee-engagement-growth-series/

https://www.speechpathology.com/articles/neurodiversity-movement-overview-for-autism-20554

https://www.psychiatrictimes.com/view/the-neurodiversity-movement-confusing-illness-with-stigma

https://neuroqueer.com/neurodiversity-terms-and-definitions/

https://www.doctornerdlove.com/how-to-make-small-talk-for-people-who-hate-small-talk/

https://www.hmhco.com/blog/what-is-productive-struggle

https://www.andimcnair.com/geniushour

About the Author

Matthew "Dr. Matt" Zakreski, PsyD is a high energy, creative clinical psychologist and professional speaker. He is proud to serve the neurodivergent community as a consultant, a professor, an author, and a researcher. He has spoken hundreds of times all over the world about supporting neurodivergent people. Dr. Zakreski is a member of Supporting the Emotional Needs of the Gifted (SENG), the National Association for Gifted Children (NAGC), the New Jersey Association for Gifted Children (NJAGC), and Pennsylvania Association for Gifted Education (PAGE). Dr. Zakreski graduated from Widener University's Institute for Graduate Clinical Psychology (IGCP) in 2016. He is the co-founder of The Neurodiversity Collective: https://www.theneurodiversitycollective.com/

Printed in the USA
CPSIA information can be obtained
at www.ICGtesting.com
JSHW010343101224
74933JS00003B/3

9 781953 360366